Content Management Systems

Dave Addey

James Ellis

Phil Suh

David Thiemecke

Published by glasshaus Ltd,
Arden House,
1102 Warwick Road,
Acocks Green,
Birmingham,
B27 6BH, UK

Printed in the United States
ISBN 1-904151-06-X

Content Management Systems

Cover Image

The cover image is a photo of the glass pyramid outside the Musée du Louvre in Paris, France. It was chosen to symbolize this book, since it is a physical example of a system that acquires, catalogs, and displays many items of content. Of course, it's also a very beautiful building!

The photo is copyright of Stan Jirman, *http://www.PhotoTrek.org*. A donation has been made on his behalf to Great Ormond Street Hospital, London, for the use of the photo.

glasshaus

web professional to web professional

© 2002 glasshaus

Trademark Acknowledgements

glasshaus has endeavored to provide trademark information about all the companies and products mentioned in this book by the appropriate use of capitals. However, glasshaus cannot guarantee the accuracy of this information.

Credits

Authors
Dave Addey
James Ellis
Phil Suh
David Thiemecke

Contributing Authors
Inigo Surguy
Alyson Fielding

Technical Reviewers
Dave Addey
Jay Blanchard
Dave Gibbons
Mark Howells
David Schultz
David Thiemecke
Kevin Vanourney
Michael Walston

Proof Reader
Agnes Wiggers

Commissioning Editor
Simon Mackie

Lead Technical Editor
Amanda Kay

Technical Editors
Matthew Machell
Daniel Walker

Managing Editor
Liz Toy

Project Manager
Sophie Edwards

Production Coordinator
Rachel Taylor
Pip Wonson

Cover
Dawn Chellingworth

Indexer
Bill Johncocks

About the Authors

Dave Addey

Dave has spent the last six years building and implementing web systems for major US and UK organizations. He is the founder and director of agant.com, a UK-based CMS and Intranet consultancy. He's had more experience of Content Management than is probably advisable, from designing and building bespoke systems to purchasing and implementing major commercial products.

To Mat & Pauline, for starting it all.

James Ellis

James Ellis is a part-time MBA student, part-time blogger, part-time web teacher, part-time freelance designer, part-time writer, part-time consultant, and full-time web thinker living in Madison, WI (by way of Raleigh, Austin, Houston, and Ho-ho-kus, NJ). He can commonly be found online, working on his Internet sites, *http://www.suite102.com*, *http://www.pinstripesuit.com*, and *http://www.supersquish.com*.

Thanks go to the beautiful Anna, my parents, Janie and Toby Ellis, and my other parents, Suzanne and Neil Lewis. As always, much love to Dan, Marrit and Jim, Katie, Charlie and Farrah, DJ Scary Mike, Kim, Kathy, Sarah Van, and Eleanor Manley. Thank you to glasshaus for inviting me to this project, and all the editors who make me sound good. A special thanks to Jeffery Zeldman for publishing "CMS and the Single Designer" in http://www.alistapart.com, the beginning of my part in this little play.

Phil Suh

Phil Suh is a programmer based in San Francisco. He worked for three years as a content engineer at Organic, Inc., where he both evaluated commercial CMS products and built custom production systems for building web sites for Organic's clients. In the summer of 2000, Phil and Cameron Barrett co-founded the cms-list (*http://www.cms-list.org*), a mailing list for content management discussion. The ranks of the cms-list have swelled to over 2,200 content management developers, users, and vendors. Today Phil does freelance production engineering and content management consulting, tends the cms-list, and occasionally speaks at conferences.

David Thiemecke

David M. Thiemecke acts as the architect for QuantumCMS (*http://quantumcms.com*), a content management solution in production since 2000 at such diverse clients as the Roswell Park Cancer Institute (*http://www.roswellpark.org*) and the City of Buffalo, New York (*http://www.city-buffalo.com*). David also guides the requirements analysis, estimating, project management, design, and software engineering processes for Algonquin Studios (*http://algonquinstudios.com*), a software consulting firm with more than 150 clients spread across Upstate New York, North America, and the globe. David is Vice President of Technology and a co-founder of the firm. Algonquin Studios performs Content Management Software and Consulting, Translation and Localization Services and Software, Enterprise Application Development, Web and Print Design Services, Web Site Implementation, and Coding and E-Commerce services. David orchestrates solutions with the Microsoft technology framework to ease transferring solution ownership to clients.

David earned a combined B.S. degree in Electrical and Computer Engineering and a B.S. in Computer Science from Carnegie Mellon University while acting as a software engineer for CMU projects with ABB and Daimler-Benz (now DaimlerChrysler).

Table of Contents

Introduction   **1**

    Who's This Book For?   2
    Style Conventions   2
    Support/Feedback   3
    Web Support   3

Chapter 1: Foundations of CMS   **5**

Defining the Problem   **5**
    Web Sites Are Hard Work   6
    The Root Problems   9
    How This Book Can Help   10
    Why Don't People Use Content Management?   10

Defining Content Management   **12**
    The Activities of Content Management   12

Principles of Content Management   **17**
    Anticipate Growth   17
    Don't Shortcut the Process   18
    Plan for Change   18
    Build On Standards   20
    Separation of Content and Design   21

Chapter 2: CMS Map: Asset Management   **27**

What Is Asset Management?   **28**

Understanding What You Already Have: Taking Stock   **29**
    Content Inventory   29
    Content from Non-Web Sources   34

Understanding What You Want To Do With It: Workflow   **35**
    The Existing Process   36
    Changing the Process   37
    Streamlining the Process   40
    Security   40
    Feedback Loop   41

Understanding How To Get There: The Enablers   **41**
    Metadata   42
    Reusable Data   45

Building New Assets   **46**
    Authors: Not a Dirty Word   47
    The User Interface or the Client Tool   48

Chapter 3: CMS Map: Transformation   55

Visual Design   56
Assess the Situation: Look At What You Did Before   56
Deriving Need   58
How Cool Is Too Cool?   58

Templates: Designing from a New Point of View   59
Template Basics   60
How Many Templates?   64
Template Patterns   65
Updating Templates   67

Content vs. Presentation   68

Thinking About Your Users   69
Everything They Said About Usability Is Right   70
Everything They Said About Usability Is Wrong   72

Chapter 4: CMS Map: Publishing   75

What Do We Publish?   75

Rendering Sequence   78
Opposing Endpoints on a Continuous Line   79
Points In-Between   80

Publishing: a Team, an Act, and a System   82
Different Requirements from Authoring   82
Operating a Production Environment   86

Publish To More Than Just Web Browsers   89
Scenarios for Content   89
Templates and Transformations for Publishing   91

Learn from Publishing   93
Hard Evidence of Who Uses Your Site   93
Monitor Use   93
Understanding Use   94

Chapter 5: Buying a CMS   99

Why Buy?   99

The Purchase Process   100
A Big Document Full of Questions   100
Show and Tell   101
Don't Think Out of the Box   101
Don't Believe the Hype   102
Proving the Concept   102
Your Role in the Purchase Process   102

Questions You Must Ask: The BDFQ   102
Asset Management   103
Transformation   110
Publishing   114

Licensing and Implementation Costs   **119**
License vs. Implementation   119
Think About the Future   121
CMS Service Partnerships   122

Chapter 6: Building a CMS   **125**
Why Build?   **125**
Are You Prepared?   **127**
Picking the Right Team   127
Choosing the Right Technology   129
Defining a Product Roadmap   **133**
Asset Management: 133
Transformation: 139
Publishing: 144

Chapter 7: Implementation   **149**
It's a Game of Two Halves   **149**
Reasons for CMS Implementation   150
Roles and Responsibilities   150
Concept Phase   **153**
Budgeting   153
Concept Phase Timeline   153
The SIS Document   155
Production Phase   **166**
Pre-Production   166
Production   167
Post-Production   168

Chapter 8: Migration   **171**
The Problem with Migration   **171**
Before You Start   **172**
Take Stock of What You Have   172
Content Review Document   173
Keeping the Style Consistent   175
Think Global, Act Local   177
About the Author   178
Migrating the Content   **180**
When Can I Start?   180
Let's Go To Work   180
Picture Perfect   181
It's Better with Meta   181
Winding Down Your Old Site   183
Are We Nearly There Yet?   **185**
Going Live with the New System   185

Index   **189**

Introduction

Content Management Systems (or CMS) are becoming a much talked about topic amongst web professionals.

In mid 1993 the Web consisted of around a hundred web sites serving, at most, a few thousand pages. Less than ten years later, Google Inc. (*http://www.google.com*) can claim to have indexed over two billion standard web pages using its search engine, the "Googlebot". This, in itself, is a telling statistic, since it takes no account of the number of additional pages that the regular "Googlebot" cannot access because they are locked within company LANs and off-line archives.

As this rising tide of content and potential content on the Web continues unabated, web professionals are more aware than ever of the need to maintain this resource. There is an urgent need to fix the emerging bottlenecks in the content publication process before the flow of new material becomes overwhelming. For this reason, content management is often quoted as the Holy Grail of web publishing.

However, definitions of what "content management" actually means can often seem unnecessarily vague. There are few clear-cut descriptions of what it actually involves, and the numerous vendors of proprietary CMS solutions do not help by offering their own slightly different answers to the problem.

Beneath this apparent confusion, however, structure *does* exist. This book will bring this structure to you.

In Chapter 1, we talk about the reasons why you may have a web content problem and how some form of content management system could be your solution. The actual process of content management is split into three activities – **Asset Management**, **Transformation**, and **Publishing** – to which Chapters 2, 3, and 4 are then dedicated.

By the halfway point in the book, you will have a thorough understanding of the key features of content management.

After the theory, we turn to the practicalities of content management. There are two main ways to go about acquiring a CMS solution: you can either **buy one in**, or **build your own**. In Chapters 5 and 6, we cover both possibilities in detail, to help you make an informed decision about which way to turn.

Once you have either built or bought your CMS solution, however, the work is far from over. It needs to be implemented for your particular organization's needs. Chapters 7 and 8 cover this process of **implementing** the CMS and **migrating** your existing content to your new system.

Who's This Book For?

Content management will mean different things to different people within an organization, be they the content creators, those who approve and edit the content, the ones who build and implement the system, or those who hold the purse strings. Depending on the size and strategies of the company, each of these people will have a different role to play in the process of providing a company with a CMS solution.

This book is aimed primarily at **web professionals**, but may also be of interest to anyone within an organization thinking of implementing a CMS solution.

You may be called upon at the decision-making stage to answer questions such as what CMS requirements exist, whether to build a bespoke system or buy one in, and, if necessary, what system should be bought. If your organization decides to construct their own system, you may be involved in actually building it. Either way, you are likely to be involved in the implementation and migration of your business to the new system. Our aim here is to provide you with enough background information for you to be confident with this process, whatever role you end up playing.

The book is light on actual code. We don't claim to provide you with a code tutorial on how to build your own CMS solution, and it would be unrealistic of us to assert that we could do so. We will, however, provide real-world advice for web professionals faced with implementing a CMS, based on genuine, qualified experience.

Style Conventions

We've used a number of styles in the book to help you understand what's going on.

We've used a bold style to flag up **new or important subjects**.

This *italic style* is used to indicate anything you'd see on the screen, including URLs, and also book titles.

To talk about code within text or to give filenames, we use this `code style`.

Essential not-to-be-missed details are found in boxes like this.

Asides to the current discussion are presented like this.

Perspectives on particular topics are displayed like this. They usually contain additional material on the current topic, often incorporating the author's own point of view.

Support/Feedback

Although we aim for perfection, the sad fact of book publication is that a few errors inevitably slip through. We would like to apologize for any errors that have survived our best efforts. If you spot such an error, please let us know about it using the e-mail address support@glasshaus.com. If it's something that will help other readers, then we'll put it up on the errata page for this book on our site: *http://www.glasshaus.com*.

This e-mail address can also be used to access our support network. If you have questions about any of the content in this book, please e-mail your problem to us quoting the title of the book, the last four digits of its ISBN (106X in this case), and the chapter and page number of your query.

Web Support

Feel free to visit our web site, at *http://www.glasshaus.com*. It features:

Downloads

The example code for every glasshaus book can be downloaded from our site. In the case of this title, there is no code as such to download. Instead, we provide a useful download of the questions to ask vendors when evaluating their CMS products, as discussed in more detail in Chapter 5.

Online Resource Center

Some books contain code examples that we show working on the site in *Galleries*. For example, for our *Usable Web Menus* title (ISBN 1904151027), the sample menu systems are shown as code you can copy and actual working examples. Feel free to browse this area and use any examples you like.

We will also be building up a definitive reference section on our site, containing all the up-to-date reference material that you'll need. We've decided to put this material on the Web rather than weighing down our books with hefty appendices. It will be added to over time, so if there is anything you feel isn't up there, but should be, please let us know.

1

- The Problems Content Management Can Overcome

- The Three Activities: Asset Management, Transformation, and Publishing

- Principles of Content Management

Author: Phil Suh

Foundations of CMS

Defining the Problem

Shhhh. As we peer through the window, we can see a figure hunched over a computer across the room. There is a steady drumming noise, like the rat-tat-tat of a machine gun. As our eyes adjust to the dim light, we can see the blur of fingers dancing across the keyboard.

Finally, the typist leans back, yawns, and stretches. Then she grabs a pack of cigarettes off the desk, and heads out of the far door. This is our chance. We slip into the room. There is the bookshelf of web design books, arranged by the color of their spines. Printouts of HTML code and e-mails, and a stack of CDs clutter the desk. Dilbert cartoons adorn the side of the monitor. On the wall, a large whiteboard is covered with boxes and arrows and scribbled lists: "Need to fix: broken links, search, left navigation…" A URL in bold lettering is splashed across the top, followed by a colon, and in all caps, the word 'RELAUNCH'. Next to the whiteboard is a large calendar with a big red circle; some sort of deadline next week.

We look, finally, at the monitor. The cursor blinks in an e-mail window, and we can read the last few paragraphs of a long, rambling rant. The sentences are sharp, bitter, and weary. I print out the e-mail – that's all the evidence we need: another confirmed sighting of the increasingly stressed, beleaguered, web professional.

Back at the office, you read over the e-mail. It's a sad, familiar story. "If only I had a dollar for every developer I saw suffering like this," you say.

"If only I had a dime for every broken link on her site," I reply. We get to work on our report.

Web Sites Are Hard Work

I'll start with a statement:

> The care and feeding of the average web site has grown (and keeps growing) far beyond the capability of most web professionals to handle on their own.

This is not necessarily a bad thing – it means that there is demand for the work that we do. While it's not exactly job security, it is nice to be needed. However, the days of a lone webmaster wrangling all aspects of a web site are long behind us.

Even if you think you have been doing a pretty good job of managing your web site up till now, web sites will continue to be challenging work, at least for the foreseeable future. Let's explore the reasons why.

Tidal Wave of New Content

The amount of content that your group or company wants to make available on the Web will continue to grow. Old content doesn't die; it just goes into the archives. And the spread of technology means that the tools to create content – music, video, and plain old-fashioned text – have become ubiquitous. Like it or not, people have always had the will to communicate and now they have the means. Your job is to get it up on the Web.

"But my web site is small", you say. And here's where I respond with one of my aphorisms: **inside every small web site is a huge web site struggling to get out**. There is probably a lot more content that your company or group wants to get up onto the Web, if it could.

Some of you may be skeptical and unwilling to take my little truism to heart, so let's do some math. How many authors do you have? How many items (news, press releases, short tidbits, calendar events, articles, etc.) does each author create or change per month?

- 3 authors @ 5 items a month: 15 updates a month; 180 per year.

- 5 authors @ 10 items a month: 50 updates a month; 600 per year.

- 100 authors @ 12 items a month: 1200 updates a month; 14,400 per year.

If we assume that we will continue to have more authors, posting on average the same amount of content, the curve of the graph will continue to go up, year on year.

It's not uncommon for sites created just three or four years ago to have more than fifty thousand pages. University web sites, with their sprawl of student and faculty publications, easily range upwards of one hundred thousand pages. Today's businesses are incredibly information intense. Corporate intranets can often have page counts in the millions.

There is no doubt that the amount of content will continue to grow. The only real question is whether you will be able to keep up with the load, the way you work now. If not, it's time to start thinking strategically and develop a plan to coordinate the production of the site.

An Ever-Changing World

Time doesn't stand still. A number of external factors make developing web sites more and more challenging. As we wait for final approval on the press release copy, technology presses on. Browser upgrades, plug-in incompatibilities, new wireless platforms, and the latest W3C recommendations come raining down. It's difficult to keep up with it all – let alone implement best practices for your web site.

When web sites carry information that is more current than other media, it can change the flow of information in an organization. Previously, some web sites may simply have duplicated print publications in an online form. Now, those web sites drive the production of print documents. One site may now export the company's print product catalogue; another may produce the documents that an integrated voice response system reads to telephone callers.

Although this book is very web-focused, content management should not be applied to web sites alone. There are many paths and destinations for content, and your content management system should be able to support the paths and platforms you choose. Technology changes the way an organization creates and manages content – it has also expanded the scope of the web development team, and raised the bar for the web professional.

Sometimes change forces its way onto your site. A search engine upgrade or adding a personalization feature to the site may have a wide impact. For instance, converting every HTML file on the site to a Java Server Page (JSP) could cause a few late nights.

As your company moves into new endeavors, it may run across new legal requirements in disclosing information about their products. A contract with a government agency may impose stricter accessibility requirements on your web site. Financial regulations may require certain types of disclaimers to be added to product pages. In manufacturing shops, ISO-9000-compliance requires you be able to roll back your product sheets to earlier revisions.

Your organization may begin expanding its reach around the world and your web sites need to reflect this new diversity of language and culture. Being able to manage web sites in different languages, different currencies, and different cultures will certainly impact how you develop and plan a web site.

Increased Expectations

There is always a demand for new features or changes. Managers want to add press releases. Designers want to refresh the look and feel of the site. Usability experts want to fix the navigation. The legal section is talking about compliance to new accessibility laws. The backend geeks are suggesting an application server and new database for reliability. Finally, the CEO wants the logo to "do a rollover and match my favorite tie" (we're trying hard to ignore him).

Users, too, are becoming accustomed to features they've seen elsewhere – on sites like Yahoo (*www.yahoo.com*) or Amazon (*www.amazon.com*), for instance. They have higher expectations, in terms of clear site navigation and a comprehensive search facility to find what they are looking for. They want to see what is new, what is popular, and what is relevant to them.

While the expectations rise and rise, the time frames get shorter and shorter. If we're going to keep up, we're going to have to utilize the best tools and processes available to us.

Success can raise expectations as well. A web site that launches and gets an enthusiastic response from its target audience can often propel an organization to create more web sites. You may find yourself creating multiple sites, with the requirement that they share content and stay in sync. The technical challenges have increased substantially, and the organization still expects the same or better rollout of the new sites.

The truth is, maintaining and growing web sites is hard work. It's not getting any easier. And web professionals and the organizations they work for are feeling the pain.

The Litany of Pain

Let's take a look at the main problems that plague web sites and, by extension, their authors, web professionals, and users. The effects are often cumulative and may follow the course we'll outline here.

Bottlenecks

First, there are bottlenecks caused because each new page of the web site has to be touched by someone. Say, the page is manually coded into HTML. Templates help, a little, but the number of new pages being asked for guarantees that the HTML coder runs the risk of becoming a bottleneck, falling further and further behind schedule.

Unintended Responsibilities

These bottlenecks create an unintended and undesirable social side-effect. As content contributors wait for you to update their content, they begin to understand that they don't control the site; you, as the site manager, do. They begin to perceive the web site as your sole responsibility and not theirs. Once they begin to identify the site as "Somebody Else's Problem", they become less inclined to contribute to it, or help fix it. Suddenly you, as the site manager, are not only responsible for the technical development of the site, but for its content.

This has disastrous consequences. If you are micro-editing/correcting the content of the site, you'll never get through the backlog of page production. You'll never have the breathing space to think strategically and tackle the more interesting, compelling problems. Worst of all, your authors will feel isolated from the site, and you'll lose the interest and support of the group of people you most need in order to make it a success.

Stale Content

As the backlog of HTML pages grows, the content that's already up on the site gets old and "stale". Updates to the home page become less frequent, so people stop checking it. Information never gets updated, so the data on the web site is deemed unreliable. People start bypassing the site altogether. You find HR sending out the new vacation policy to everyone in the company as a Word attachment because it's easier than waiting for a web page to be updated.

When the marketing folks want to change the design of the site, the web team will tend to dig in their heels. They're behind as it is, and don't have the time. Even simple site design changes can be painful, requiring a couple of weeks of overtime from the team. Of course, during that time, it's nearly impossible to do regular site updates. Your Perl guy is laboriously tweaking the script he wrote, changing "*Register*" to "*Sign up*" on every page of the site.

Inconsistency

The Perl guy is worried because he knows the site is inconsistent. There's been a succession of programmers, who all preferred their own tools and have their own coding styles. Different areas of the site handle navigation slightly differently and the site doesn't feel cohesive.

There's always one person on any team who can recite the history of their web site. "This," they may say, "works weirdly because we hired that one contractor before the Christmas redesign two years ago..." There were 'good' reasons at the time why short cuts were taken, and corners cut, but the team just never had the time to go back and clean up. So the site struggles on, somehow working, but underneath it's a patchwork of hacks.

The inconsistency isn't always hidden behind the scenes. A company's brand identity often suffers online. Without a web-oriented style guide and a template system that enforces it, the presentation of the company brand can be distorted by business users whose expertise is in content, not in managing and protecting the brand.

There is another reason for inconsistency. Often the site grows piecemeal, with different groups within the organization publishing subsections in an ad hoc manner. Little fiefdoms of power emerge, and there is a lack of clear leadership.

Low Quality

The inconsistency ultimately manifests itself as a **Low quality** site. This has two separate effects:

- The site just doesn't look good or work well – reflecting poorly on your team and your organization. It's not fulfilling its potential to communicate, and this translates, in the language of the bean counters, into poor return on investment (ROI).

- The site is no fun to work on. Low quality hurts the morale of your web team. If they don't feel that they are working on something that is inherently worthwhile, then it is hard for them to care about it, and if your web team doesn't care about the quality of the site, who will?

Inefficiency and Inflexibility

All the above problems add up to a site that is difficult to maintain. Its fragility makes its owners (rightly) fearful that it will break, so they hesitate to make improvements. Time is spent fixing broken links and tweaking design, page by page, that could be better spent elsewhere.

A brief example: I once consulted with the web team of a large, high-profile web site. Posted on the wall was a chart where they tracked the number of broken links (found using third-party link-checking tools). They had a campaign to scour the site and fix these links by hand. I took this to be a **bad** sign. While they should be applauded for doing their best to fix problems on the site, it was a terribly inefficient way for the team to be spending their time. Yet without a content management system in place, this is what they had to resort to.

The Root Problems

We've looked at the reasons why web sites are hard work, and the problems behind them, but *why* do these problems arise?

The root cause of many of these symptoms is that the site uses a **handcrafted approach**, which **doesn't scale to bigger teams or larger amounts of content**. In the Internet Age many of us are still, curiously, using production techniques from an earlier era.

Coding pages in HTML by hand is a useful skill. In some cases, it approaches an art. However, coding *every page* in HTML by hand is a tremendously inefficient and unpleasant way to spend your working days. Manual production of web sites is a leftover from a simpler era (1994) and it doesn't make sense for a modern production site.

Those of us who've spent so much of our creative energy in building the Web may be uncomfortable with applying Industrial Age automation techniques to our web sites. After all, doesn't it cheapen and devalue the skills we've developed, and isn't there a danger that we'll be replaced by machines? The short answer is that automation hopefully will lighten your load of monotonous, repetitive work, and free you to plan and implement redesigns.

A notable legacy of this handcrafted approach is **inter-dependency between design, code, and content.** Most often this is because, early on in the web site's life, one or two people did everything. Today, this is seldom the case. While core web development teams are still small, successful developers work alongside writers, editors, designers, and production artists to create their web sites. The effort is larger, more collaborative, and more complicated.

When design, code, and content are mixed together, it becomes extremely difficult to manage or change them independently of one another. If your web team audibly groans when a redesign effort is announced, it's probably because they intuitively understand that the process will be slow, painful, and error-prone. But a redesign should not require weekends of hand coding. Although it takes more effort to keep content and design separate, the payoff during the eventual site redesign is well worth it.

Another legacy of the handcrafted approach is **lack of a production process**. There is little need for a process when you are the only one working on the site, but the instant you start working with others (developers and content authors, for instance) you need to define a process and have the tools in place to enforce that process.

Finally, **no site can thrive unless there is a clear vision of its message and audience**. While not a technical problem, lack of strategy and direction influences the quality of the technology, content, and design choices made throughout. Let me rephrase: if you don't know what you want, you're not going to get it, but you will waste a lot of time, effort, and money trying to do so.

How This Book Can Help

It's no fun to work on a web site that doesn't work. This book is about how to stop the hurting. It proposes that a philosophy, methodology, and practice known as **content management** will provide web professionals with hope for their projects, and the pride of shaping a web site that not only works, but is continually getting better and better.

Content management applies technology to automate the most tedious parts of the old handcrafted approach. It helps you define a system for maintaining your site designs separately from your server code, which is kept separate from the content created by your authors. It provides the means and the opportunity to make your site into what you want it to be: usable, attractive, localized, accessible, fast, and up-to-date.

Our task in these pages is to explain what content management is, and how to apply basic principles of content management to your web site. Ultimately, I hope to help you make good choices about content management.

Why Don't People Use Content Management?

In the next section, we'll define what content management is, but let's just pause to ask ourselves why more people don't have content management systems in place already.

A Leap in the Dark

Committing to a particular content management strategy is somewhat akin to getting married, in that, hopefully, the choice will work for a lifetime. An organization may be inexperienced with content management, however, so they have to commit to a substantial relationship without understanding exactly how it will impact them.

It's Hard To Change

It takes effort, courage, and money to change the way things work. Frankly, although people understand that the changes need to be made, the status quo is preferable to an uncertain future.

Planning and implementing content management is a high-level strategic activity. Selecting a content management package is perceived to be a job for CTOs or the heads of the IT department, largely because of the high cost of the tools and because these are the people such tools are marketed at. Additionally, many web professionals are so busy trying to stay afloat that they don't have the time to consider a content management system.

However, as a web professional, you'll often have the best view of the challenges and impact content management will have, so don't be afraid to speak up and help shape the decisions about content management. No matter what happens, a content management system will impact your work significantly, and it's best to get your input in at the start.

Content management affects many people in an organization. Getting all of those people moving in the same direction and working together is hard work. The impact on the organization is often not widely understood – depending on your goals, it's possible that everyone in the company will be affected.

The Market is Confusing and Immature

For those who have decided to buy a solution, there are many vendors trying to carve out a niche in this growing market. Many agencies that have written a CMS for a client are now packaging it as a product. Some of these are nowhere near 'product' quality, and those that are industry leaders are, in many cases, only there because they made the jump early.

It is difficult to compare the content management products available because of the widespread use of jargon, buzzwords, and marketing babble. While there are some basic similarities, the approach and metaphors used by one software product often do not match precisely those of another. Content management tools may only implement a portion of a full content management strategy, but market themselves as a full end-to-end solution. This confusing and complex marketplace leaves customers frustrated, quite rightly.

There is also trepidation about picking a product that will be a winner. In uncertain economic times, in such a competitive, untested marketplace, it is hard even to know who will be around next year. We have yet to see which companies will do well and survive, and which will fade away.

Products are also distributed unevenly. Products available in Europe may not have support in the US, while support for CMS products throughout Asia is generally weak.

Content management vendors are on an uneven footing when it comes to advertising their products. The big vendors can afford to saturate the market with advertising (one prominent US vendor sponsors the replay at my local ice hockey arena). Smaller products – even if they have a reasonable feature set and price/performance ratio – are often lost in the noise of the market. It's hard for vendors to differentiate themselves.

Furthermore, the vendors are experimenting with all sorts of business models. Some license their products per server or per CPU; I've even seen a license based on the total CPU speed in megahertz. Others have a base server fee on top of which they charge per-seat costs. Furthermore, per-seat costs may be based on concurrent users or include a separate fee for developers and administrators.

11

There are open-source consultancies that charge for significant professional services. Other products have a hybrid open-source model – they still charge for their product, but you do have access to all the sourcecode, and they have an explicitly open development model. Then there are application service providers, who will host a CMS for you that they have built or licensed from a vendor.

The result is that licensing costs are difficult to compare. (The one common license element I've seen from commercial vendors is a yearly maintenance and support fee that averages about 20% of the initial license fee.)

Content Management Can Be Complex

Ultimately, the practice of content management is about getting disparate parts working together. Those disparate parts are both the people involved – authors, editors, and developers – and the technology that supports them. Content management is a group activity, and requires collaboration to succeed. Putting in place a technology infrastructure that will support that collaboration is non-trivial. It requires coordination across disciplines.

In many organizations such inter-departmental cooperation is unheard of. And even though this is a failing of the organization and not one of content management, this is the situation into which content management may well be introduced.

Content management is also complex because it tries to prepare us for an uncertain future. There is no guarantee that we will use the same browsers and systems to view our content in the future. The compromises that need to be made between preparing for the future and still getting something that works today (and on today's budget) are not easy to make, and sorting through the various options can be complicated.

Defining Content Management

Most people encountering the term *content management* for the first time are confused by the various definitions. In some ways the expression has completely lost meaning, because it's used by so many different products to mean (often) completely different things.

It is probably best to think of content management as a broad concept that covers all aspects of publishing content with digital tools. But a 'broad concept' does not begin to approach a definition that we can understand and use.

The Activities of Content Management

Content management can be defined more precisely in terms of activity: it is appropriate to ask, "What do I need to do to manage my content?"

In its simplest form, content management does just three things:

- **Asset Management**: Organizing units of content

- **Transformation**: Presenting that content

- **Publishing**: Delivering the content to your audience

Personally, I call each unit of content an **asset**. Day in and day out, we *create* and *manage* these assets. In order to get those bits that seem worth broadcasting to a wider audience published, we submit them to a process I call **asset management**, which formalizes and prepares the assets for the next steps.

> Don't confuse asset management as used here with Digital Asset Management (DAM) which is a usually refers to the cataloging and storage of multimedia – movies, audio, and high quality photographs.

Once we have some content assets available, we then make choices about how to present that content. Usually we have some sort of design, and we attempt to shoehorn our content into those design templates. Indeed, most people refer to this process as **templating**, but I prefer the words **content transformation**. "Clothes make the man", the saying goes, and I think that the right application of design to content does more than just make it look attractive; it enhances its effectiveness and impact.

Once we have created the right content, and dressed it properly, all that remains is to *deliver* the message. This **publishing** step considers our audience and makes sure that the content is available to them, in whatever formats they may need (HTML, WAP, database feeds, for example) for various devices (browsers, wireless devices, or legacy systems). This phase is primarily technical and logistical. It deals with getting the transformed content out to the intended audience. This might mean deploying static web pages, or updating a content database for an application server. The publishing phase is heavily impacted by the choices made in the previous two activities: we either enjoy the fruits of our labor or learn from our mistakes.

While the focus of this book is on web site development, content management has benefits for all possible output formats. A well-implemented content management tool can become a company's primary system for publishing to print, web, CD-ROM, and wireless platforms.

One thing to note: as you progress from asset management to transformation and finally to publishing, progressively fewer and fewer people are involved in the process, while at the same time the level of technical knowledge needed by these individuals increases.

These three activities will form the basis of the following three chapters (Chapters 2, 3, and 4), where we will explore them in more depth.

Workflow

The glue between the human processes and the technical infrastructure of content management is known as **workflow**.

> Workflow is a predefined series of tasks that facilitates the progression of content assets through the asset management, transformation, and publishing activities.

Workflow makes human processes explicit and systematic. For example, your organization decides that authors will have their work checked by an editor, who then sends it to be approved by the legal department, after which it is published. Workflow simply codifies that process.

Content management tools have a variety of approaches to workflow. But the basics are the same: the application of *rules* on *users* and *tasks* to enforce a process.

While the basics are the same, they will be applied differently in each organization. It's important to have a workflow tool that is flexible enough to accommodate your needs. Needless to say, if you don't have a process defined, or don't understand the process, no amount of workflow tools will help you.

It's important to realize that workflow extends outside the world of content management. Content management may just be a small subset of tasks inside a much longer and more complicated workflow in your business.

A good workflow tool will automate the mundane reminders that shepherd the content assets through the entire process. It will generate a log so that we understand what is going on, what the status of each content item is, and where the (often human) bottlenecks exist.

Technical Infrastructure

Every content management tool is structured slightly differently, but the basics are the same.

Users typically add content via a **browser-based interface**. This interface often mirrors the look and feel of the web site, and provides rich text editing capabilities. The interface also allows users to edit existing content, look at and compare versions of content, and to approve content for publication – all the activities of asset management are handled within this interface.

There are other ways to add content. Some systems offer integration with desktop applications such as Microsoft Word or Macromedia Dreamweaver, for instance, while others provide a custom client-side application – either for a richer editing environment, or for administrative tasks. An **application programming interface** (API) may also allow technical users to add or manipulate content that is stored in the repository, via scripts.

That **repository** can take many forms: a database, a closed file system, or a mixture of both. It can even be a virtual repository – one interface to numerous backend data sources. The repository stores both the content and any associated metadata.

Metadata provides information about the content. For instance, common metadata values would be the author of the content, the date it was created, the date to publish it, and the date it expires. Metadata provides context to the content and enables the content management tool to deliver more precise searches, generate topic-based navigation, create links to related pages, and track workflow status.

A **template engine** applies design elements to content, in order to produce the desired output document. The templates themselves usually contain placeholders for content from the repository. More powerful schemes can allow inline code to be interpreted in the templates. While more flexible, they are also more complex.

Link management refers to how the tool tracks and maintains internal links and site navigation. Sometimes this is driven by an internally maintained glossary of unique content IDs. Other systems handle it by referring to a user-created **site structure**, which is also used to create navigation. The site structure is simply the hierarchy of files and folders within your web site. (This can be a logical hierarchy, or physical.) Much is made of the separation of design and content; structure is also an element of your web site that needs to be maintained.

The site is then **published** and deployed. Publishing can occur ahead of time, that is, pages are created statically (a more colorful term for this is '**baking**'), and then deployed to the server. The dynamic approach (called '**frying**') is in reverse: content is first deployed to the server (probably to a database). Then, when a request for a web page is received, the template engine is invoked to apply the design. The difference is primarily in server load and administration: a dynamic server requires more processing power, but is useful for presenting constantly changing or frequently updated content.

Workflow helps manage the flow of content through this technical structure, and makes sure that the human structure approves and is aware of what happens throughout. **Version control** helps people track changes to the content, providing a safety net to roll back changes. The administrator can assign users and groups to certain roles and actions: this is sometimes referred to as **user access control levels** (ACL).

Products that offer this technical infrastructure are commonly referred to as **content management systems** (**CMS**).

Tools or Systems?

The term "content management system" is often used generically to refer to products that offer the basic technical infrastructure: a repository, template engine, and an asset management interface. However, it is sometimes useful to draw a distinction between the tools or products and the broader context – or system – in which those tools operate.

We'll discuss such tools, and the process of buying and building them, in Chapters 5 and 6

You may want to think of the products that are marketed as "content management systems", as **content management tools** (or **CMS tools**). Making this distinction leaves room for a broader definition of content management systems themselves as the organizational context in which the activity of content management occurs. It has three qualities:

It Occurs in the Business Environment

The surrounding environment includes the business' goals, company culture, and the decision-making processes. Content management does, in some ways, reflect the people who undertake the activity. It does not happen in a "clean room".

This has a couple of corollaries. First, content management is **a people-centric activity**. In the broadest sense, as organizations and people, we use web sites to communicate. While that communication is not the same as speaking on the phone or writing a letter, it is, ultimately, person-to-person communication. Content management is about facilitating the technical aspects of this type of communication.

The second corollary is that content management is also **a people-intensive activity**. Although the focus is often on the technology and the products, the aim is to apply that technology to help people get their jobs done faster and more efficiently.

In this book we will examine the technology, but we also talk about our experience with applying technology to real human problems. This means that you'll need to train people, and explain what the content management product you purchase or build does. You'll need to set expectations, and you may have to do some internal evangelism.

Successful content management implementations always take account of the human aspect.

It Is a Set of Processes

The processes involved marry and merge the human and the technical. While most vendors would have you believe that their technology can solve all your content management problems, the nature of the problem is such that a product on its own cannot solve the problems you may have with your people processes.

In any organization, there are agreements about how to get work done. Content management is no different – it is an agreement between people. An agreement or contract concerning how things get done is not new to business or programming. But in content management the agreement has to be more explicit and the enforcement of the process needs to be programmed into the workflow.

This workflow enforcement can also change the nature of the agreement. In many cases this can be an improvement – a simpler process can emerge, for example. In other cases, the technical enforcement of a poorly conceived workflow serves merely to calcify it.

Business processes change all the time. Once workflow is introduced, and people rely on it, it's important that the workflow reflects the current business agreements. It follows that accurate, flexible workflow tools are a must.

It Is an Infrastructure

This infrastructure supports the many mundane tasks of content management. For instance, reminding people to submit content, approving the content, and pasting it into a template. By using tools to automate as much of that as possible, we can support the most important aspects of content management and allow people to work at a higher level.

Authors can focus on what they write, rather than on waiting for a production person to make changes for them. Designers can think about site navigation, usability, and redesigns, rather than tedious, repetitive HTML coding. Developers can tweak the system for performance and improve their code, rather than getting called in to fix a broken deployment of the site.

Premeditation

Despite what the sales people will tell you, content management cannot be installed as an option, with some new piece of software. Planning is the key to successful content management, and you can't buy planning in a box. Content management is a **deliberate** process. This may seem obvious, but let me just make it clear that you *have* to plan.

Planning involves:

- Thinking about and identifying what your problems are

- Listing what is needed to solve these problems

- Developing a process to move forward and meet your requirements

It consists of knowledge of the issues, and a philosophy of how to handle problems. It implies some understanding of technology, and how to apply that knowledge to solve problems.

Implementing content management requires lots of choices. Do you buy a product, or build your own? How much training will be necessary? Which technology approach is the best fit for your organization?

From your plan will emerge a requirements document describing what your needs are, and a process to guide you. The actual choices of content management will then be much clearer.

As I said earlier, we'll spend an entire section of this book looking at the three activities of content management, but before we do, we'll spend some time talking about the philosophy of content management.

Principles of Content Management

Many people approaching content management for the first time ask what features a particular CMS product has. In my opinion, that is the wrong place to start. Every organization has different needs, so every content management system is going to be different. Your choice should be driven by your needs, not what you may be able to do with your own or some third-party piece of software.

Comparing content management systems is not like comparing different models of cars – it's more akin to evaluating different modes of transport, such as an airplane, a bus, or a train. These are different ways of getting you to where you are going and your choice is based on things like where you are now, how far you have to go, and when you need to be there.

While each web site will have different requirements, there are some general principles to help guide us as we search for the right system. These are:

- Anticipate growth: be ready to cope with huge amounts of content

- Don't shortcut the process: content management is not a product, but a journey that takes time

- Plan for change: architect the system for flexibility

- Build on standards: don't reinvent the wheel

- Keep content separate from design: work upstream from integration areas

We'll take a quick look at these now – the ideas will be expanded upon in future chapters.

Anticipate Growth

As mentioned earlier, one of the challenges for web professionals is the growing quantity of content on their web sites. Not every web site will become large, and many don't need to, but the potential is always there. Web professionals who recognize that potential also plan for it.

Anticipating growth means exchanging the minute-to-minute handcrafted HTML coding for a production content management system. Good content management tools will improve upon the by-hand page production of the past, and eliminate production bottlenecks.

Create templates that work well with your content management system. Balance the desire to customize each page's look and feel with the imperative to reuse templates as much as possible for efficiency and consistency. Relish the challenge of creating visually fresh templates, but always design for both reuse and flexibility. Think about how a constantly growing body of content will impact navigation design elements, for instance.

Smart web professionals know it's not possible to anticipate everything. So they monitor their progress, and regularly do an inventory to take stock of their web site. They view the server logs. They talk to the content contributors who use the CMS tools. They regularly evaluate the health of their content management tools and the way people use it. They watch to make sure that as the site grows, it can still be managed easily.

Content management tools require care and feeding. Make sure that colleagues who contribute content understand how to use these tools. Spend time gaining an understanding of how each tool works, so that you can exploit its strengths and account for its inevitable weaknesses. As the site grows and the number of users increase, you will have to make constant adjustments to keep things running smoothly.

Don't Shortcut the Process

Content management is a process, not a product. It is about getting people to work together, and it takes time and sustained effort to coordinate people.

With this principle in mind, what can we do?

Avoid Expecting Instant Results

Understand that this does take time. And make sure you let everyone who will be impacted know what to expect. Tell them that change will occur, that there will be a somewhat painful adjustment period, but that things will get better. It's best to communicate this early and often.

Keep the Vision Alive

Life is hectic, and it is hard to keep long-term goals in mind. It is easy to get sidetracked in the pursuit of, say, the quarterly sales figures. Spend some time with your boss or an ally in a position of influence who understands (or can be taught) what content management is, and why it is important. This will be an immense help to you as you make decisions about which products to purchase or build.

Be skeptical about products that force you to change your current process completely. Going cold turkey is a great way to send your organization into shock and to ruin your chances of success in the long-term. Forgive me for being a little cynical, but when was the last time you installed a multi-user software package and had everything work correctly the first time?

Fortunately, content management is a practice that provides practical benefits, so be sure to keep reminding people of those benefits. Keep them motivated and **track your success**. As the content management effort proceeds, it helps to be able to tell stories like: "It used to take twelve burly men three long days to publish this content, but now I can do it by pressing this small orange button." Given that the process of managing and publishing web content in most organizations is simply awful, the upside is that the potential for improvement is enormous.

Take It in Easy Stages

When you line up all of the content management challenges in an organization, they can make quite a daunting list. Adapt a strategy that allows you to make changes in an iterative manner and allow for small adjustments along the way. Try to start with the low-hanging fruit by finding the largest points of pain in the system and fixing them first. Don't expect everything to work right the first time. As you learn from your mistakes, apply that knowledge to the next portion of the project.

Plan for Change

For better or worse, the world has changed dramatically in the past few years. Technology has driven a fair portion of that change. However, technical projects are usually impacted most by changes in the business climate, new legal requirements or the turnover in staff and the changing structure of your teams.

Planning for the future *is* planning for change. Our challenge then, is to design and build systems that can survive change.

Examine Your Assumptions

It seems prudent not to assume too much about the future. It is perhaps wise to take a moment to examine our current assumptions.

We put a lot of effort into creating web sites these days. This assumes that the primary vehicle for the content we publish is the web browser and that the primary technology we use for publishing will continue to be the web server (the HTTP protocol). In five or ten years, will we still be using HTTP and the web browser? Probably, but on the other hand, will it be the *primary* delivery platform for our data? Perhaps not: by then, there may be another preferred networked experience.

While the web browser is not going to disappear overnight, it's instructive to think about what would happen if it did. Would you be able to shift your content to a new format? How difficult would it be? What changes to your content format, or to your template system would make this easier?

Of course, our content management system must serve our needs today. It's impossible to plan for every contingency, but it is possible to choose a system that works today that has a better chance of responding to future changes. Understanding the underlying assumptions in our CMS tools helps us to be ready.

More importantly, the business environment constantly changes. The company adds a new product line. They merge with a competitor. The marketing department gets restructured. New laws require product safety information to be publicly disclosed.

Build Systems That Can Adapt

If you build your own CMS tool, compose your system of distinct components. There is a natural seam between the asset management, repository, transformation, and publishing parts, for instance. Make sure that each component is fairly independent of the others, and that the connections between them are either simple or standard – preferably both.

Pay attention to how the transformation step of the system is handled. In my experience, the most powerful content management tools allow great flexibility inside the template system. This flexibility is key to surviving major changes in the site: whether it's a new navigation design, completely reorganizing the page hierarchy, or changing the site technology from, say, PHP to JSP.

If you purchase your CMS tool, you obviously have less control over how the tool is put together. Still, you can evaluate how *well* the system is assembled. In particular, you can look for a CMS tool that is built as a framework, with a robust, easy-to-use application built on top of that framework. These days any CMS tool that you pay for should consist of more than merely a framework; you should not have to develop the actual functionality yourself when you pay for professional services.

Some systems are developed with a monolithic approach. They make assumptions about the entire content management process, from managing assets to the final publishing steps. The all-in-one approach is attractive (get your site set up in days, not weeks!), but can be brittle. If there is a problem, it often takes more time to locate the cause of the breakdown.

A modular approach can help you make the inevitable changes and improvements, without worrying about a small change having an unintended side effect somewhere else in the system. A modular approach also makes it easier to understand how the entire system works, so that you will be able to respond to problems that arise.

Build On Standards

Standards-compliance consists of two things. There are technical standards, such as XML, XSLT and SOAP, which any content management system you use – be it your own, or a proprietary one – should employ. Then there are common elements of the feature-set offered by each proprietary CMS ("commodity standards", if you like), which will allow easier migration between different systems, for instance.

The technical standards were largely developed outside the CMS world. For instance, XML is an excellent markup language developed by the W3C for creating structured documents. There is now a large array of tools (many of them free-to-use and open-source in nature) that can understand XML documents. This means that, once you get your data into XML format, you can capitalize upon the work of others to manipulate your content in powerful ways.

One of these is XSLT (*http://www.w3.org/Style/XSL/*), a stylesheet language for transforming pure XML documents into other XML formats. XHTML, WML, and other common content formats you will handle are subsets of XML, and so XSLT is an excellent standard to use for templates in the content management world.

While the uptake of XSLT has been slower than that of XML (many vendors had already developed their own templating schemes before the XSLT 1.0 final recommendations came out in November 1999), developers are now beginning to adopt XSLT and it is the closest thing to a bona-fide standard for content management.

Meanwhile, in the Java world, efforts are underway to define a standard for data repositories. The relevant Java Specification Request 170, titled "Content Repository for Java technology API" (*http://www.jcp.org/jsr/detail/170.jsp*), is a fascinating proposal, in a technology area where there had previously been no standards. However, it is still too early to say how widely it will be adopted. The proposed schedule for the publication of the final recommendation is June 2003, and it will take time for vendors to implement once the standard is in place.

There are also implementations of good ideas found in other areas of technology, upon which CMS tools happen to touch – for example, the use of LDAP for user authentication, and the use of common data access methods, such as JDBC or ODBC.

Because the content management field is still immature, the commercial vendors have been experimenting with different features to gain a competitive edge. As their customers begin to understand what features they really want from their systems, vendors have begun to respond, and standardize. This means that they have to work a little harder to support a standard, and then even harder to differentiate themselves from competitors whose systems also support that same 'commodity' standard. Eventually, customers will have an easier time understanding what to expect, and also have some basis of comparison between products.

Of course vendors are going to try to lock you into buying more of their suite of products. It's to their advantage to make it less desirable to use any tool but theirs, once you get started. However, there is a difference between a superior fit between products from the same vendor, and being handcuffed to their products and locked away from your data.

Building your own CMS tools would seem to be the best way toward vendor independence, but this isn't necessarily true. Consider that, when you build your own content management tool, you essentially become the vendor. Under these circumstances it is even more vital to use standard interfaces wherever possible to avoid the risk of being stuck with a piece of proprietary software that isn't properly documented or supported.

Separation of Content and Design

We all have our own recipes for building web sites. We use different editing tools, different imaging tools, and have our own preferences for indenting HTML tags. We have our own JavaScript variable conventions, and our own unique conventions for file and folder names. As we mix our content and design they become intertwined and one of the great strengths of the Web is the ability to mix text, images, movies, and sound, and display them on this canvas we call the browser.

However, while content and design are always baked together before they get to the browser, they absolutely must be stored separately. A good chef naturally keeps his salt and sugar and flour separate until it is time to cook.

The main reasons for keeping content separate from design are:

- The two are different in nature

- They are managed by different groups of people

- They change independently of one another

- It makes it easier to reuse them both

Whenever I see that a site hasn't been redesigned for a while, I often wonder if it is because the content is tangled with the design.

We build changeability into most other parts of our lives. Our cars feature interchangeable parts – oil filters and batteries are designed to be replaced. Our clothes are easily exchangeable – we use zippers and buttons to make clothing easy to wear and remove. If content and design on our web site changes so often, why use a system that is difficult to change in a similar way?

Content and design are fundamentally different things. Content seeks to communicate a message; design aids this communication by providing hints and context. Note that it is often not a balanced relationship – sometimes the design *is* the content. More often though, good design serves the needs of the content.

Content and design are also managed by different groups of people. Writers and designers are both creative, but use their own tools, and have their own distinct ways of looking at the world. A successful, people-oriented CMS will take this into account, and provide ways for different groups to work together without making them wait for each other to get their jobs done.

It's worth taking a moment to reflect on how content and design get muddled together. Many web sites start out life with one person with some HTML knowledge running the whole show. They write the copy, do the HTML design, wrangle images in and out of an image editor, and have an FTP account to post the web page up to their server.

As one person working alone, it is natural to concentrate on the details of each page. Each document is handcrafted, the links are double-checked, and the spacing and layout are perfected. Working on a page-level is enormously satisfying; perhaps because seeing the changes you make show up in a browser offers an immediate satisfaction, and because the tools we use, such as Dreamweaver or FrontPage, are very page-oriented.

Because the individual who manages the copy also does the templating, the content very easily becomes entwined with the design. Naturally, people work in ways that fit their skills, knowledge, and the time they have available. Many web sites survive with this way of working, but it doesn't scale when the site becomes larger and the workload too big for one person to handle.

Working Upstream

It makes more sense to separate the various parts of the web site and manage them at their source. By **working upstream** of the points of integration, each aspect of the site is easier to manage. Rather than having one huge, complex dam at the coast, smaller stations up in the mountains control the flow of assets into the system. Working upstream offers a number of advantages:

- **Separating out the types of work makes it possible for people to work on those parts of the site at which they excel.** Authors can write articles, designers create templates, and programmers can integrate code. Everyone can focus on their jobs and not worry about getting in each other's way.

- **It scales better.** We can all appreciate the web developer who is a jack-of-all-trades; but as web sites become more complex it means that it becomes increasingly harder to find people who both understand the technology involved and know the ins and outs of your particular web site. By dividing the work into reasonable chunks we lower the skills required for people to work on the site. For business people, it means that the organization can utilize more of its people to help manage the content. For overburdened web developers it means working fewer late nights or weekends.

- **It is easier to make changes.** In fact, a small change made upstream will have a far larger impact downstream. For example, adding a simple 'Last-Modified' metadata field to each article on the site in the asset management stage, enables many new features on the published site. We can add a listing of recent items. We can sort all articles by month or year. We can, of course, display the date stamp at the top of each article. And we can have our search engine index that date information.

- **The entire system is more robust.** That is, if there is a problem with one aspect of the site, it doesn't break everything. Errors made should not cause the entire system to stop. For example, editors should still be able to add content to the system, and authors should not have to go back and redo their articles.

Of course, mistakes and errors propagate downstream rapidly, too. For instance, a few days before the launch of a major web site I once worked on, a harried project manager greeted me at my desk. A previous night's site rebuild had generated a couple thousand broken links. In this case, however, I was able get everything fixed in a few minutes because all I had to do was find the typo responsible for the error in the template and rebuild the site.

The cause of the error had been a mistake (mine) in a single template. Of course it was disconcerting for my project manager to see a completely broken web site, but because we managed our templates separately from our content, it was a relatively simple fix and my mistake did not impact anyone else's work. I refer to this story as "the time I fixed a few thousand bugs in half an hour". (Of course, I had managed to generate those bugs in the same amount of time, but I usually don't mention that part.)

Of course, at some point, content and design will be combined for presentation to the client's browser. How and when to do that is a subject for later chapters, but by choosing to manage content upstream, and dividing the work into common-sense portions, we simultaneously make our problems easier to manage, while increasing the ease with which we can make changes.

As your web site matures, you'll want to extend this separation principle to other aspects of the site. While content and design are the two main ingredients of your site, they are by no means the only ingredients. Code and structure also play a role.

Managing Code

For people who run a web site that dynamically interprets pages on the web server, it is often useful to manage snippets of code as well. Web sites that run ColdFusion, PHP, ASP, or JSP often feature complicated templates with repeated bits of code in them.

For example, at the top of every page there may be code that checks to see if the user is logged in, and if they are, display their login name, and, if not, show a *'Login'* button. This bit of code is an independent unit, repeated throughout the site, but it may need to change as the site develops, so it would be a good idea to abstract these bits of code out and manage them from within your content management tools.

Managing Structure

The structure or hierarchy of the site is something that often gets overlooked by both web professionals and content management tools. Perhaps because it is implicit – structure typically gets created by the way we place pages into the file systems of our servers. However, it is still a very important part of any web sites.

The structure of the site is often reflected in that most fundamental UI element of any web page: its URL. The URL can give the user valuable contextual information:

```
http://www.example.com/products/beer/
http://www.example.com/products/coffee/
http://www.example.com/products/guns/
```

However, one of the problems with placing our content into a strict hierarchy, by placing files into a **physical** file system that reflects our site's structure, is that the structure may change as the site grows. If we place files in a hierarchy, then we start to break URLs and (perhaps) have to start doing redirects on the server. For example, say the company's new marketing vice president wants to re-brand products as solutions:

```
http://www.example.com/solutions/attitude_adjustments/
http://www.example.com/solutions/morning_productivity/
http://www.example.com/solutions/productivity_enforcement/
```

Many database-driven web sites, on the other hand, eschew the whole structural issue altogether. In the database, everything is a record. While this has advantages, it forgets that humans like to organize data into a hierarchy. What we're often stuck with are URLs like:

```
http://www.example.com/template.cfm?pageid=110167
http://www.example.com/template.cfm?pageid=112671
http://www.example.com/template.cfm?pageid=022066
```

This tells us nothing about our site structure.

It is possible to have the best of both worlds by creating a **virtual structure** that is flexible. Systems that can decouple hierarchy from content by using metadata allow the content to then be stored in either a file system or database, and the hierarchy mapped to it, based on that metadata.

There is another benefit to managing the structure of your site separately from its content. Managing the structure gives you a control point for all the link information for every page of your site. Some content management tools take advantage of this and provide **link management**: the ability to create and track every link within your web site easily. Implemented properly, this feature can completely eliminate broken links within the web site.

Summary

The term 'content management' really represents a broad family of ideas and issues. It's the latest response to an age-old problem: managing human communication.

Content management is a concept with many facets. It should be a **people-centric activity**, which supports their style of working together. It implies having a plan, understanding the problems, knowing the requirements, and applying the appropriate amount of technology to help people in their work.

Content management happens in distinct phases: we define a process called **asset management** to create and organize assets, we **transform content** by applying design and structure, and we **publish** it on the most appropriate platform and format for our audience.

There are other principles that help us succeed in content management. Smart developers anticipate growth; they plan for the future. They understand that content management is a process, not some out-of-the-box product. They employ standards, and they work upstream, managing content and design separately.

2

- Knowing Your Information Assets

- Workflow and Metadata

- Creating New Assets

Author: James Ellis

CMS Map: Asset Management

You have your reasons for looking into Content Management, and one of those reasons is likely to be that your site is getting too big to handle the way it is. Maybe you have too many authors creating pages and they end up working on pages at the same time without realizing it. Maybe it takes weeks to make a change in navigation because you have to populate thousands of pages with the new information by hand. Maybe you have a stack of press releases online from your first Internet redesign (was 1997 that long ago?) that no one reads anymore.

The real issue is that you have too much stuff worked on by too many people. The key underlying issue here is **asset management**. If you think of all the pieces of information you have as assets (and you should), how you deal with them is asset management.

Think you understand what's on your web site or even just your section of the web site? Think again. Take this little test:

- How many pages are on your web site right now? (Please be exact. Do not round to the nearest hundred.)

- How many pages contain out-of-date or incorrect information?

- Are there any pages that have not been looked at by users (real ones, not search engine bots) for more than a month? Six months?

- Name everyone who has contributed material to your web site.

- Name everyone who has the ability to upload material to your web site.

- When was the last time someone uploaded a page (be exact)? Who was it?

- How many broken links/404 errors exist on your site? How many times do people click on broken links?

- How much time does it take to train a new employee to create a web page? How much does it cost?

- Does every page on your site look like the others? Are there pages or entire sections that look like they were designed by other people?

- How long does it take to get a simple web page from an idea to being published online?

If you were honest, you probably didn't know the answers to all these questions, and the results weren't great for the answers you could give. It's all right; you're not alone. In fact, most organizations with web sites bigger than a hundred pages have these issues. But knowing this kind of information is crucial to making your web site efficient, useful, and valuable, which is what this is all about, right?

Think of your information assets as boxes of money. If you had a room containing all your boxes of money, you'd know how many there were, right? You'd know who had the key to the room. You'd install a few cameras to see who was entering and leaving. You'd make it really easy for people to drop off new boxes, I bet. You'd want someone you trusted checking each box to make sure it didn't have rocks in it instead of money. And you'd have some sort of emergency response system, so that if something went horribly wrong, you'd be protected. If you accepted any less, you'd be looking for a job. If you treat your information assets in the same way, you'll be a lot happier. We'll be revisiting this metaphor a lot in this chapter.

Many content management projects fail because people assume that you just buy the software, install it on a server and a couple of clients, and you'll be managing your content. Or they hire vendor consultants to come in and redesign your business processes and procedures to sync with the software's idea of how you should run your organization. Don't you know your business and assets better than they do? Your software should work for you, not the other way around.

Most of this chapter will deal with processes and models for dealing with your assets, rather than specific software issues. Don't skip it; this is foundation material. Once you understand what we're doing and why, you can make your software and systems bend to you, rather than having to bend to what the software thinks you should do. Understanding the theory will allow you to get a lot more out of your system, turning it from a potential money hole into a key component of your business.

What Is Asset Management?

Information asset management is just like any other kind of asset management. It involves goals, such as:

- "I want to add pages and change pages on the site very easily"

- "I don't want everyone and their dogs to be able to post web pages"

- "I want web content to be current, accurate, and obvious"

The content management system is the tool that will get you there, but the tool won't work unless you've done all the groundwork. You need to understand what information you actually have.

You need to do a Who, What, Why, Where, and How of your assets – an **asset analysis**. Once you know that, you can **define the processes** that touch the information. Defining these processes is the secret to making content management work. It's not a very well-kept secret but, because it involves a lot of work, content management vendors don't really talk loudly about it. This process will let you decide things like who has to see information before it gets uploaded, and how to streamline the authoring process. It will help to standardize the rules and regulations of your web site, making it easier to administer and maintain.

If you got hired to manage that big room of money, and they showed you a room with boxes piled to the ceiling in a haphazard fashion, people just walking in and out, boxes coming in half-filled with money, people yelling at each other as to what they were supposed to do and not supposed to do, what would you do first? Aside from making sure your resume was current, you'd get those boxes straight.

Understanding What You Already Have: Taking Stock

During high school, I did some sort of weird fundraiser for the debate team (make your jokes now). The team hired itself out to a large department store to help do its quarterly inventory. We showed up, geeks en-masse, at 10:00pm and we went through every piece of clothing in the men's section that night, finishing bleary-eyed at 4:00am. We checked it, made sure the tag was on it correctly, scanned it, and put it away in its proper place. Our "earnings" were spent on hotel accommodation for the state championships.

That kind of inventory is standard operating procedure at most retail stores and warehouses. It lets you verify the things you thought you knew about your inventory. Think you sold all of your T-shirts? Then why is there a box of them in the corner? Will you find a pair of acid-washed jeans on the clearance rack that have been marked down 30 or 40 times? Hey, no wonder these shirts aren't selling, they've got ink stains on them.

When a distribution company moves to a new distribution system, step one is to do a hand-count of the entire inventory. Always. How else are you going to know if what your reports are telling you is correct?

The same goes for a content management system. Before you move to one or swap, get to know your inventory. Maybe you'll find that pages you thought were gone just got moved. Maybe you'll find that one of your departments has gone overboard publishing to the Internet and another pretends it doesn't exist. Remember, it's probably been a while since you knew every single page on your site. Time to get re-acquainted.

The inventory process, together with other processes involved in migrating content to a CMS, will be discussed further in Chapter 8.

Content Inventory

A content inventory is a dull, tedious, meticulous, time-consuming process, let there be no doubt. But every hour spent at this stage of the game will pay off in saved days and weeks later on.

A web site is a messy place. It's not just a bunch of pages on a server. It's a web, remember? Think about every link on every page. Think about every paragraph and image. Think about how one department has a wide, shallow site (like the first figure below), but another has a narrow, deep one (similar to the second figure below).

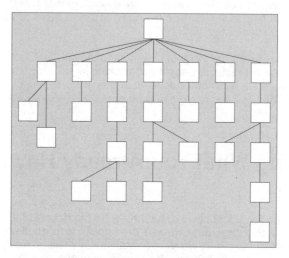

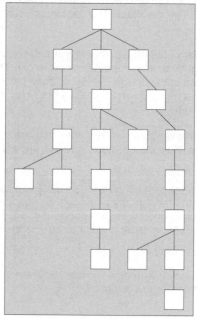

Think about the people who never got the hang of optimizing their images, so little pictures are 100KB. Think about every single executive bio, press release, legal contract, form, map, image map, PDF, spreadsheet, Word document, logo, bullet, invisible spacer... the list goes on. Now, think about the stuff in your web server that isn't used, like old versions of logos and images that didn't get written over, and sandbox areas where people tested ideas, but never took them off the server. That's a lot of stuff.

While a content inventory is tedious and not particularly pleasant, it does have a lot of serious benefits.

Obviously, you will be able to weed out bad information. Every misspelling, every awkward sentence, every discontinued item, every old Special, and everything else that no longer needs to be on the web site can get yanked out.

Also, you may find that some departments or people were not abiding by company standards and guidelines. They may have personal material on the server (you laugh, but I know of someone who was able to host the web site for their sister's daycare on the company servers without anyone knowing). They may have posted other non-work-related unmentionables: keeping material like that off your publicly available servers could save someone a lawsuit.

Probably the fastest way to find unused files is to use the standard command-line tools to list files by "last accessed" date (the specifics are dependent on your server operating system and production/live server arrangement). It's a safe assumption that anything that hasn't been accessed in the last few months isn't actually on the live server, as users or search engine bots would have accessed it more recently. If you can cut out 10% of the pages that are useless and unused, you will be able to free up valuable server space.

If it helps to ease your stress levels, you will not be doing this yourself. A good content inventory should take place from the "content expert level", meaning that each department should look at its own material for inaccuracies, expired offers, and inadmissible contracts. You do not know the information as well as they do. If *you* do the inventory, your life will be spent calling the experts up and asking if that policy is still in effect or that offer is still valid. It should be the job of the content experts to bring all their content up to speed and up to snuff.

As each department goes through their own material, they may use the opportunity to re-evaluate what direction they want to go in. A new tone, a new feel, or a simple re-organization of content would be a great bonus.

How do you do a content inventory? Excellent question. Of course, there are many ways in which you could run this process, but you may choose to do something like this:

Start from the top. Run a server report to give you a broad overview of the site. Look at the structure. How many pages are there? Are they distributed among 5 folders or 500? Is your site broken down by department, topic, idea, or consumer role? Look for large chunks of pages. Think like a surveyor, getting the sense of how big or complex the project is.

Make it manageable. If you can, this is a good place to break the site into smaller sites. Each site is different, so you'll have to be the judge as to which level of granularity you will deal with. For the most part, in my experience, most web sites can be broken down into between 5 and 10 discrete sections. You could break it down by departments, for example. But maybe your site could be broken down into 10 or 20 different projects. Again, you'll have to make the call.

Assign a leader. Unless you have a small site, each section should have a team leader. That person will be in charge of making sure that the work is getting done. They will make the judgment calls for their content, so they should know the material very well. The teams will report to their leaders with problems, questions, and successes. The leaders will report to you.

First report. Once the team leader has assembled a team, they will need a list of all their pages from the server. If your teams are broken up by directory on the server, this job is easy. For example, the contracts team will get the server reports for the contracts directory. If you are breaking your sections in a different way, you should configure your reports to reflect this. If you can't, you are going to be missing your most basic asset: a comprehensive list of files. Think long and hard about how you have broken your sections up, if this is the case.

One at a time. With the list of files in hand, each team should go to every file in the list. Check for accuracy, spelling, punctuation, topicality, and freshness. You aren't looking at the design or navigation here, just the content – your assets. Remove pages that are stagnant or useless – since each team should know the relevance of the content they review, it would be up to them to decide what stays and what goes.

Each team should be given a list of their files, ordered by popularity. They can then see, in stark black and white, how many hits each page gets. I can almost guarantee that they will be surprised and even shocked at how different reality is from their expectations. If pages are not getting hit at all, either remove them or think about where they would do more good. If pages are getting sporadic hits, they may not be getting the visibility they need. This may be an indication that your navigation needs some re-thinking.

The name game. Your teams will have to give each page a name, but you should determine the naming convention. Note that these names will not become names of actual pages, visible to end-users. They are merely mental placeholders, ways for you and your teams to talk about the same page without having to resort to long, description-based names. For example, "1-1-7" is a lot easier than "In the X section, Y subsection, page called Z."

The name can be anything. Some people suggest that you use a numbering system, which is a great solution (see *Perspectives* opposite). However, a name and a location should be considered at the same time, as they will probably depend on each other. Some people assume that the name should be the same as the title (between the `<title>` tags), which is not the case. In fact, that may be the absolute wrong answer – using the same page title instead of a more abstract system may bias your team when redesigning the structure. They will tend to put pages where they previously went, instead of really thinking about where they should go.

Map makers. Once you have names in place, you should start to build a map of your site. Think of the home page of each section as the top of the pyramid. Everything on the second level is everything you can link to from the home page. Each page should show every link to every following page that is deeper in the hierarchy. You shouldn't show every possible link; otherwise you may have to draw a line from each page to (for example) the home page, which would be a mess. See this map for example:

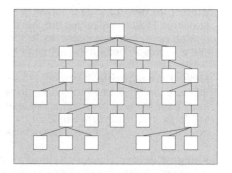

This will give you a sense of how your site looks. If you want to create this map by hand (which is time consuming, but can be a revelation to anyone who has to do it) you can do so with tools such as Microsoft's Visio. Alternatively, you can use a shareware program to search your site like a search engine bot and map it out for you, though results do tend to be cluttered. If you design and manage sites with a high-end WYSIWYG like Microsoft's FrontPage or Macromedia's Dreamweaver, these programs will have functions that map your site out, based on the pages you've created in them.

Realize at this point that the map you make will determine much of the navigation of the site. If you've looked at any usability materials yet (and you should have), you've seen how important an obvious, consistent, and structurally sound navigation is. Many organizations will stop at this point and do a card-sort usability test. A card sort is where you put the topic or function of every section on its own index card. Then you shuffle the cards and hand them to a willing and friendly participant. That person must then lay out the cards in a hierarchy, hopefully similar to the one on your map, but without seeing yours first. Do the two maps (yours and theirs) look at all alike? The card sort test shows you what a user would expect to see and how your navigation would logically work.

Where it's at. It's time to think about the content's place in the world. You will need to give each page a location. Now, this can get tricky. When we talk about location, this can mean either its physical location on the server, or where in the navigation it lives. For example, you may say a page about Product XJ7 lives in the "*products*" folder and the "*xj_series*" subfolder on the server. Alternatively, you may say it lives in the "*Family Value Products*" section in a subsection called "*Home Office Supplies*" within the navigation.

My suggestion is that you go with the latter – the navigation location. Not everyone will be familiar with the folder structure, but they will be fluent in the navigation, especially of their section. That having been said, if you choose this kind of name/location, you should solve any and all navigation issues first (see *Map makers* opposite).

Perspectives: Names and Locations

Consider a numbering system for the name and for the location of the pages together. That way, the location is the name. For example, if a page is called 2-1-5, that means from the home page, choose the second in the list of the navigation. From that page, choose the first in the navigation list. From that page, choose the fifth link in the navigation list. That way, if you get the name of any page, like 1-1-7, you know exactly where that page lives in the navigation structure. Also, this gives each page a unique numbering system.

In order to avoid the confusion that would ensue if you moved a page after it had been named, name your pages in the following order: put the pages in the structure you want them to be in, then apply the numbering system. If you have to move one later, put the old number in parenthesis, for example 1-1-7 could become 1-1-5(7).

This number system is only a logistical tool until you and your teams have hammered out the structure of the site. Once you've done that, you can toss the numbering system away.

However, the number system is not for everyone. If you have a very large site, you may want to try creating the site structure with groups of related pages. For example, instead of showing the Products page getting linked to every individual product page, you could link to the Economy Products, Commercial Products, and Luxury Products pages. Within each group, you can build a structure like a separate site.

If your site isn't that big, using contextually named pages with obvious labels may be easier. But if you are worried that confusion of page names might be an issue, try the numbering system.

Results. Once each group has reorganized their section, they should present their results to the other team leaders. This will bring everyone back to the real reason you did this exercise in boredom: **knowing your content**. It will also give each team leader a chance to see if their section matches what other sections are doing. What you want to avoid is making each section unique, so that it looks like your web site is run like a series of fiefdoms with no central guidance. It will confuse users if in one section the site map is linked to from every page, but in another, it is only linked to from the section's home page.

Page types. Something else to think about at this stage: if you had to boil all the pages into a few "types,' could you? Your basic type might be a page with mostly paragraphs of text and some small images. Another type might be a page with large images or maps, or a page with a screen-sized table or image. Think of types not as the kind of information they convey, but the amount or shape of screen space they will require.

Remember, all this information is going to be filling templates, as we'll explore in detail in Chapter 3. If each page is so unique that you will require a new template for it, you are defeating the purpose of content management. Without considering things like section logos or headers or colors, but concentrating on the layout of the pages, can you find five or so types of layout? We'll talk about it later when we cover templates, but you should definitely be thinking about this early on.

Content from Non-Web Sources

Most organizations end up stuck in ruts. Once a process has been developed and proves to be successful, why change it? With this attitude, if your company has set up a method by which content is written by authors only when a page is needed, you may be missing a lot of content. There are huge amounts of information locked up in people's heads, in their desks, in their computers, and not on the Internet. So far, we've only talked about revising current web pages, but adding a content management system is a great time to think about what your web site is missing. Do you have all your product documentation on the Web, or just on paper? Could you turn manuals into PDFs and publish them to the Web? Members of ongoing projects tend to keep notes and materials to themselves. They could publish minutes of meetings, as well as diagrams, action items, tasks, roles, and decisions that need to be made, to your intranet for everyone to see.

Databases are rich sources of information that often get overlooked. Sure, you know that putting the database of trouble calls from customers online lets customers know that you care, but some people in management don't like the idea of showing the world that (gasp!) people sometimes have problems that involve your product. Content management and some basic data-level type security could create a password-protected area for customers, where only they can see the status of their issues.

Maybe you have a headline database for your area. Connect it to the Internet so people can look up news by city, date, or subject.

Databases shouldn't be limited to external web pages. Think about how great it would be if your Human Resources department could put the employee handbook online in the company's intranet or extranet. That way, HR wouldn't have to print a bunch of paper copies every time they make a revision, and they won't have to bother you to make changes to their web pages. You should encourage everyone to look for "hidden" information that might be of more use in an electronic format.

Perspectives: How a Bunch of Text Becomes a Web Page

You need to get your information from where it currently lives to the content management system. Depending on the format of your material, it might be easy, or it might be very messy. Below are some hard-won pointers to help in your battle of conversion.

Copying information from a text editor or an ASCII e-mail client to a CMS author interface is very easy. ASCII or text doesn't recognize formatting, so it just leaves it out. If your page had a lot of bullets, it means you'll have to re-insert them, but otherwise, not much else. However, tables are worthless through a text editor – don't bother.

Copying information from a Microsoft product like Word can be very messy if you don't do it the right way. If you run the document through the Save As Web Page *command, be prepared for unnecessary XML and stylesheets, and ugly HTML. Note that cutting and pasting from Word into FrontPage does the same as* Save As Web Page. *To copy a Word document into FrontPage, use the* Insert | File *method.*

If you are using Dreamweaver 4 and above, cutting and pasting from Word is OK. Dreamweaver knows the horrible things Word can do and is prepared for them. It has a command called Clean Up Word HTML, *which does a wonderful job.*

If you are given a web page converted from Word via Save As Web Page *and you don't have Dreamweaver, there is a web site that will clean up the HTML. From Dean Allen, a web-based Word HTML cleaner will do the trick at:*
`http://www.textism.com/resources/cleanwordhtml/.`

Microsoft Excel, like Microsoft Word, also has the tempting function Save As Web Page. *Do not be tricked by this – it will make your life much harder. Take a look at what it does to a Word document.*

Macromedia's Dreamweaver will not understand Excel's .xls file format. Your best bet is to re-key or copy and paste each cell. If you have FrontPage, open a new web page and use Insert | File. *Choose the appropriate Excel file and FrontPage will convert the spreadsheet to tables fairly well. Go over the code to check for any glaring problems, but generally, this works.*

Understanding What You Want To Do With It: Workflow

Your web site is not static. I'm not talking about database-driven pages or dynamic HTML. I'm talking about the site's content. How often does your content change? How often would you like it to change? Every week? Every day? A few times a day? It doesn't matter what your answer is because, if it changes at all, it means adding new pages to the current site or changing existing pages.

But you just spent a month (probably more) getting the current material in shape! Adding new stuff would disturb the beautiful elegance of your structure, but pages *must* be added or changed. Since you understand how the site was redesigned, maybe you should make the changes. Do you really want to do that?

No way. So we have to design a whole bunch of rules that determine who can write material for the site, who has to approve it, which template it can go in, where the page should live, and how it should appear in the navigation.

The rules by which pages get created, approved, and added to the site are called **workflow**. Workflow is the key to maintaining a site without going crazy. A well-defined workflow means everyone knows the role they play in the creation of pages, that no page goes up without all the proper authorizations, and that you have a log of the path each page took, from idea to HTML. No two organizations' workflows are the same. Depending on the number of people involved, what their roles are, and how much or how little approval process is involved, page creation could be as fast as a few hours, or as long as a few days. But make it clear to everyone that workflow guarantees that page creation will be faster than before, with better accountability and fewer problems to slip through the cracks.

> ### Perspectives: It's All About the (Work)Flow
>
> *When you start talking to content management system vendors, they will talk about how easy it is to get the system installed and ready. They may be right. It may take an hour or two to install the software, and another few hours to connect it to the network. But the real work happens on your end. Building a workflow might look like a pain, but it is the most valuable step you can take when moving to your new system.*
>
> *If you have your workflow and roles and all that painful preparation work done when you start talking to vendors, ask them how much time and work (and cost) it will need to implement the system to your specification. You will find that the answers you get are much more honest. Workflow is just the process content goes through to become a web page. Knowing the workflow is really just determining need. Until you have that figured out, asking a vendor how much a system will cost, let alone comparing costs, is useless.*
>
> *Aside from helping you choose a vendor, workflow helps you understand your organization. It will guarantee smoother content creation, and ease executive worry that an expensive system upgrade makes content creation faster and less error-prone. It will also ease their worry that more and more people will have access to publishing via the web server.*
>
> *If you get your workflow right early on, the benefits are real.*

The Existing Process

Again, we begin all change by understanding what exists now. If your site is big enough to have different sections, go to one of your team leaders and ask them to create a page (or have a page created) and track it. If your site is smaller and this process usually falls on your own shoulders, do the same. Ask the following questions:

- Who has the power to authorize the creation of a page?

- Who creates the text on the page?

- Who creates the images?

- Does anyone proofread the page? (Who?)

- Does anyone verify the page's correctness? (Who?)

- Who designs the page?

- Does anyone approve the design? (Who?)

- Once the page is made, who sends it to the server?

- Does anyone have to verify or approve the page before it goes live? (Who?)

- Who puts it on the live web server?

- Does anyone check the page once it's live? (Who?)

- Is there a record of the process moving from one person or station to the next?

- If something goes wrong, how can you backtrack to find out where the problem is? Is it possible to go back to a previous version if you can't fix a problem?

Document the entire process in full and build a flowchart to show people. Does the process match what you thought it was? It's okay if it doesn't, because we are going to redesign it from the ground up to make sure that problems get eliminated and you can see what stages of production every page is in at a moment's notice.

Changing the Process

Changing a process like workflow is a big deal, and you shouldn't try to tackle it on your own. Get your team leaders together (I hope you picked team leaders that you can handle seeing every few days) and look at the flowchart you created. Explain that this is the way pages are created, but that together, you will be designing a better way.

Your first instinct may be to simply add a bunch of approval steps, but the whole process is bigger than that. You need to think about what the most crucial steps are, and design the process around them.

Authors

The basic building blocks of content are the authors. They create the text that filled the site. What do they need? They need a topic or idea. They need someone to say, "I want you to create a page about 'X' and I need it pretty quick." Who is allowed to tell them that they should create a page?

Your authors may be in the marketing department, or from other departments. There may even be authors who write for more than one section of the site. The best processes put content experts in the role of author. If Marketing writes material for brochures or ads, let them be the people who write the web page to keep a consistent voice. If the page is about technical support, let someone in technical support write it. They don't have to be accomplished authors (you can build in as many layers of editing as it takes to make it readable); they just need to understand the content.

Don't worry too heavily about teaching authors how to actually enter text into the content management system. A good system will have a simple method by which almost anyone can add content without any knowledge of the Web. Gone may be the days of WYSIWYG training for authors and complex clients on their desktop. Let authors focus on the text. The designers will build templates and do the visual layout of pages that require special attention.

You want to get as many people to write as possible, because they are the owners of knowledge (see *Perspectives* below). Either everyone should take a class before they are allowed to author, or you should build in extra layers of editing to polish their work.

Perspectives: The Best Part of CMS Is That It Begs You To Add Authors

The thing I love the most about good content management systems is how they let more and more people publish to the Internet. It's even better than swappable templates or meta-tagged data or accountable processes for publishing pages.

Think about everyone in your company. Think about all the knowledge and wisdom locked in their minds. Think about the guy in building maintenance who knows the secret to fixing the printer. Think about the office manager who knows all the codes on the telephone. Think about the designer who knows more about layout than anyone. That information is just sitting there, waiting to be used. But if every time the printer jammed or you forgot how to transfer a call you had to walk down the hall for help, none of us would get much done in a day.

Content management says, "Don't teach everyone FrontPage! Let them compose in a simple interface within the browser!" It's easy. Everyone can create information for the Web. And almost everyone should. Granted, there are layers of approval and a central authority to handle where each page goes, but the burden of technical knowledge gets much lighter.

Sure, you want your legal staff to go through legally binding documents with a fine-tooth comb, but wouldn't it be great to let the sales staff publish a daily column called "My favorite product" to the Web? They can talk about the products everyone overlooks, or unusual features or uses.

Look at a company like Macromedia. They told a bunch of their developers to go out and put together web logs about the products they worked on. The developers can now post anything they want about the products (including installation issues and bugs) without the parent company watching over their shoulder. Aside from building enormous goodwill, the web logs let the customers talk directly to the people who built the products.

As much as it may terrify some of the people in your organization, you will want to build better communication between customers and your staff. Perhaps the technical staff can post their top ten fixes to the Web for customers. Perhaps production and design staff can ask customers what they want for the next version of their product.

Content management puts the rank-and-file staff closer to customers and vice versa. Think of all the knowledge you could let loose!

Editors

There may be authors writing, but do you want all those people to be able to post content? Of course not. There needs to be a team of editors to do things like check spelling, punctuation, grammar, and to make sure authors are complying to the right styles. You could set up a system that has one editor for each section, who would cover for each other when one is sick or goes on vacation. Alternatively, you could have a centralized team of editors for all pages. You will have to decide which is right. To make your decision there are a few things you should consider.

First, if you put an editor in each section, will they be a full-time editor or a writer who edits on the side? Editors should never edit their own material (the more eyes that see the material, the fewer flaws it will have). Will that editor have enough time to do their other jobs and still edit? Putting the editors in a centralized setting tends to mean that they are full-time copy editors (who do excellent jobs keeping us all from sounding like idiots). Full-time should mean that they will have adequate time to do the job.

Second, full-time professionals are more expensive, even though they will probably do a better job. Companies like IBM and Blockbuster have full-time copy editors, and magazines like Salon and Time already have a staff like that. You'll have to make that decision with upper management, presumably.

Editors should not be afraid to send text back to authors for fixes. Your content management system will allow them to send the entire text back with revision notes and possible amendments. In a professional setting, copy will commonly go through more than one revision, so pick editors who are willing to back up their decisions.

Approvers

Once you have text that your author and your editor are both happy with, it has to get approval before moving to the next step. Approvers are the gatekeepers of content. They should be looking at the text with a content-critical eye. Does a choice of words sound slanderous of the competition? Does the text make claims that are unverifiable? Does the information portray the organization in the correct light? Approvers should be managers who have the authority to make decisions like these every day.

Approvers will also have the ability to send text back to the author for fixes. Because your approvers are probably managers, they shouldn't have any problem with sending material back.

How many approvers should you have? It's hard to say. Clearly more than one, in case someone gets sick. But you may need one for every section. This decision should turn on the question of how many new pages you think will be created in a day. If it's just one or two, then a minimal number of approvers will be fine. If you'll be creating more than two or three per section each day, then maybe use an informal approver within each section.

You might decide that you need multiple layers of approval. Should all pages go through managers, then through lawyers? There may be some good instances where this is the case. Do you pass pages through the president or CEO? Should Marketing see everything that they themselves didn't write? All of these approval processes need to be thought out in advance.

While you can change the approval process on the fly, setting up as much as you can before you let everyone onto the system will save you time and hassle. Planning it out beforehand will avoid the patchwork approval process you had before.

You will also need a list of terms that denote where in the process it is. If a page is waiting for the editor to pass it on, it could be a first draft, a resubmitted draft, or awaiting answers to a question from the approver. A common vocabulary is very beneficial when you have to say that the page is waiting for approval: the page may have already been to the approver, who had a legal question and sent it to the lawyer, who made a suggested amendment and sent it back to the author for the fix, who then sent it through to editing where it now waits. You won't make a term for every possibility because there will be too many, but distinctions should be made between, for example, first draft to the editor and third draft to the editor after a manager changed their minds on an issue.

Streamlining the Process

Executives or upper management may ask you to design a process with many layers of approval before anything can be considered for publication. This, of course, will slow down the publication process considerably, which is often a reason for using a content management system in the first place. You may see that the assumptions you designed some of the processes with were incorrect. This is natural. No amount of planning will allow you to see all the problems.

As the weeks roll by, keep a notebook or list of all the things that seem redundant or slow. Don't enact them yet, as one change may cause other problems. Once you feel that the system is working as well as it should be, ask management to allow you to streamline the processes. Show them that fears of people posting to the Web without approval are unfounded. Show them how you are able to track each page through the system. Show them how some streamlining will further speed publication.

Remember, you had reasons for designing a process a certain way. Just because it seems slow doesn't mean it should be removed. If you create another flowchart (like that shown below) to see how a page is now created and put it next to the flowchart you created for the old workflow, you will see how much farther along you are. Test your new system. Remember that any streamlining you can do improves efficiency which will lead directly to the bottom line, and the managers should be financially predisposed to trim layers of approval as close to the bone as possible.

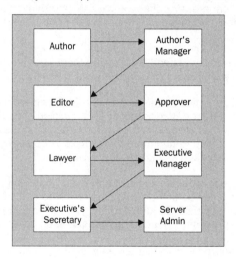

Security

If you had a room with boxes of money, you'd keep the doors locked, right? You'd know exactly who had a key and when they entered and left the room. With all this new information moving around the company, and a bevy of authors, editors, and approvers, you need to keep a "lock" on where pages are within the process.

For example, the Vice-President of Marketing is wondering what the hold-up is on a page they requested yesterday. How can you give him or her a solid answer without asking the author and the editor and the approver what the situation is? Your content management system should be able to tell you who the last person to touch a page was. Maybe the author sent it to the editor, but the editor is on vacation and forgot to tell anyone.

Another example: the president calls and asks why a certain page includes the phrase, "no one will read this". They want to know who wrote it and how it got on the home page. You need to be able to look at your reports to see who the author was, who the editor was, and who approved the page without reading it!

This is the kind of security your information needs. You want people adding and polishing information, and you don't have the time or inclination to edit and approve it all yourself, but chances are you are in charge of the web site and all problems with the authors, editors, and approvers end up in your lap. Your system's reporting tools will let you keep your eye on what everyone is doing (and should be doing) and keep you from getting into hot water.

Your system also affords you a little security to restrict people from doing certain tasks. You could determine that authors can only write within their own sections. You could decide that authors and editors do not have the authority to delete a page. By defining people's work roles within the workflow, you will be able to keep everyone in their assigned areas.

Feedback Loop

After a few weeks, ask your authors, editors, and approvers how they think things have improved or gotten worse. Find out who the slow or less competent editors are, or who is too strict with their approval. Find out which authors need more layers of editing or class time. Remember, your goal is to make the process as smooth and easy as possible. If you've got someone taking too much time, you need to figure out how to solve that problem.

Get as much feedback from your users as you can. You should focus on your administrative role and let your authors, editors, and approvers do the heavy lifting. Do what you can to help them, but let them tell you what they need.

Don't think that the feedback loop is a one-time-only proposition. The best way to find problems and uncover little areas of inefficiency is to do regular checks with your authors and editors. Let them tell you what they think would be improvements. They live inside the system, so they will be the best people to report to you.

Understanding How To Get There: The Enablers

Again, back to the room full of money. Workflow design lets you know how boxes are added to the room. It guarantees that the boxes are full of money and that when your boss calls and asks where a certain box is, you can find it quickly. We've set up enough security that we know where a box goes and who is using it. We've gotten the room pretty much done.

However, a few more enhancements need to be taken care of. In order to manage the boxes (you know, to do things like restack the boxes in a different order, or put the old boxes in front or back), we need to make the boxes a little smarter.

In the distribution world, most companies print barcode labels for each item and stick them on. That way, when they sell an item, they just scan it and it will remove itself from the inventory. The barcodes may have locations on, so you can find anything in the warehouse, no matter how big and complex the space may be. Basically, the items are smarter: they know what they are, their quantity, their location, their age, and perhaps their size and weight. You can use the barcodes to see who you ordered the item from and how long it took for the item to arrive.

We need to make our information smarter as well. We need to be able to know everything about it, like what it is, where it came from, where it belongs, and how old it is. We also need to know how we can reuse it wherever possible.

Metadata

Metadata is really data about data. It's the information that tells us what the information is. For example, if I had a box called "Address", it would be the metadata that would tell you it meant street address rather than, say, the Gettysburg address. The metadata can tell us whatever we want to know about the data, provided that we've been smart enough to create any metadata in the first place.

This section will be very theory-heavy. We will leave discussing "how to create metadata" for the later section, *The User Interface or the Client Tool*.

What Is Metadata?

There is one kind of metadata that you already capture: server logs. It can tell you many things, such as what browser an end-user is using, the operating system, the time they looked at the page, where they came from, and how long they were on the page. Whether or not you actually do anything with that information is up to you, but it *can* be used to calculate how long it took for a document to be written, who wrote it, and when they sent it off, etc.

There is another kind of metadata; a more formal kind (often seen in the form of XML), which allows you to define the kind of information you'd like to gather and what it should look like. For example, we said "address" could mean a street address or to speak (as in, to address someone). We can also define what we are looking for within an address. We can break the address into Number, Street, City, State or County, and Zip or Postal Code. We can go a step further and say that the Number preceding the Street should be a numeral. We can say that the State (if, for example, we know the address is in the USA), is a two-character abbreviation, which can even be defined ahead of time (so that the person or system inputting the information doesn't have to remember if Wisconsin is WI or WN, or even Wn or wn – the possible options are already specified).

This is called a **data dictionary**: what the information you are looking for is, and how it should be given. A data dictionary should know that my name isn't "James 445" or even "jAMES eLLIS", and my phone number isn't "hello-6418."

Every system will build and use this data dictionary and metadata slightly differently, but the idea is the same throughout.

Why Use Metadata?

There are a number of reasons why metadata is so important to a content management system. Like an envelope for a letter, the metadata will know where a piece of information came from, who it is supposed to go to next, and when it left. If you think about all your authors' and editors' and approvers' offices, the content management system is like a mail system for your web pages. When the author is done writing, he or she applies some metadata to the chunk of information and sends it on its way. The system acts like a post office, looking at the information, deciding who it goes to next, logging the time and date, and sending it to the right person.

Metadata can be used for much more. If you tag some pages as "Internet" and some pages as "extranet", you can decide to only let people (like vendors or customers) who have a password see the "extranet" pages. If Marty is coming up for review, you can pull all the web pages Marty has written over the last six months to see how she's been doing. You can tag information as having an expiration date (for a special deal or other time-sensitive material) – when the date comes up, the system can be programmed to remove the page and all links to it.

You didn't have to use metadata before because when your site was small, you just read the page and knew everything you needed to know about it. If it was a Special that ended next week, you could read the page, and put a note on your calendar to remove the page on that day. However, now that the site is so big, you should let the system take care of it. The system isn't smart enough to read the page and say, "Gee, this page looks like it should expire tomorrow because it says so in the body text." You have to have a "slot" for that information and a program that knows what to do when it sees that information.

Metadata can also help you build customized web pages. You can ask users to register and log in. When they register, you can ask them what kind of user they are, and then, using metadata, present only information relevant to them. For example, say you run a site that sells gardening equipment. When each user registers you can ask them questions like, "What is your favorite plant?" or pull out the state they live in from their shipping address. If you then create a page that is part of a Special on certain plants, you can have that page pop up for people whose favorite plant is on the Specials list. Or if the user is from a state that is suffering from dry weather conditions, you can put a link on their pages to special offers on irrigation equipment. If you didn't take metadata, you wouldn't know to offer that Special to that person.

What Type of Metadata?

What kind of metadata should you be creating? Well, the system will create a fair amount all by itself. Based on the workflow rules you've set up, it will know things such as who started/wrote the page, who edited it, if it went back to the author, if it went for approval, when it got approved, who put it on the live server, and what time and date all of these things occurred. Is that enough metadata? Not even close.

You should collect metadata on things like:

- What section is this page going to live in?

- What pages should it link to?

- Should every page be available to everyone?

Think about what you would like your pages to do, and collect information that would help the system do that. If you want to show certain pages to specific people, how would you determine which people? That's the kind of metadata you want to collect.

If the CMS was bought from a vendor, read the manual and ask other people who have the same system what kind of metadata they have set up. If you are creating a homegrown system, there are a lot of resources for you to look at, including the features pages of retail systems, list servers, and web sites. While I have tried to list a number of great ways to use metadata, it is by no means a conclusive list. System administrators are amazing sources of knowledge on these kinds of subjects, and you should use them as best you can.

Note: you have to determine what metadata to collect before you can use it. If you decide a month after you set your system up that you want to show certain pages only between 5:00pm and 7:00pm, you have to make every page say, "I can be seen at any time" or "I can only be seen at a certain time." You can make a site-wide edit to set all pages to say, "I can be seen at any time" and change only the few pages that have special needs. Of course, that may be an easy change. If you have a piece of metadata that is more complex than "Yes" or "No", or for which the value is evenly divided between your pages, you'll be spending a lot of time making the changes by hand.

Where Is the Metadata?

Where does the metadata live? Without a content management system, the metadata would have to live in the pages themselves, inside the `<meta>` tags. These have limited use for anything more than keywords, description, and authoring info. However, your CMS may store the information in other ways such as:

- As a chunk of XML inside the page (for example, in the header).

- Within the same database, if the content is stored in a database by the CMS.

- As a complementary document. This is usually in XML format, but it could be nothing more than a universally structured text document. The system will remember that the document corresponds to the page, though the user will never see it.

You don't have to apply metadata to a whole page. If you have some of your content broken up into smaller pieces, your system should allow you to add metadata to just parts of the content. For example, if you decide that a certain image (say, a logo or special offer illustration) should only be seen by certain people (recent buyers, for example), you can add this as metadata to the image.

Who Creates Metadata?

While this is different for every system, generally what happens is that during the creation/editing/approving process, metadata is added to the page. The author putting the text together may decide that the material should expire on a certain date or be used in the Contracts section. The author is likely to also add keywords so search engines can find the content, and labels for things like sitemaps and links. The system should automatically capture author, time, and date. The editor could refine existing metadata or add more. Approvers could decide if the page should be viewed by everyone, if it is linked from the home page, what kind of prominence it gets within the navigation, etc.

So, anyone who helps to create the document can and should add metadata. However, remember that authors and editors will have a more localized view of the web site than you and your web team leaders. Imagine if you specified a piece of metadata that answered the question, "Will this content require a link from the home page?" How many authors wouldn't want their page to be linked to from the home page? You will need a governing body to determine site-wide issues like that.

Different people will be better suited to make certain decisions on metadata – be sure to build those people into your workflow. Maybe you need to be an executive to decide if the page should be publicly viewable or live behind the extranet wall. Maybe you need a lawyer to decide if the page needs a legal disclaimer. Maybe human resources would like to add metadata to a "help wanted" page. You and your team should create the data dictionary (as defined earlier) and determine who adds what metadata to the content. Then, as it moves through the workflow, the metadata can be added.

Remember, the better you build your workflow and train people within the workflow on their roles, the less work you will have to do, because policy decisions are built into the system. You don't have to worry about covering yourself in the case of controversy and taking anything even remotely controversial to the lawyers and executive leadership. The system, if the metadata is sound, will route the page to the right person and take care of those decisions for you.

Reusable Data

The key to surviving in college, as I am told, is not plenty of coffee, or making friends with someone with a car, but about making sure that everything in your room has more than one use. It's not just a refrigerator; it's a nightstand. It's not just a pile of textbooks; it's a stepladder. You reuse your materials as often as you can. Submitting a paper from one class to another? That kind of re-usability might get you expelled, but it's exactly the kind of trick that will save you time and energy.

The same holds true for content management. You want to be able to reuse headers, footers, navigation, and even advert space. Aside from saving server space, it allows you to change something once and see it get populated out to all the other pages. Better yet, reused data is consistent data. And you definitely want to save time and energy at work, don't you?

We're going to talk about two ways to reuse your information: chunking data (or grouping data), which is very common, and restringing data, which is not.

Grouping Data

Chances are you've already looked into some means of chunking your data. By this, we mean thinking about your web page as being chunks of information all laid out on a page, for example headers, footers, primary navigation, secondary navigation, content, adverts, a search box, other utilities, and even images. If you could break your pages up into such separate pieces, you could standardize each piece. Maybe your footer has standard material on it, such as legal information, a privacy policy link, a contact link, copyright material, etc. You could build it once, and attach it on the fly to all your pages as they get sent from the web server.

Content management systems will allow a more complex and powerful way of chunking material and swapping it in or out of the page depending on the metadata. You could create a subsection of navigation (search, home page link, contact us, site map, etc.) that would appear under the left-hand navigation of every page. Maybe every contract page should have the same boilerplate material at the top and bottom. Perhaps every press release should have the same "who we are" information. The more you look at grouping data, the more you will find that there are plenty of areas you can do it: navigation sections, *Next* and *Back* buttons for applications, pull-down menus, logo sets.

If you group and reuse material, not only will you speed up the process of creating pages because authors don't have to type it every time, you also guarantee that the material is correct, accurate, and the same throughout the site. An author in the Contracts section may have the boilerplates saved in a Word document on their desktop, and just copy and paste them into a page. That doesn't keep them from turning "Acme Industries" into "Acne Industries" for fun. You may want to separate as much of the web page from the author, editor, and approver as possible. Chunks such as headers and footers usually get approved by managers and executives – you don't want copy editors fooling with that stuff.

Restringing Data

Where chunking data stops, restringing data begins. I will admit that there are not many sites that do this for more than forms or applications or news sites, but it is a really neat idea if you can make it work.

Restringing means breaking up your biggest chunk – the body text – into smaller chunks, and then restringing them into new pages. It would be like taking your favorite book, cutting it into paragraph-sized pieces, shuffling them up, and calling them a different book. Obviously, it doesn't work very well unless you have special data.

If you ran a news site, you could use this restringing technique to create the front page of the site using summaries of all the current news stories. Perhaps, if the news story was stored using XML, you could tag all summaries of your stories with `<summary>` tags that the system could look for and pull out. Alternatively, you could have the system simply grab the first paragraph of every story.

If you have a complex form on your site, you could ask the user a few basic questions, each correlating to a set of deeper questions. For example, on a B2B site, a user would register as a seller. The form could provide a list of types of products and ask the user to pick all the kinds of products they sold. Then, on the next page, the user would find in-depth questions about all the items they sold, but no questions on products they didn't (the full list of questions being automatically restrung to a list of suitable questions).

Restringing data is gold dust if you have this kind of specialized data. Otherwise, don't spend time worrying about it.

So, as a recap, we've rebuilt all our web site's content from the ground up. Our room full of money boxes is safe. We know exactly how many boxes there are, who is allowed to enter the room, who is allowed to make new boxes, and who has to verify that the boxes are complete. We have security to make sure boxes don't go where they shouldn't and smart labels on each box so we can quickly find and use them when the time comes. We have documented and implemented a workflow so that everyone knows their role in the process, and built plenty of reporting tools to see if everyone is doing their job. We have also decided to have quarterly reviews so everyone is doing the right job, problems are brought to everyone's attention, and tests are done to determine if decisions we made now are correct for the end-users.

We have set up the room to be secure, reliable, and smart. Now what?

We make more boxes and more rooms to put them in.

Building New Assets

There's a scientific principle somewhere that states, "All creatures will seek to minimize the amount of work they have to do." It's the rule that says, "I fixed it. Let's not bother with it anymore." We all end up abiding by it if for no other reason than the fact that we're all too busy putting out fires to actually go and start a few.

The installation of a CMS is a great opportunity to clean the slate and start afresh. All that time you spent trying to figure out all the subtleties of browser compatibilities is no longer necessary as the system will give the correct pages to the correct browser (see the next chapter on *Transformation*).

All the workarounds and patches to make your web site do what it's supposed to do and look like it's supposed to look? Gone. Not to mention all the processes you built to keep your work in order, what you've taught your authors about the Web, and all your secrets for uploading files. They're history. New problems loom, but progress is being made.

You've got the opportunity to do all those things you have wanted to do for months and years. For every time you said, "I could probably make that easier" or "That's not quite right. I should take another look at it", this is the time to improve things. You're teaching everyone new skills, building new workflows, adding new authors, and wiping away all the remnants of the old.

Let's start with the frontline of this brave new world, your authors.

Authors: Not a Dirty Word

In a lot of places, authors are looked on as annoyances, problem children, issues that always have new and interesting ways of interrupting your busy life. Sure, in your organization, that's not the case. But let's just admit that we've all got friends or ex-co-workers who have that problem, okay?

For all the flak authors get, they are doing a job most people don't want or can't do: they write (hopefully pretty well). So, why do many of us perceive authors as bothers? Because they are overlapping on our territory (web authoring), but are generally woefully prepared for the task. Give them a copy of Word and they're ready to roll. Open up a copy of a tool such as FrontPage, and most of them will start to get the shakes.

For all its flaws, a program like Word works. Fonts work, bullets work, colors work, and images can go in the middle of a page without having to build complicated table structures. Word makes sense. If something happens you weren't expecting, you can always run the "*Hidden Text*" option and see how Word sees your document.

But the Web is vastly different. Without getting into super-complex stylesheets, you can't do half the things you can do with a Word processor. Have you ever had an author ask why, when a document moves from Word to the Web, the font is different? And when you explained that users need a copy of the font, they suggest we simply send everyone a copy? What about making really funky bullets? Or kerning control or making words flow around an image? Clearly, most authors and web professionals come from two different worlds.

So who are the authors? How can you make content management help them?

Who Are "The Authors"?

Authors have a job to do every bit as vital as yours. You have to find a way to work together, with a common vocabulary and an understanding of each person's role within all these new workflows.

In my experience, there are two kinds of authors, and they each have different sets of needs and different expectations of their role and yours. There are basic authors and advanced authors, and they will both need extra help.

Basic Web Authors

Every time you see a statistic about how huge the number of people on the Web is getting, take a second and do a little math. Recently, it was determined that almost one billion people had used the Web. That's a huge number… until you subtract it from the five billion or so people on the planet. Fully four billion people have almost no exposure to the Internet. And they aren't all trapped in places without electricity or phone lines. Some of them may work in your organization.

Basic authors are people who have low, and in some cases no, experience with the Web. These are the people for who technology like WebTV was invented. Some people just don't think the Internet is interesting. Some people (like a friend's grandmother) think it is nothing but porn and bomb recipes. And some people are actively afraid of it.

So, you should treat your basic authors with care: make them understand that they are safe and remind them that they are to focus on the content. Then show them the client for the system. It will have far fewer buttons and options than Word or FrontPage. Explain that the client will keep them from using functions that won't work on the Web. By removing unnecessary features like line height control or font face, most users feel like they won't screw anything up because they couldn't if they tried (you might want to make that point for them). We'll talk more about client interfaces for the system a little later.

Advanced Web Authors

Advanced authors sound like they would be easier to deal with. You don't have to answer questions like "Why are my paragraphs spaced so far apart." But advanced authors sometimes go the other way, being too knowledgeable for their own good.

They may have taken a class or read a book, and based on what they learned, they may feel like they can do your job, whether that's the case or not. An example would be an author who read that cascading style sheets (CSS) allow web designers or site administrators to make site-wide changes to the design instantly. You know that a site has to be designed with CSS, and that even so, changing the stylesheet is dicey business. We want to teach them the best ways to use the Web, but be on your guard. While they respect your knowledge, they may be waiting for you to slip up, so they can show off how knowledgeable they are. Keep one step ahead of them in public situations or you may wind up with egg on your face.

An advanced author may need to feel like they are in control of their page, so when confronted by a somewhat limiting client, they may balk. Your job will be to wean them off the idea of design, and explain how much faster the new system will be for their page creation. They should be more creative with their prose, not their designs. After all, that's what their job description says they do.

The User Interface or the Client Tool

Think about the cost of adding a new author to your old system for adding content to your site. Did you have to hire people who already had lots of web experience? Then do you have to pay them a lot more every year because of it? Do you send them to class so they can learn a skill they might not be interested in learning? Those classes are not cheap, and they don't turn everyone into web experts, or even good WYSIWYG users. You could have your web designer convert text from a word processing format to HTML, but that takes up the web designer's time and you pay him or her to do other jobs.

Why did it have to be such an expensive process? Because you had no way of separating the author from the template. If authors wanted to add a page using the template, they would have to use whatever tool the template was designed in. Even a tool as user-friendly as FrontPage can have a steep learning curve. But content management gives the author an interface that is simple, useful, and uncomplicated. It helps them do their job without having to spend as much time learning as with a complex new tool.

The client is the main interface between the people who make content and the system itself. Getting your authors happy with the client is key. Most systems have customizable clients, so talk to your authors about what their needs are, then talk to your vendors to see how they can make it happen.

Web App vs. Desktop App

Clients, luckily, are fairly simple applications. For the most part, a client is a nice big area to type text, a few formatting buttons (for example, for bold, underline, and italics), bulleted list buttons, and maybe a way to apply a predetermined font style (like "big" or "red" or "big, red, and bold"). You'll have a place for adding metadata (for more details, see below), and a way to submit finished work. If your workflow requires it, there may be a way to submit the page to a specified person (for example, an approver may have to be able to choose to send it to legal, back to the author, or off to the web server).

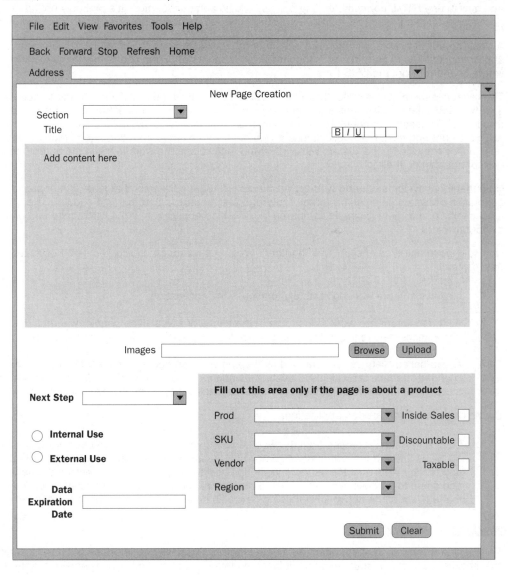

If (as is likely) you've already decided that all your web site content should be the same font and size, those options will not be available on the client. That way, your authors and editors don't have to worry about them. The same applies to kerning, letter spacing, margins, header sizes, etc. Your designer picks all of those things beforehand. All your authors have to worry about is the text, and some very basic formatting. Simple.

Note that some content management systems allow HTML to be used in the text field. Do you want that? For some organizations, letting users enter their own HTML is like letting them design their own page: things can get non-standard in a hurry. For others, users are disciplined enough to know when and how to use HTML correctly (editing bullets, adding comments, etc.). It's probably not an urgent decision, but it might lead to a loophole in your structured authoring process, so do bear it in mind.

A **desktop client** is an application like any other that is installed on the computer. Once installed, the application just has to be told who is logging in (so it understands the user's role in the workflow) and where on the network the CMS lives.

The client is generally so simple, that it isn't even always a desktop application. Many systems offer a **web-based client**. This client is an application that lives on your intranet server and is ported through HTTP. Instead of double-clicking an icon on their desktops, users just open a browser and go to the right address. The application is a web page with all the formatting and authoring tools they need. Once they log in, the system will understand their role in the workflow and the author, editor, or approver can do their job.

Note that most systems offering web-based clients will require the use of at least fifth or sixth generation browsers (Microsoft Internet Explorer 5 and Netscape 6, to name a couple). The functionality of the client is simple compared to a desktop application, but it will require one of these newer browsers.

How to choose one type of client over another? Well, that's a tough choice to make. For a web-based client:

- It allows authors working remotely to access the application.

- All the maintenance work tends to be in the hands of server-type people, whereas desktop applications tend to live in the area of help desk support or, unluckily, web support.

- A web-based client can be changed on the server, when necessary, meaning that the changed interface is available to everyone when they next log on. For a desktop application, a change in the interface involves having to reinstall the application on every desktop.

On the other hand, for desktop applications:

- They don't take resources from the web servers (which, as we all know, never really have 100% up time). If the server does go down, web-based client authors will not be able to see any of their work until the server is back up. Desktop applications connect via the network and seem to be down less often. Some desktop clients will allow users to store work locally in the event of the network itself going down. Of course, desktop computers crash as well.

Metadata

The client is where much of your metadata gets entered. Typically, the interface will have a series of checkboxes, pull-down menus, and text fields to enable the author, editor, or approver to enter the metadata information.

While the simple interface to a client lets you skimp on a lot of the training for authors, one place not to skimp is the metadata. It must be well labeled and explained carefully to every author. If you can, standardize all the data values that can be set. For example, if the author is supposed to choose a section for the content, don't make them type it in – put all the section options in a drop-down menu. That way they can't misspell anything.

Also, a short guide to your metadata might be a good idea. Give a screen capture of the client, list all the pieces of data you are capturing, and an explanation of every option. Examples would be better. Appoint a judge to rule on how to choose a metadata value if there is any question, and document the decision. You don't want to decide one way and have someone else go another way.

Management of the Workflow

So, all this information is moving from author to editor, back to author, back to editor, off to approver, back to author, again to the approver, and to the system for indexing and publishing. The process can take hours, days, or even weeks for some items. How many new pages will be in this larval stage at any given time? Lots. How will you keep track of them? More to the point, how will each author, editor, or approver know where his or her pages are? Each system is different, but a common method for managing all these pieces is e-mail.

An author writes their text and submits it. The system notes the date, time, and the author. It will change the status of the page (within the metadata) to reflect that it is waiting for the editor. An e-mail goes to the correct editor (how does it know who? Workflow rules determine that) saying that a new page has been created and needs to be edited. Some CMSs are set up to provide the editor with a path to the right page. When the editor opens the page, from a sandbox-type area on the server, the system updates the status and notes the time, date, and editor. The editor does what editors do. If the text needs work, the page can be sent back to the author with notes. The server keeps track of the change in status and sends an e-mail to the author to let them know that changes need to be made. The author opens the page, makes the changes, and resubmits the page. This time the editor is happy with the changes and submits it to the correct approver. All of this information is duly recorded by the system. The approver gets the notification e-mail, goes to the page and can approve it, which would send it to the server to be prepared for publication, or send it to someone else (legal, human resources, sales, etc).

Some systems will use an application-based To-Do List to let each person know that a page requires their attention. An editor would open their client application and see how many pages have been submitted to them for review. Aside from the method used to alert the user to the work they have to do, a system like that would act just like the e-mail system. In fact, some To-Do List style systems allow you to connect the system to your e-mail server, so that e-mails can be sent alerting users that new work is in their To-Do List.

You can see that the system does a good job of keeping track of where the page is and who's touched it. At any point in the process (and after, depending on how long you choose to keep your logs), an administrator can go into the system and look at the log for the details. They can even calculate things like how long each person worked on the page (just subtract the submitting time from the opening time) or how long it took someone like the editor to get to the page. They can see how many people had to work on the page and its path through all the layers of approval.

The ability to get an overhead view of how pages are being built and moved around is key to getting work done. A workflow designs the process, but this kind of management is like looking at the factory floor to see who's working and who's letting things pile up.

Summary

Content Management Systems are nothing without content to manage. Converting content from your old site is a huge hassle with little glory, but it is the jumping-off point for everything else you do with your system. Messy though it is, converting from existing content is faster and more productive than having to start from scratch.

We'll cover the migration process in detail in Chapter 8.

Building a process by which you build new content will also make your life easier in the long run. Better delegation of tasks, better definition of roles, and the means to do the job will make your authors, editors, and approvers more efficient and more useful. Workflow stops bottlenecks and disagreements before they start.

You data is secure, and only created and moved by people who are authorized to do so. You have seen a little bit of content nirvana. Now it's time to wrap all that content in attractive, easy-to-use templates. Are you ready to talk about designers?

3

- Visual Design

- Templates: Designing from a New Point of View

- Thinking About Your Users

Author: James Ellis

CMS Map: Transformation

The Web started as a way to pass academic documents between large universities. These documents were not exactly chock-full of cool motion graphics and whiz-bang designs. In fact, when you look back into history, you realize that it wasn't until 1991's Mosaic (later Netscape) that web browsers could even see anything but text.

In terms of sheer volume and speed, you can't beat text. It's the most efficient way of getting information from one place to another. If you took away text, would anyone be surfing the Internet, no matter how good the Flash animation is?

But as important as text is (where would CNN, the New York Times, or Yahoo! be without it?), visuals serve an important function. Just as images, colored fonts, colored images, and basic layout were key to getting the public interested in the Internet, visuals are key to branding, identity, and e-commerce.

Content management is a system to separate content and design, so that they may be independently created, edited, and used. In the previous chapter, we looked at how you go about getting your information ready for content management. Now, we are going to look at how we wrap that information in a visual blanket, to give it "look and feel", to make it identifiably yours, even at a glance, and to make it look like what it's supposed to be. Basically, this process is a transformation, usually achieved through the use of **templates**.

The design of your site, from your font choice (face, color, size, kerning, and line-height) to your colors, to your logos, and every image in between, is more than interior design. There are a lot of things to consider, not the least of which are usability and accessibility. There are also things to consider that are specific to your content management system.

The visual design is the container in which your content lives. If you build a container that makes sense, is easy to use, and can be used by anyone, it is more likely that people will use your site. If you sell great food, but your take-away box is impossible to open, you'll soon lose all your customers. So we want to build attractive, well-branded templates that are easy to use.

Visual Design

Designers have a heavy load to carry through this life. It doesn't matter if they are graphic designers, web designers, interior designers, or car designers. They are charged with the task of taking whatever the world has put together and making it run better, work better, feel better, and look better. They are the ones who clean up our mess and make it usable and saleable to the world.

To make matters worse, most people think they could have been, with a little more schooling or the time to practice, a great designer. What's so hard about picking a font? Color choices? No sweat. You have a flair for design, right?

Imagine if everyone you worked with labored under the assumption that you had the cushiest job in town, that you spent your days debating image choice with other designers while sipping sherry (or whatever). You'd feel a little frustrated, too.

Of course, in an organization where the web developer and designer are the same person, things are a little different. With one foot in each camp, the developer knows what would make the content work in a great way. The designer can understand the underlying ideas of the content and can make templates which show that content in an aesthetic way.

Before this little lecture on the horrors of being a designer wears thin, let's keep in mind that designers are going to make the site look good. How does a designer give you the best they can when you are setting up your templates? Let's start at the beginning.

Assess the Situation: Look At What You Did Before

Your web site did not appear out of thin air. Over the years, what started as a brochure and some executive biographies may have turned into an e-commerce center, a magazine, a sales site, or a government agency information site. It didn't happen in one day, it grew organically: when you had a need for a new section, you built one. If you're lucky, maybe you've gone through a site-wide redesign or two, but part of your site has some resemblance to the brochure you started with.

Some of the things you did were grounded in the fashion of the day, for example HTML frames. Page by page, section by section, idea over idea, you've built a patchwork quilt. From that patchwork we will be able to see some of the underlying themes for your web site, and pull out the best parts to transition to your new site.

So many organizations make spur of the moment decisions and allow them to become de facto policy. Don't let the cry of, "This is how we've always done it," keep you and your team from throwing out all the bad design choices from your site. Let the content management system play the bad guy. Tell people who say, "It's policy," that to implement the new system, you had to change policy. Otherwise, you'll end up shackled to old ideas and processes.

What Was Wrong?

Since 1995, which some regard as being the birth of the Internet boom, there have been a lot of ideas as to what makes a great web site. Technologies or theories or schools of thought that lasted little more than a matter of months and then went away, can be thrown out first.

- **Frames**. At the time they were a great way to show a lot of information in a little space. But then problems with page indexing, search engine rankings, wrapping (when someone wraps their frame around your web site, portraying it as their own), and navigation made frames less attractive. Frames have made a bit of a comeback, but are generally considered bad mojo.

- **Pages with a lot of navigation or images**. There was a time when a million images and tons of navigation were the way you made a "killer site". Even large news organizations who upload dozens of images a day have learned to keep images small and out of the way.

- **Motion graphics**. Without siding against the Flash camp of developers, most Flash and shockwave animations are not meant for business web sites. (If you are building a site to display more creative ideas, such as for a movie, a rock band, or an advertising studio, Flash can be used effectively and beautifully.)

This list doesn't take into account the real horrors from 1997: the `<blink>` tag, multi-colored text on black backgrounds, unnecessary JavaScript and Dynamic HTML, "star field" and "crushed velvet" backgrounds, and scrolling text. We can assume you know that that's wrong.

What else is wrong? Well, it wasn't long ago that the guideline was for all colors to be one of the 216 web-safe colors. If your logo colors were not originally one of those 216, you had to adjust the colors. Now, you may have the same logo all over your site in a variety of subtle color choices.

Did you switch from Arial to Verdana without applying the change to all the pages? Does the left-or right-hand navigation have a consistent width across all the pages? Is the image you use for your buttons exactly the same across the site?

Don't be too embarrassed, it happens to a lot of sites. That's why we're managing the design of the site at the same time as the content.

What Was Right?

Okay, we've survived the litany of horrors with all our hair intact. However, swallowed up in the dead-ends of new technology are some pretty good ideas. It's probably not going to be easy to find them, though. You may have trouble seeing the really good stuff right in front of your face.

Was there a color combination or an image or header style that you thought worked well? Maybe you thought the breadcrumb trail one of your designers made was pretty cool. (A **breadcrumb trail** is a way of displaying your current location in the site as a list of links back up the site tree.) Was there a button type or a pull-out menu that caught your eye?

Remember that you are not always the best judge of what works. Convene a panel of people who have no stake in the web site. Strangers would be best; maybe you can get people from an organization next door, or pay college students a few dollars for an hour of their time. Otherwise, people in-house who aren't designers or in the marketing department, IT department, or executives will do fine. Ask them to look over the site with you. Ask them questions like, "Can you find a certain product?" or "Can you register easily?". These people will clue you into the hidden gems of your web site.

You are likely to want to keep any forms or registration processes. They tend to get fixed and edited and fiddled with until they are refined to their purest essence. Don't throw them out until you're sure they aren't usable.

Another item to keep hold of are your logos. You've taught your users to recognize what they mean so, unless you can come up with spectacularly better ones, it's best to stick with what you have.

Using old design material is like choosing a favorite tool: you know it works. It's been tested in live conditions and deemed useful. Reusing it is not cheating, it's about getting the most out of your designs.

When you find pieces you like, get a screen capture of them. Crop out all the other stuff, and start a kind of catalog of "cool". It will be useful to you or your designers to remind you what worked. Not everything will get used, and some stuff may end up as a springboard to something different, but it's how you build a visual vocabulary.

Deriving Need

There are plenty of books, magazines, and web sites telling you how a web site should look, act, and be. The templates we design will showcase your content, so they should "match" the type of content you have. Should your site be image-heavy, text-heavy, design-oriented, bare bones, funky, professional, news-oriented, community- and interaction-based, or personal? We're not just talking about the "look and feel", but rather what the goal of the site is. You don't want to design a site that looks like the New York Times or the International Herald Tribune if it's actually to showcase the albums of a rap group.

Things like picture galleries and audio-clip galleries require special design – you can't just throw them into any old template and expect them to work. If you are selling products, how do you show your products, and against what kind of background? Boring products against exciting colors and patterns will cause your end users to run. A religious site that looks like a heavy metal fan's home page won't portray the right image. If you run a news site, you don't want to have the eye drawn to the colors and layout – you want to focus on text readability and structure.

A smart shortcut is to check out the competition, so to speak. If yours is a B2B site, go look at what other B2B sites are doing. Look at their layout and navigation: can you find your way around easily. Can you find a specific product in less than three or four clicks? Can you see why you can? Now, how would you use that knowledge on your site? Do you advertise services and educate people about what you do? Go and look at the big consultants and services sites. Is it clear what they do? Do the sites give you the feeling of competence, professionalism, and achievement? Can you see why?

The theory among some web thinkers is that you should copy what everyone else does, because it helps build the mystique of standards. Debate it all you want, but knowing how your peers and competitors designed their web sites can give you great ideas on how to do your own. Of course, you don't want to steal entire layouts and color schemes, but if someone else has found a clever solution to a problem you're having, figure out how you can use it. Don't bother reinventing the wheel.

However, remember that there is sometimes a lot to be gained by being different. If you expect to get a lot of traffic from people looking for the cool new web site, don't even think about borrowing designs – start from scratch and go wild.

How Cool Is Too Cool?

There was a time, not too long ago, when "cool" was the coin of the realm: you had to be cool to even be worth looking at. In the days of one- and two-page "web sites," making something new and interesting was the best way to bring traffic your way. The idea of "cool" turned into the "killer web site," a mix of visuals, colors, JavaScript, and anything else people could throw in. Huge, 60KB rotating logo in 3D letters? Must be a "killer site". You may not have seen many of these lately, because they have gone the way of the dodo.

Well, sort of. Today, many web sites have replaced JavaScript and Dynamic HTML tricks with Flash and DOM tricks. Endless fly-out menus, colorful advert banners, and never-ending Flash splash screens have many people scrambling for the "*Skip Intro*" link.

It may almost seem that web designers have replaced one bag of tricks with another, with little benefit. Too much of a good thing can end up bad. How cool is too cool?

Determining Shelf-Life

The best way to see if something is "too cool" is to determine how long it has been seen as an interesting technique, and how long other people think it will retain its novelty. This is a technique's shelf life.

If you use a new technique on your site, can you replace it quickly, or does your whole site depend on it? Think about all those organizations that bet on frames, only to have them turn into "inaccessible". That didn't mean a site fix, it meant a site redesign.

So, if you want to try something new, use it in small doses.

Nothing On the Web Is Forever, Except Mistakes

There is a web site referred to as the Wayback Machine (*http://www.archive.org*). It has archived much of the Internet historically. Where Google (*http://www.google.com*) lets you search for a site, the Wayback Machine lets you see versions of a site as it changed over time.

What does this mean? It means that every mistake you've ever made in terms of design is out there. Sure, it's funny to think that there's an old version of your page where you have the motto of the organization dancing around the cursor like a flag. If adding it brought a hundred thousand people to your site, then that's great. Laugh at it, knowing that it was goofy, but it served its purpose. However, if you could do it over again, would you reconsider knowing it would be there for all eternity?

Templates: Designing from a New Point of View

On the most fundamental level, content management is based on the idea that one person creates some content, someone else makes a template, and when the page is asked for by an end-user, the server puts the content in the template and sends it out. It's kind of like going to a fast food restaurant: one person makes the hamburger, and someone else makes the bag. When you order a burger, they assemble your order, putting the right burger in the bag with ketchup and napkins and a receipt, and deliver it to you. Well, if you're lucky. We spent a lot of time talking about the burger... er, content, in the last chapter, but now we're going to discuss the bag.

Templates are not new. WYSIWYG software packages often have their own template feature. But those templates are for developers and designers to fill with content. The web professionals are smart enough to put the content in the content area, the navigation in the navigation area, and put the right title on the page. However, content management is supposed to help the web professionals avoid having to fill the empty spaces. We need to program these pieces into the system.

Templating depends, like so much in content management, on proper planning. Do you know what content chunks need to go in which pages? Does a page have one or two navigation areas, or does it have four or five (don't laugh, have you really looked at some of your pages)? The designer in you may be champing at the bit to put together the visual design (colors, layout, fonts, images), but there's more to templating than picking the right colors.

Template Basics

Your pages, to put it bluntly, are not all the same. When people start talking about templates, they think of the rigid, staid structure of a WYSIWYG template: everything stays the same except the content, no matter what content you have. A template may have a content column of 370 pixels. That's fine for your simple pages, but what about pages with maps, org charts, spreadsheets, financial data, or other images that are wider than 370 pixels?

Templates can be as rigid or as flexible as you want. As we'll soon see, few sites really use only one template: they use a variety of templates that all have the same look and feel to them.

Structure

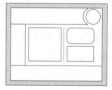

Does this look familiar? This basic layout structure could be one of a few million web sites online right now. It is referred to as the **"inverted-L" layout** (because the navigation and top header lines make it resemble an upside down L), the workhorse of web designers everywhere. Why?

- It's easy for your designers – half the job of design is done.

- It's easy for your users – they are used to this layout. They innately understand where content, navigation, and headers are because they've seen and learned it from lots of other web pages.

Aside from that, it is also a simple structure. This is how a lot of web pages start, so we'll use this as a kind of structure model for our web page.

> **Perspectives: The Inverted-L**
>
> *The L is about as easy as web design gets. You put your headers, logos, and primary navigation along the top in a series of horizontal rows. Then, you put the rest of your navigation along the left-hand side. How hard could that be? It's foolproof! Wrong.*
>
> *The inverted-L works because it makes the structure obvious. It just about yells at you to put content in the middle and less-important things like adverts and sign-in forms on the right. But it is not infallible. If you don't put enough material in the middle or to the right, your page will look unbalanced. If you spend days building the images for the top, and only a few minutes on the rest of the page, the page will be top-heavy. If you slack off on the header, but your content is really complex or riddled with images and maps, your page will look... odd. Let someone else look at your design for balance before you turn your "simple" inverted-L into a published page.*

There are a lot of things content management can stuff into your bucket, such as body content (multiple types if you want), navigation, logos, titles, footers, and images. So where does it put it all? Think back to our content chunking in Chapter 2: each chunk is a block. Where do you put the blocks?

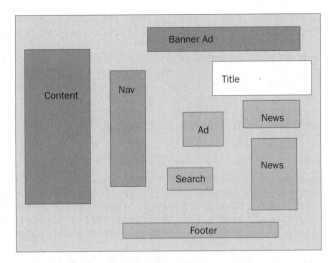

Let's use this material as an example. Well, using a process of elimination, we can see that the Title has to go at the top and the Footer at the bottom. What's left? Content, navigation, search box, and the news can go anywhere else. We'll follow convention, putting the navigation on the left and the content in the middle. The search box can go in the top-right and the news below that.

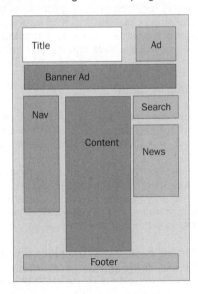

So we're already halfway to designing our page layout. If you have different pieces or different ways you'd like to arrange them, feel free. This is just an exercise so you can see how the process works.

This is the visual structure of your page. Knowing where the content and navigation go is crucial, because now you'll be able to tell your content management system where to put the pieces as it builds each page for the end-user.

Whatever layout you end up with, don't think it's the only one you will ever use. It's likely that you have some content or some sections that will require special consideration. That's fine. You want to design a structure (and therein a template) for 80-90% of your site. Unless all your content is very similar, you'll have to make a special template or two for the small percentage of pages that can't fit in your default structure. Go back to the fast food metaphor. If your store's bags are all the same, you'll feel silly selling someone an order or french fries and putting them in a huge bag. Conversely, if your bags are all small, you'll be using three or four per order. Having a variety of templates will allow you to display a variety of content. The system will be able to use the template that you chose (the one that best suits the content) and make the content work.

Modularity

Of course, your chunks of content are not all the same. Some chunks are always unique, like your body content. Some chunks are always the same, like your footer, with all the legalese, contact information, and privacy policies. Some chunks are in between, like your header and navigation. Maybe your header changes with each section, and maybe your navigation is the same on pages within a section. The level of uniqueness determines how modular the content is.

Your footer is a great example. If you build your pages using the XHTML/CSS model, you can just create your footer text, and have the system stick it into the bottom of every page as the server requests it. Even if each section of the site has a different color scheme, the text will appear as if someone typed it in by hand with whatever background color showing through.

If you've used Server Side Includes (SSI) before, the process is the same: the system will add whatever material you want to wherever you want it. If all your chunks of content were the same, you might not need a full content management system: you could just use a series of SSI to run your web page. However, since few people have chunks that are all the same, SSI-style inserts are usually not feasible.

Perspectives: Server Side Includes

Server Side Includes (SSI) are one of the first steps web professionals took towards modularizing content and building web pages on the fly. Think of them as ancient (in web time, anyway) ancestors to content management systems.

A line of code (perhaps one that looks like this: `<!--#include file="header.html" -->`) is added into a web page's HTML, for example, `index.html`. The server begins to send out `index.html` to an end-user. It sees the line of code, gets `header.html`, and copies this into `index.html` wherever the line of code was. Then it sends the complete page out, so it looks like the header was there all the time.

The bonus is that you can put the include code for the header in every page on your site. When you change the header, every page will start using it as soon as it is saved to the web server and it looks like you've done a subtle redesign in a few hours. It saves time by making pieces modular.

What about navigation? If you have a simple site where the navigation is basically the same for each page, you can treat it like you would a footer. You would have the navigation built as a chunk of information and the server would add it (in the right place) on every page. However, most sites have contextual navigation: navigation based on where you are in the site.

Perhaps each section or subsection has its own navigation? As the user builds a page, they should decide where in the site it should "live" (that is, what section the page should be in). Based upon the rules you've designed, the system should then add the generic footer and the correct semi-generic navigation when building the page.

Another way to attack this kind of problem is to simplify your templates, but let server-side variables choose the correct header and footer, the logo, and the navigation. The system can then build the right template for each page.

The body content itself can be further modularized to smaller paragraph templates, which we'll see more of in Chapter 5. Perhaps the author wants to add content that is just text, or has a small image to add alongside their text or a section. Creating paragraph templates that specify how the paragraph text and any images are laid out and allowing the author to choose which paragraph template is suitable for their content gives them more control over their work.

Customization

As we discussed earlier, 80-90% of all your pages should fit within your default structure. However, what about the other 10-20%? Since those pages won't work in your basic template, you should make a few secondary templates.

If you look back at the inverted-L layout, your body content column is not that wide. If you are building a page that adheres to some basic accessibility principles, that column may be as narrow as 400 pixels (we'll talk about usability and accessibility later in this chapter). That's fine for an all-text page or a page with small images, but if you have an image that's wider, you can't just throw it out.

The map would fit if you got rid of all that material on the right-hand side (news and utilities), right? If the material on the right-hand side was secondary, your content should "out-rank" that material. In other words, your content in the middle is what people came for. They might not be surprised (or even notice) when the navigation disappears to make room for the content. So, make a template exactly like your default one, but remove the material on the right. When an author encounters a need for that much space, they can simply choose that template.

Note that, in your workflow, you should consider making a rule that says if an author decides to use a template other than the default, it should go to a manager for template approval. If all your users could pick whatever template they wanted, it might give them more freedom than they need. Remember that your goal in using a content management system is to maintain consistency across all pages (old and new). Limit authors' use of the other template to achieve better standardization.

But what if you have a very big table or spreadsheet, one too big to allow your standard left-handed navigation? Perhaps make a third template structure that does not have any extra material on the left or right. As above, make sure it is not easy for authors to use this structure; otherwise they may be tempted to build their own page layouts. Alternatively, you might try using pop-up windows, containing nothing but the extra large content and a logo, that appear in front of the existing window. You could even put the content in a PDF document and link to it. The PDF solution is particularly effective if you expect users to print the material.

If you have some material that is generally slightly wider or narrower than the 400 pixels of the content area, you can make a template at around 350 pixels or 450 pixels to allow for subtle adjustments. However, this template should only be used when you use standard-sized graphics, such as for products. Pages that just contain text or small images should fit fine within the default size, otherwise, it shouldn't be the default structure.

Remember, all your templates should maintain a consistent look. If you build each template from existing designs, it will help users feel that they are on familiar territory, as well as guarantee that the templates maintain a consistent look and feel across the site.

How Many Templates?

You may have noticed in the last few sections that I've been talking about structures rather than templates themselves. When you are thinking about your chunks of content and your structures, you shouldn't get too hung up on the idea of "how it will look." Not yet, anyway. Why? Because one of the truly great functions of content management is its ability to choose the templates you are applying to a chunk of content. You can have different templates for different uses of the same content. Why would you need different templates for the same content? There are a few obvious reasons.

By Browser

Browser issues have been the central theme of frustration for designers for years. Most designers would love to build pages that fully utilize the DOM and CSS: it means smaller file-sizes, cooler pages, and easier maintenance. However, some 8% of the Internet population use older browsers like Internet Explorer 4 and Netscape Navigator 4, whose implementations of DOM and CSS are basic at best.

Here's the solution. Make a template for older browsers that doesn't have any bells and whistles, uses basic table layouts, watered-down font controls, and the like. Make another template that uses CSS, `a:hover` rollovers, and `<div>` positioning. When a user with an older browser comes to your site, the server will detect the browser automatically (as part of the HTTP request that gets passed from a user to your server when they navigate to your site), and the system will give the user the content they requested using the simple layout of the simple template. If someone with a later browser, such as Mozilla 1.0 or Internet Explorer 6, comes along, the system will put the content in the super-modern template so the user gets the latest and greatest design.

To take that a step further, think about users who use Lynx (a text-only browser) or a screen reader (which reads aloud your web page). You can put your content in a really stripped-down template and send it off, knowing that the user will be glad to see a page free of clutter they can't use. PDAs and WAP phones, as well as other Internet appliances whose screen size and resolution are much smaller than even the older monitors, also need special templates. If you view the site through a PDA, you'll see that the images are less important. On WAP phones, they are virtually useless. Your template for these browsers should reflect that.

By User

Recall that in Chapter 2 we discussed the fact that metadata could be used to store information about end-users so that special chunks of content could be delivered to them based on that information. Well, you can also deliver special templates to special users. If you have an extranet site (a subsection of the intranet which outsiders can see, usually specially registered users who must log in to see the content), you might want to consider using a special template for those users, with a different logo, different colors, and navigation that takes them to places other people can't find. If you have a B2B site and you have a few high-volume buyers, you can put their logo on the site when they view it. If you have a co-branding agreement, you can alter pages for users who came to the site through your partner.

You can probably think up a few good ways to separate your users into groups for their own templates. Users love to know that they are special, and this is a smart way to show them.

You can even make templates for authors and editors, based on their needs. An author for the legal department doesn't need any tools for images, and the editor for the sales department probably doesn't need as many metadata options. You can build templates so that these internal users can see only the tools they need, making for a trimmed-down, efficient interface.

Template Patterns

Over time, designers learn what works and what doesn't because they see what other designers do. Thus, we have patterns in design. Following these patterns is an easy money bet. It's not a sure thing, but generally, these patterns have emerged for a reason.

E-commerce Sites

Obviously, e-commerce sites are designed to get users to buy. Rather than rock the boat with cool design, most e-commerce sites keep to a simple inverted-L structure, with a listing of all product categories across the top. A handful of e-commerce sites have pushed the envelope (Dr. Marten's shoe web site in 1999 was a notable example, though MAC cosmetics in 2000 was also very different), but those sites generally catered to a younger, more web-savvy crowd.

Look at Amazon (*http://www.amazon.com*). They helped to forge the standard, and are still the best example of it. The broad navigation sections (Amazon calls them "stores") are across the top. The ability to drill down through categories is on the left. They use a three-column layout: left for the navigation, middle for the most important content, and right for less important content. If someone is using a 640x480 resolution, the less important content to the right gets chopped off, but the best material is still visible. Amazon has lots of links in the content area, and lots of small images that can be made bigger by clicking on them. If you put your mind to it, you could name five major shopping sites that share those same properties.

E-commerce is dominated by the idea of usability: if a user can't find a certain product or group of products, that's a lost sale. It would be as if you put an unusual handle on the front door of your store – it's not locked and you could figure it out given a minute or two, but why should a shopper spend a second trying to figure out the door handle. They'll shop somewhere else.

Information/News Sites

Information sites aren't specifically trying to get you to spend money (though they may have ways to collect any cash you're offering). Success isn't based on sales; it's based on a looser metric sometimes called "ability to find information". That kind of metric is hard to define or measure, so rather than count sales, information sites generally have to rely on usability tests and focus groups to determine if people are able to find the information they're looking for.

News sites have the benefit of a built-in structure (world, local, sports, features) and a full-time editorial staff. They know how to group stories together and how to rotate new stories into old ones. But that doesn't mean that news sites are always easy to design. There are plenty of smaller newspapers that seem to make it impossible to find the newest stories or archives. Presumably, the thinking is that they are publishing to the Web, but would rather users buy a paper copy, where they see more revenue.

Examples of great news sites are the New York Times (*http://www.nytimes.com*), the BBC online (*http://news.bbc.co.uk*), and the International Herald Tribune (*http://www.iht.com*). The latter gets special recognition for understanding that it is a global paper (albeit in English), tries hard to make getting the news easy for everyone: one or three column layout, changing font size, and printable versions make it easy for users on the oldest modems and monitors to get the news.

Information sites are a broader category. Government sites, non-profit organizations, and community groups need to put out the same kind of information as a news site, but without the guard rail of established sections and editing. The best solution for these sites is to arrange pages in an order a user would want (you should be asking them, repeatedly, what they want and how they want it), and build pages in a way that focuses on the content. Don't worry about splashy design, as it often irritates users looking for a specific piece of information and they have to wade through (and on a dial-up modem, wading is the right term) your design. Spend more time on your search function (how it works and where it's located – it should be easy to find and useful for the user) than on, say, your color scheme or pop-up windows.

Examples of useful information sites are *http://www.evolt.org*, *http://www.webstandards.org*, *http://www.texas.gov*, and *http://www.irs.gov*. These sites focus on giving you the information you're looking for. The designs vary greatly, but the structure and templates should be based upon the content and user needs alone.

Personal and Community Sites

Personal sites deserve a mention primarily because a lot of the "cool" design work is being done there. Few personal sites will actually require a full-scale content management system, though many are run with **web log** (or "**blog**") software like Movable Type, Blogger, and Radio, which are really just simplified CMSs.

Blogging is a recent phenomenon, wherein individuals get simplified input screens to capture their thoughts. Just like a CMS, blogging eliminates the need for authors to worry about the HTML, so they need only focus on the content once the site is up and running. All these software packages even come with default and sample templates, so no knowledge of HTML or design is ever needed.

Because these sites usually don't get the kind of traffic a large e-commerce, government, or news site would get, the focus tends to be on experimentation and expression rather than structure and usability. Blog software is cheaper, and often easier to use, but cannot always handle the load of a large site.

Examples of personal sites are: *http://www.diveintomark.org*, *http://www.bostich.com*, *http://www.whatdoiknow.org*, and *http://www.littleyellowdifferent.com*. The sites are wildly different, but do reflect the personality of the designers.

Community sites share the same homey atmosphere and care that go into personal sites. They are usually designed like personal sites, but have a more powerful content management system since more authors and content is involved.

The real difference between a community site and others is that it thrives on content from the outside. A community site like Slashdot (*http://www.slashdot.org*) relies on people who aren't employees to add content to the site. They have web interfaces that registered users log into and add links, reviews, commentary, and opinions to the site. In that regard, the idea that someone who isn't on the payroll and can't be fired can still post publicly to the site is unusual.

Community sites are really amateur news/information sites with external authors. As such, these sites need to make sure that their registration process and posting process are easy to use. No matter how avid the fan, if posting is a chore, they will find some other channel to get their information.

Updating Templates

Once you have your site all set up, what happens when you want to change your templates? Well, that depends on whether you bake or fry your pages.

As we defined in Chapter 1, baking is when your system builds pages beforehand. The template gets filled with content and saved to the web server, where it waits to be called by a user. Frying happens when the system builds the pages when you request them. The content and templates sit separately, waiting to be built, up until a user clicks on a link to that page.

If you bake your pages, and you update your templates, you will need to resave the created pages onto the web server. This may bottleneck any changes you make to your templates. Bear in mind how long this process will take.

If you fry your pages, any changes to your templates will be publicly available as soon as you save the template to the web server. Because the pages aren't made beforehand, changes are used as soon as they are available to the content management system.

Perspectives: Updating Templates

Let's do a little math. You've got three structures (a default structure, a wide structure, and a structure with no left-or right-hand navigation or news) and a handful of special templates (one for your site map, one for your search results page, etc). These need to be supplied to three groups of users who need browser-based templates (one that conforms to the latest browsers, one that conforms to earlier version 4 browsers, and a text-only version). Finally you need a set of templates for your extranet (you're lucky here because you've required in the user agreement that anyone in the extranet has to have Internet Explorer 5). How many templates would you have to design?

Hmmm, let's see. Three browser-based templates for each of three structures is nine templates. Plus another set for the extranet, so add three more. And we can't forget the special pages, which will need special versions based on the browser. How many is that? 15? Wow. That's a lot. Now, once you've set up your system and everything is going well, a new project is announced and they need a new set of templates (times three for each browser). And a few months after that a new line of products is rolled out and the marketing department would like to highlight it with a new set of templates (times three). So, a year from now, you might have as many as... 21 templates? Yikes! Now, a year after the content management implementation, your boss comes round to tell you that it's time to do a redesign, and that because of the system, it shouldn't take long at all. A few days should suffice, right? For 21 templates.

The trouble with templates is that they reproduce like rabbits. You may start with a well-defined set, useful for any occasion, but someone will decide they need a new one (which is really three). And they add up quickly. Pretty soon, you're up to your ears in templates.

You need to nip this problem in the bud. You may decide that you will draw a line in the sand and that no new templates are to be created. You won't win any popularity contests this way, but if you can pull it off, bully for you.

Perspectives: Updating Templates (Cont'd)

Or, you can find ways of building "newness" into your templates. For example, you can make a spot for a chunk in your structure in which you can place a second logo. When your organization puts out a new product line, you can signal the template to show a second logo for the product line on all pages about that product. Imagine an empty area in the top right-hand corner. Sure, you could put your search bar there, but you let it lay fallow. Two months from now, when someone asks you to build a new series of templates for the Widget, you can offer up the location. A Widget author creates a page, and sets the metadata for "Widget." When the page is served to a user, the template grabs the content, the navigation, the headers and footers, and the logo for the Widget, which it then places in the top right-hand corner. (Amazon.com does a great job with this. Did you see their Gold Box application? One day there's nothing in the top right-hand corner of their page, and the next day there's a little logo inviting you to special deals.)

Or, you can designate a color of background to each section. The author tells the metadata which section the content is for, and the system tells the stylesheet controlling background colors that it should show the "Widget" color (perhaps a nice slate blue?) as the background. This works well in templates for newer browsers, and makes it look like you have hundreds of templates on hand, ready to go.

These tricks should be considered during the early phases of the project, otherwise you'll have to rebuild designs and author interfaces to capture and use the correct information.

Content vs. Presentation

Content management hinges on one basic principle: content and presentation are separate until they are put together to build a page. Some of the technologies available to you in this task are:

HTML: HyperText Markup Language. This is the building block of the Web. Although its original intention was to enable designers to tag content as to its purpose (heading, paragraph, etc.), it is often used to tag content for its visual design instead (color, line breaks, etc.). It's difficult to completely separate content from design with HTML without the additional use of CSS.

XHTML: Extensible HyperText Markup Language. This is the next iteration of HTML. It's pretty much just HTML with a much stronger control of the syntax – sometimes referred to as HTML seen through XML's eyes. Its better syntax means better coordination with CSS for design and layout.

CSS: Cascading Style Sheets. A stylesheet is the visual instruction set for the Web (for example, CSS will say things like "all fonts 12pt verdana."). It's flexible, can be centralized or decentralized (for local control or site-wide control), but isn't perfectly adopted by all browsers, even newer ones. The future of web design perhaps, but the future is still a little… imperfect.

XML: Extensible Markup Language. This is the triumph of content over all else. It enables content to be tagged based on its meaning. Tags aren't universal (meaning that what I call `<name>` is not necessarily what you call `<name>`). It primarily relies on CSS or XSLT for all formatting and visual design.

XSLT: Extensible Stylesheet Language for Transformations. An XML language that can be used to convert any XML document into another XML document (including XHTML).

For a full explanation of what all these technologies do and how they work, try *http://www.w3c.org* for a technical description, or *http://www.webmonkey.com* for a friendlier approach. The W3C is the body that makes recommendations about what technologies and languages should be used on the Web.

These are the basics. Don't worry about the part where it says that HTML and XHTML do a bad job separating content from design – your content management system is going to do the separating and combining of the content and design for you. You can build templates for your older browsers in straight HTML (no stylesheet magic) and your templates for newer browsers can be built with XHTML and CSS. Increasingly, your content will be stored by your content management system as XML (though plenty still use databases), so that it can easily be output to even the smallest PDA, oldest browser, and any other format you can think of.

Thinking About Your Users

Five years ago, no one cared about their users.

Ok, that's an overstatement. They probably cared about their users, but were struggling with the inherent newness of the medium. Designers tended to focus on the cool technique of the moment – frames, or Dynamic HTML, or JavaScript, or whatever was cool and new. People even went so far as to put small banners on their site saying that it was "optimized" for such and such a browser. If you didn't have Netscape Navigator 3, you couldn't get frames (and instead you got an obnoxious page telling you to upgrade). If you had Internet Explorer 3, you couldn't see the `<blink>` tag (which is not such a punishment, actually).

When the money started to flow into the Internet, people had to figure out the best way to sell items over the new medium. In order to make buying on the Internet easy, e-commerce site designers started to think about their users.

Thinking about your users may sound boring, but it is key to reaching as wide an audience as possible. This means making a site that anyone with any type of browser can see (**accessibility**), and which it's easy to use (**usability**). You want to give your telephone nice big, easy to see and press buttons. Otherwise, some people won't bother trying to call you on your phone.

Since usability became a pressing concern, designers have fought back, saying such pages are boring, unattractive, and a waste of time. It's nice to have big buttons on your phone, but wouldn't a sleek and small phone be better? The ultimate goal sounds simple, but is hard to achieve: useful, usable, accessible, and desirable. Making compromises between the four is what web design is all about.

Focusing on "being totally accessible" is not always the right solution. Not every site needs to cater for every user. Getting the most people using your site is a good target, but a better target is getting the people who your site is aimed at using your site. Are there small changes you can make that do not detract from or dull your site's style, but still make it more usable? The issue of style getting the right balance between accessibility and usability is a central issue for web designers. It is too big to say that we will discuss it here exhaustively, but these ideas should be considered.

For more information see Accessible Web Sites *(glasshaus, ISBN 1904151000) and* Usability: The Site Speaks for Itself *(glasshaus, ISBN 1904151035).*

Everything They Said About Usability Is Right

Building in a standards-based, usable, and accessible way means that your pages are ready for the next generation of browsers. Standards and usability are becoming more and more prominent and widespread. Getting into the swing of things means being a little ahead of the curve and setting yourself up for the future of web development.

Save Time and Money

The first thing managers should love about accessibility and usability it that is can save your organization time and money.

For one thing, it speeds up design because it allows designers to focus on the standard technologies they can and should use to ensure their sites are accessible.

Usable pages mean fewer help calls from users who can't figure out how to use the site. If you sell a product online, a percentage of your customers will need phone support to complete the transaction. Building a usable site means the number of calls will decrease: task paths will be more obvious, error messages will make more sense, more users will be able to complete transactions without outside help.

If you want to do business with the American federal government, all your pages must meet the strict Section 508 Accessibility Guidelines. Maybe this falls under the category of "making more money" but, clearly, many firms would like to have the US government as a client or customer. To read more about the 508 accessibility standards, take a look at *http://www.section508.gov*.

Finally, your users will be happier to use your site. Think about how easy Amazon is. It makes sense, simple as that. You are happy to buy from or use a site like that. Compare them to any number (I won't mention names) of sites that are hard to navigate through or make it hard to get information from. How long would you, as a consumer, stay at a site like that?

Make Everyone Happy

Well, maybe you can't make everybody happy, but you can at least *reach* everybody. Accessibility, boiled down to its simplest form, is the idea that anyone and everyone should be able to view your web site. Even if your users are visually impaired, on a slow modem, or using a seven-year-old browser, they should be able to read your page.

Extend Your Reach

In order to maximize your web site, getting it out to as many people as you can, you need to implement some serious accessibility functionality.

Older Browsers

Netscape 4.7 and its older cousins own a good part of the magic eight percent of people who can't see much of what's on your web page. When it was released it was a solid browser, but that was 1997 – at least five years ago.

After its release, problems slowly became apparent. If you nested too many tables, the page didn't load. Background images for tables would get "inherited" by the table they were nested in. Tables didn't line up properly. Some table cells would become empty. Its implementation of CSS was spotty at best. At the time, these things were cutting-edge ideas for the Web. Today, they are old hat.

The problems were so bad that Netscape decided the problems couldn't be fixed. Instead, they started their next browser from the ground up, a process that cost them two years in development time and gave Microsoft plenty of time to make Internet Explorer a solid browser and take over a lot of the market.

Some designers and coders will moan so loudly about Netscape 4.7 that most simply decide to pretend it never existed. They ignore it. They forgo reaching that section of their potential audience as "too expensive or time-consuming to reach".

Building accessible pages with a content management system means that if a user with Netscape 4.7 couldn't even begin to read your "cool" page, they could at least get the watered-down one. Netscape 4.7 users are not looking for cool (otherwise they would have updated their browsers long ago); they are looking for information that you can now provide to them.

Text Browsers

You don't meet people who like to surf the Web via a text-only browser every day. Most of us can hardly stomach the idea of not getting images, JavaScript, Flash, QuickTime, or any design or layout features at all in our web surfing. But think again. You'd get no pop-ups, no adverts for wireless cameras or inexpensive plane fares, no annoying Flash adverts covering up whatever you want to be reading, or advert banners. You'd just get pure content. Sound appealing?

Raw text is an amazingly flexible format. You can make the font nice and big, you can download it quickly, and you can copy it to any device you like.

Screen Readers

People with visual impairments need the Internet more than many. Given the difficulties they may face the moment they leave their homes, getting vital information, shopping via e-commerce sites, and visiting online community sites can make their lives easier. That is, if web sites were even remotely navigable and accessible to people using screen readers.

Screen readers like JAWS (*http://www.can-we-talk.com/jfw.html*) look at the information on the screen and "speak" it through the computer's speakers. The reader starts at the top left-hand corner and works its way down. Readers benefit from the use of:

- `alt` attributes, which tell the reader what the image is, whether it's a logo or a portrait or a bullet.

- `longdesc` attributes, which allow you to describe in depth what an image is of, including conclusions the image proves or where the image was taken from.

- structured pages using header tags and skip-able navigation. Navigation is often at the top of the page which sighted users generally skip; visually impaired people need to move past the navigation to hear what the content of the page is.

Screen readers have got much better in recent years. They can be programmed to skip bullet points, invisible GIF images, and navigation. But they still often falter when they encounter a complex table-based layout (the reader can't tell the difference between a table of data and a table that keeps your images on the right side of the page). This is why a text-only page that uses header tags for structure is so much easier for people who are visually impaired to use.

Benefit Power Users

Much has been made of users who are visually impaired or users with old or unusual browsers as being some sort of second-class Internet citizens. Usability and accessibility helps those poor, helpless users.

What a load of rubbish.

Usability and accessibility is not pity, it is a way to make sure that everyone can use your web site. Even power users get a big boost. To avoid pop-up windows, many power users turn JavaScript off. So, if your site uses JavaScript fly-out menus, they won't be able to get around, even with the best browser.

Building pages to utilize 1024x768 monitors is also a fool's errand. Even with 1280x1024 or 1600x1200 monitors, power users with monitor resolutions that high use the space for extra windows, not bigger windows. Designing for 800X600 with a liquid layout is just smart design.

Even power users appreciate things like obvious navigation, breadcrumb trails, buttons big enough to click quickly, and a well laid-out page. Thinking that power users actually enjoy mystery navigation and colors with no contrast between text and its background is crazy. No one is happy to see unusable or inaccessible pages.

Everything They Said About Usability Is Wrong

Jakob Nielsen (*http://www.useit.com*) produced one of the first popular books on usability, and has since become its most outspoken proponent. He certainly has done a lot for the industry and identifies real problems with the usability of sites. However, to some people Nielsen's view of what is usable tends to be a little on the extreme side. Reading his books and articles, one might get the impression that every web site should look like and feel exactly like Amazon.

So, let's clear up some myths about usability and accessibility right now.

Myth: Usability Is Boring

Some usable web pages may be kind of boring. However, that's at least partly because the drive for usable pages is fairly recent. Usable sites shorten the amount of time someone needs to be on your site to do a given task (buy, register, find information). If users think it's easy to use, they will come back and use it often.

As more organizations realize it is in their best interests to create accessible web sites, designers will be forced to dive deeply into the minutiae of accessibility ideas and find ways to add a bit of cool to your site. It's already happening at places like *http://www.diveintomark.org*, where accessibility is combined with a series of different stylesheets to control the look.

As a content management system administrator, you can build accessibility into your templates, making sure that anyone who visits your site and needs accessible pages can get them.

Myth: Users Are Dumb

In some respects, usability has gone a little too far. What once was a plea for pages that made sense is now a demand that all pages be stupid. The current "rules" about usability say things like, "Users don't read, they scan" and "Users don't scroll". Maybe that was true years ago when everyone was still new to the Internet, but today, it's not completely true. Millions of people do read online newspapers and magazines, and complex articles. Sure, they scan for the content they want, but when the information is there, they read. You want to make information easy to find, but the information itself should not be oversimplified.

Usability is not about making your pages or your information dumb, or even assuming your users are dumb. It's just about making things easy.

Summary

As the middle of the three content management activities, the transformation process may be the one that web professionals are most used to. As we have seen, all the usability and accessibility issues that you should take into account on any site you create are just as relevant when designing your CMS templates.

Templates, arranged in areas into which chunks of content can be automatically added, allow you to display the content provided by the authors of your site. As well as providing different designs for different types of content or different areas of your site, they allow you to provide content to browsers with different functionality and personalized content to different sections of your audience.

We next turn to the final stage of the content management process – publishing your content within the templates.

4

- Delivering Your Content
- Production Environments
- Thinking Beyond Web Sites

Author: David Thiemecke

CMS Map: Publishing

Until now, we've spoken about how content management systems assist us to separate content from presentation. Now we're going to talk about publishing: the process of putting them back together. This is the last step in the critical path started in Chapter 2. If you make it a bottleneck, you can fail to reach your audience.

This chapter covers what we mean by publishing, and the issues that arise from it. We'll cover:

- What we publish

- The rendering sequence

- How publishing is different from authoring

- Techniques to operate publishing as a production system

- Publishing to multiple platforms

- Feedback from your site, and how it can improve publishing

What Do We Publish?

What appears on your web site? Your audience might use event calendars, news indexes, product catalogs, frequently asked questions, shopping carts, file exchanges, and threaded discussions amongst other things. Which of these are "content"? You could answer, "events, news, products, questions, files, and posts". Can you use any of these without sorting, searching, and navigating through them in calendars, indexes, catalogs, carts, exchanges, and discussions? No. You made your site out of applications that present your content.

Content management is just one application, but it is often linked to others like threaded discussions, file exchange, streaming media, games, e-mail lists, and enterprise applications. Content management must coexist with these other applications. Sometimes, you'll find that the other applications don't even use your content. For example, your contributors may write stories for the news index and each one passes through an approval process in your content management system. In contrast, your audience posts messages to the threaded discussions, which get handled solely by that application. Your audience navigates between applications seamlessly on the same site.

Is content management an application itself or the coordinator of applications? That depends on your site's business needs. For example, to minimize the effort needed to maintain your product catalog site, you could attach content to each product area. When managers create a new product, the system provides a place for literature about the product. Content management supports the products in the catalog. If you loosely tie content to your site, you can replace it more easily later. Your publishing system must feed its output into the managing application, in this case, a product catalog.

In a different scenario, imagine you manage a sprawling city government web site. You add a threaded discussion application to each city department subsite, where citizens can discuss issues openly with officials. The content management system wraps the threaded discussion application in its "look and feel". Picture your threaded discussion application occupying one slot in a template, while the CMS draws navigation into another slot. City web managers can place the threaded discussion where they like within the department subsite content. If content management coordinates all the applications on your site, you can organize your site easily, but you'll depend on your CMS much more. Your other applications must provide all their input and output to the publishing system to present.

Not all applications appear through the web site, either. Consider a site that offers content to web browsers, FTP file exchanges, and an e-mail list. The web site supports access to these resources, but does not present them.

When you use content management to coordinate your site, what kinds of applications do you publish?

Content

In Chapter 2, we defined content by the kinds of assets you manage on your site, including documents, streaming media, images, and files. Publishing responds to requests for the content by presenting the assets in an appropriate template. It only chooses assets that match the requirements for public content. For example, your publishing system may present only current content, available through navigation, which has been approved and fits in the same locale as the audience member.

Remember, content includes metadata, too. Although search engines vary in the value they place on it, would you choose a publishing system that ignored `<meta>` tags on your pages? Metadata extends to cover things like the way you classify your content for browsing relationships, also known as ontology. In this second case, you may access the ontology through an embedded application rather than publishing it directly as content.

Embedded Applications

What do we mean by an embedded application? Your site search is an embedded application. It accepts a query from a form appearing in templates throughout your site. It searches the database and returns results for the publishing engine to return. Despite interacting with the search engine, users remain in the part of the site they were in when they requested the search until a selected result takes them elsewhere. Other examples include e-mail forms, surveys, e-commerce applications, maps, and custom database queries. The application may have access to the publishing state, such as the identity of the user and what content they requested.

Make sure your embedded applications handle their own faults and convey you back to the content system. In the simplest case, content management either fulfills requests for pages or tells you it could not find your request. Embedded applications extend the set of exceptions to requests on your site. Can your content management system resolve a failure to authorize a credit card because the processing server went down? No, but your embedded application can produce a helpful message for this situation. The publishing system can present this to the user on behalf of your embedded application.

Authentication and Personalization

Authentication determines who your audience members are and whether they have permission to access resources on your site. Personalization applies an audience member's profile to tailor the site to their needs. Think of these as special cases of embedded applications that impact publishing. Due to popularity, your content system may integrate them. For example, customer extranets frequently use authentication to prevent one customer from prying into the business of another.

Just like any embedded application, beware that authentication and personalization may limit the scalability of your site. Can you cache pages that contain a unique "look and feel" for every user? If each protected area of your site has its own logon, you'll interrupt your user and force them to keep each account synchronized. That's a recipe to lose audience members. I suggest you share the same authentication system across all areas and applications on your site. You'll benefit from having less software to manage, having only one interruption for the user, and you can produce reports correlating users across areas.

Syndication

Think of syndication as a special case of publishing content to other automated systems. Your own site may already draw content from other systems to provide weather reports and news, but you can multiply the audience for your content by enlisting other sites to syndicate from you.

How does this work? One site imports a feed of content from another. The two parties involved agree on the format, selection criteria, and permissions up front. For export, you must configure which content you'll syndicate, just like marking content for public viewing. For import, you might supply content to an approval process or just publish it, depending on your trust in the source. What would this look like? Here's an example:

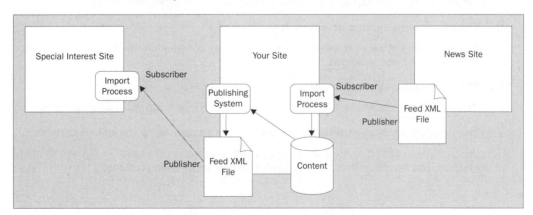

Your site subscribes to content published from a news site. The news site periodically produces an XML file containing the approved feed of content permitted for your site. Your import process makes an HTTP request for the feed file, receives it, cleans it, and adds the feed content to your own content. At the same time, your site could in turn publish content to other subscribers, like a special interest site. The editors on your site mark content you'll forward to the special interest site on their next request. Your publishing system exports the feed file, anticipating a request.

Rendering Sequence

As we mentioned at the start of the chapter, publishing is all about bringing content and presentation together, and sending the result to the user. The following is the typical execution path of a publishing system. We'll avoid any particular framework: your publishing system's unique implementation may include additional steps or exclude some of these.

1. **The publishing system receives a request from a user's browser.**

   The publishing system detects the user's browser and retrieves other session context surrounding the request, like the user's profile. The publishing system adapts its response to fit the context of the request.

2. **Optionally, the publishing system checks its cache for precomputed responses.**

   If a precreated response matches both the request and the context, the publishing system returns this cached response and we skip to Step 8. Why is this step optional? Dynamic publishing systems usually omit this step, while purely static ones always try to find a pre-cached response. We'll discuss this further opposite.

3. **The publishing system selects a template to fill.**

   Based on the request and interactive features of the audience member's device, the publishing system chooses a template. The template both answers the request and provides supplemental features like site search dialogs and navigation.

4. **The publishing system fills content into the template.**

   For each container in the template, your publishing system executes database queries to retrieve matching content, and places the output of embedded applications.

5. **The publishing system selects a transformation.**

   The publishing system chooses a transformation by considering the template and rendering features of the user's device.

6. **The publishing system transforms the template into a page.**

   The publishing system converts a stored content document into your outputted page.

7. **The publishing system returns the page in its response to the user's browser.**

   Any activity logging that the publishing system performs occurs here. At the end of this chapter, you can learn how this information can help you tune your site.

8. **The user's browser renders the page.**

Many browsers start rendering the HTML page before they've finished receiving the full response. However, if your page includes JavaScript navigation and other client-side applications, the browser may not begin to render them until it gets the last byte from the server. These factors tie your user's perception of site responsiveness to the content on the page, rather than the efficiency of your publishing system.

Opposing Endpoints on a Continuous Line

When you evaluate publishing systems, you may find a variety of ways to render pages that fall between strictly static rendering (sometimes called **baking**) and strictly dynamic rendering (sometimes called **frying**). What do these two endpoints mean?

Static Rendering

Static rendering engines attempt to get the most out of Step 2 opposite. As an archetype, they work in one of two ways. In the first case, they precompute and save all the pages on your site for each of the possible request contexts. This is like exporting a directory structure full of static HTML files from your content repository, in advance of any requests. You can take this static site and load it on a cluster of web servers. On a request, the web server locates the static page, and sends it straight out to the user. Periodically, you rerender the whole site.

For the second case, an audience member makes a request of the publishing system, and the system looks in its cache to see if it handled the same request before. If so, it returns the static copy. If not, it evaluates the result, returns it, and saves it to the cache. Periodically, contributors create a new page causing the cache to discard affected content. You probably noticed that in both cases the publishing system must render the result at least once. For that reason, static rendering is an added feature to a publishing system, elaborating on dynamic rendering.

What are the benefits of static caching? On most web servers, your fastest possible response draws from static HTML files placed on the local file system. If you export your cache, you can cheaply distribute your site to many publishing servers, without licensing more copies of your publishing system. A variety of third-party caching tools exist to support you, too.

On the down side, caching becomes an extra step in publishing for you to manage. Caching requires extra logic to keep your site current. It could lead to problems where you have new content but your web servers haven't received updates. Leftovers from prior versions may appear. If you purge your cache, any inbound links to that purged content will cease working. As you increase your use of request context in your site to do things like personalization, you'll increase unique user requests and prevent matches from occurring in the cache. This makes it difficult to cache embedded applications.

Dynamic Rendering

Dynamic rendering engines publish the most current content permitted for your audience member from the content repository. As an archetype, they follow the whole sample rendering process described above, except Step 2. This makes them ideal for handling unique user requests to embedded applications. You'll treat all embedded applications and content uniformly, simplifying support. Some consultants argue that in the long term, dynamic rendering offers more value to the publishing team. Their argument says that static caching exists because of hardware limitations, not to address audience requirements. As hardware capabilities increase, these caching concerns decrease, emphasizing flexibility to treat your audience individually.

In contrast, dynamic rendering may repeat unnecessary computations on each request. This unnecessary work limits scalability by wasting processing power that you could apply to serve additional users. For many publishing systems, you pay for each instance on each server, making it costly to distribute your site to a server farm. To improve the speed of your rendering engine, you may compress content repository calls into as few as possible. Over time, you may decrease the modularity of your dynamic rendering engine and increase the customization required for each site you build.

Points In-Between

Few publishing systems reside at the archetypical endpoints described above; most compromise on this issue, placing them between the endpoints on a continuous line between static and dynamic rendering. Consider the position along this line a function of how many user requests result in unique outcomes. Sites with the same request details across all users are easy to render statically. Most dynamically rendered sites require more unique request details. Your site could use a combination of the two strategies.

How? Your site might partition your templates into static and dynamic areas or chunks. Precompute some or all of the outcomes of embedded applications (for example, top search terms and the current calendar). The benefits to your site will vary based on the application and use. Site searches have few user-specific variables, making them a good candidate for caching. Your returns diminish on infrequent queries, so concentrate on caching the top queries. Your benefits from caching will vary with the amount of customization. A chat application most likely defies attempts to cache the results of the person on the other end. It's an absurd example, but useful for illustrating the point.

What strategy do you get by default? That depends heavily on your publishing system and the software and hardware that underpin it. You need to investigate this. For example, Microsoft's Internet Information Services (IIS) web server caches static HTML files retrieved from the file system. It also caches the interpreted form of Active Server Page (ASP) scripts, but not their execution results. If your site renders its output to static HTML files served from IIS, your site will be statically cached. However, if you require ASP scripts to run, those pages still execute dynamically. Lots of other technologies exist for caching, including third-party services that cache requests to your site from users around the globe on the server nearest the user (**"last-mile" caches**), proxy servers, site crawlers, precomputed OLAP databases, and so forth.

Don't forget that you can change strategies to adapt to exceptional use for some reason. CNN (*www.cnn.com*) refocused their home page throughout the day during the terrorist attacks of September 11, 2001 to handle the onslaught of traffic. When it was first hammered at 9:00am, CNN still had many dynamic features on their site. Last-mile caches may actually resolve the page you retrieve from CNN, so a combination of static caches and dynamic rendering denied service to most users. As the day progressed, CNN gradually stripped all the dynamic features off their pages as well as returning to a simple static HTML page to shrink download sizes. This improved CNN's responsiveness to last-mile caches and reduced the traffic jam from last-mile caches to you. You can do this by switching templates and updating your cache if you have one.

Perspectives: My Audience Complains About the Slow Site

Miscommunication creates the most stress between your CMS team and the people who operate the solution. How? One of my clients has very technical staff throughout its organization. They grew more vocal about the slow speed of their web site as we improved it. On asking them for more detail, they stated that if we could improve the speed by 100%, why couldn't we go further? Why does a site that runs their intranet run slower than Google, located all the way across the Internet? Later, they found that supplying two arguments to the rendering engine made the engine return results faster in their eyes than if they supplied only one argument. Again, we asked for more detail, and learned that they tested by counting "one-one-thousand, two-one-thousand, ..." while operating a variety of browsers on a variety of desktops throughout the day.

What lessons did we learn? First, we learned to ask, "Who owns the issue?" If you concentrate on people who are not accountable for responsiveness, you won't solve the problems of the decision-maker. Identify perceptions: who says the site is slow? I learned that the decision-makers placed a low priority on addressing the impressions of the technical users. Make sure you preserve ownership of the issue in the hand of the person accountable for the site. I performed a suite of tests that the client never used, because we did them on our own to satisfy our curiosity. The client did not commission them, and therefore did not know what to do with the data. Just facilitate the client's troubleshooting process and advise them on your perspective.

Work with your client to define acceptable behavior. If you don't, you'll never know how much improvement is enough. Identify infrastructure and perception issues that may dwarf any solution you can control. You could work for months optimizing your database calls, only to find out that the network is so slow that your gains get lost in transit to the database server. Agree on tests with your client. Take their problems and ask them what information they need to make a decision. You can suggest tests and relationships, but make sure your client agrees. Create prototype solutions to evaluate. If you find ideas that could improve a site, characterize the improvement by implementing it on a limited scope. It's better to fail early and get up again than to invest a lot of effort and fail permanently. Consider prioritizing those improvements requiring the least drastic changes.

In general, I've found that you can improve dynamic publishing systems by reducing round-trips to the content repository. You can collapse many calls into fewer calls by optimizing calls for your templates. To move to a static publishing system from a dynamic publishing system, first consider exceptions. What stuff can't you cache because it requires too much context? If you want to improve a static publishing system, identify where benefits from larger cache-sizes cease. How close to the user can you position your cache?

In my experience, resource-heavy pages may displace users. They take too long to load, and consume resources others could use on your site. Infrastructure issues may dwarf any software solutions you can perform. Do you have control over infrastructure issues? Everything between the content repository and the audience influences opinions about responsiveness, not just the server or the browser. Consider other applications that consume resources available for your site, such as enterprise applications that eat network bandwidth.

Publishing: a Team, an Act, and a System

Your audience reads everything the authoring team collects, edits, and approves. Everyone can get to your content, day or night, anywhere on earth, in the browser and language of their choice. That takes work. The publishing **team** owns these issues, operating your site so your audience can get to it. Each time an audience member makes a request, your site **acts** to respond. To respond to threes, tens, hundreds, or thousands of requests a minute, the team uses a publishing **system** made of software, hardware, and networks.

In practice, you'll find that operating your publishing system in production is a constant activity, seeking consistency. Much of your publishing effort is related to operational problems, not increasing the quality of your content.

To keep everything live and responsive, we'll talk about how to plan in advance. Yes, your authoring system also runs in production, but you have a small, technically sophisticated group of authors compared to your public audience. We must find ways to manage your audience's expectations, and match them.

Different Requirements from Authoring

Publishing has different requirements from other parts of content management systems.

For example, the authoring interface provides tools for contributors to create, refine, and place content. Your contributors return frequently to continue their work. You trust them to participate in an approval workflow. Your staff might only need authoring tools during the working day.

In contrast, your audience is the primary user of publishing. Every day, your audience attracts new members with no knowledge of your site. The audience includes people you may not trust, who in turn may not trust you. To conduct business, your audience may depend on your site for current information around the clock.

However, you'll find some facets of publishing are similar to authoring. Your audience requires usability, integrity, consistency, and durability, just like contributors. These requirements underlie the whole content management system. How do you know which requirements are most important?

Your audience evaluates your site based on a number of common qualities relating to publishing:

- Responsiveness

- Availability

- Scalability

- Interfaces

- Fault Tolerance

- Security and Fraud Prevention

Keep in mind: great people force terrible systems to work, terrible people struggle with great systems.

Responsiveness

When I ask for a page, does the site respond when I expect it to? Do I expect the page to process when I enter data into each field, or when I save my changes? Has the site timed out if it fails to meet my request to save in twenty seconds? Is the site fastest before I go home at night, long after I needed it?

Your audience gathers their opinion of how your site should perform from their experience with other sites, especially those they perceive to be similar. Would you return to a search engine that had the same coverage as another engine and worked the same way, but took twice as long to get you results?

Who says it's slow? Responsiveness is perception. Know who's asking and how they're measuring. You'll learn a lot about their needs, and cut down on chasing speed from wrong assumptions.

Availability

"Can I get to the site when I want to?" your audience asks. Taking a system down for maintenance at night in the US is fine if you only have users there, but what if you have international users? That same downtime may cause loss of access in the middle of the day for some European users. Think about how it will affect their workflow and opinion of your site.

Availability is also about expectations. When does your audience anticipate downtime? How do you tell them gently to try back later? If you have a reputation for being unreliable, you'll spend a lot of money to recover your audience later. You might guess that experienced audience members tolerate more downtime than new users, but how long would you stay calm if your business depended minute-by-minute on a site that had been down for an hour?

Can I still find something I saw last year with ease? Some of your content benefits from age. Imagine that you publish a scientific journal where authors gain prestige when others cite the papers they based their work on. If you purge a paper too soon, you'll prevent others from being influenced by it. To learn more about how long your content should remain available, monitor the referring links to your site. Inbound links tell you how long you need to preserve old content before you purge. Remember, purging too soon causes links to rot on others' sites, as they gradually lead to unavailable content.

Scalability

We already mentioned that most sites attract far more audience members than contributors. Can you afford to post content that will attract twice as many users as you have today? Will your publishing engine crank out enough responses to keep everyone satisfied?

Each feature you add to your site impacts use. Content attracts attention in varying ways. Some extremely compelling work, such as broadcasts of breaking news events, will keep users on for long periods. Jokes may cycle through far more people but only once each and for tiny fractions of time. Examine how your next change will impact requests, and plan for capacity to handle it. As we discuss below in the section *Learn from Publishing*, you can read your site logs to observe requests.

In many content management systems, you'll find a setting to limit the maximum number of concurrent users. Why? As more people use your site, it keeps getting slower for everyone. Each additional request interrupts and slows responses to others. Eventually, nobody will get answers, so nobody benefits. Placing a cap on the count of concurrent users denies access to excess audience members while adequately serving those you have room for. This cap allocates scarce processing and memory resources to give your publishing system enough to satisfy part of your audience. Consider your core audience and provision your site's publishing tools accordingly.

Ideally, your publishing team has enough resources to add capacity to your publishing system. In that case, invest and capture them all. If your team lacks the time and money to cover all the traffic you'll get, you need to compromise. Defining your target audience is one way to make a trade-off.

Your target audience consists of the people you care most about reaching. If you succeed in covering them, your team may earn enough to expand the target audience. The trade-offs we'll discuss throughout this chapter help you adequately serve members of your target audience, at the expense of those outside it. Remember that you may possess resources to cover only a portion of your target audience. That's OK. At least you'll satisfy those people.

Interfaces

How does your audience access the site? Their devices could include desktop computers, notebook computers, palm-tops, cell phones, adaptive devices like screen readers, and so on. Each of these has different bandwidth limitations, presentation issues, and input requirements. Your content could fit on all of them, but is it worth it?

You can read this issue another way. What set of devices covers my target audience? A surface of compromise exists. Place cost on one axis, audience coverage on another, and list platforms on the third. Each point on the surface represents a combination of these. Find your target audience and your cost, and you'll get a set of devices to support. Here's an example:

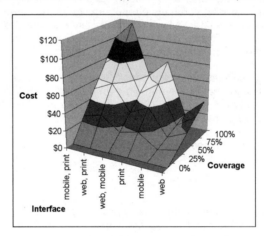

Fault Tolerance

What did your users think about the error they received on that page? An error could drive away your audience by ruining confidence in the information near the error. How many times have you felt uncomfortable when you caught an arithmetic error in your shopping cart? Keep in mind that support is much further away for audience members than for contributors. For help, they send a request to someone they've never met.

Consider the sources of errors that impact your audience. Hardware errors occur when a hard drive fails or the power goes out. When a user supplies characters where your application expects numbers, your software raises an error. Software errors can even pop up from correct operations from more than one user, like two audience members editing the same value at the same time. If an engineer incorrectly routes traffic, network errors could prevent your publishing system from reaching the content repository.

How do you handle these errors? Plan recovery techniques that don't interrupt your site, like RAID 5 arrays for your publishing system's hard drives and redundant power supplies. If you must interrupt operation, manage your audience's expectations. Ask your authors to post navigation messages informing your audience of the outage and expected return to operation. If the error prevents your whole publishing system from functioning, plan in advance and provision a backup publishing system, even off-site. If you roll out changes to one system, test it thoroughly before upgrading your backup system. Many books and web sites document testing and fault-tolerance techniques for software systems.

Security and Fraud Prevention

Just as faults undermine audience confidence, so do fraud and privacy breaches. Unlike many of your trusted contributors, audience members access your site over a public network. Others might snoop on their requests and responses. Worse, your firm may share audience member profiles without seeking consent.

Compromise about employing security techniques that burden the audience. For sensitive information, you can publish an extranet where each user authenticates first, to share only permitted content. Will your audience register for accounts with you, taking their valuable time? You can configure your publishing system to communicate via Secure Sockets Layer (SSL), to encrypt traffic between the user's browser and your publishing system. Will your audience use browsers that support your encryption technology? You can indirectly burden your audience too. If the capacity of your publishing system reduces because of the added strain of encrypting every page, you may decrease responsiveness.

Above, we spoke about how your trust of your audience varies depending on the site. To reduce the chance of your publishing system being hacked, place it behind a firewall. Although the firewall permits traffic to specific ports like your web content, it prevents would-be attackers from connecting to other ports like Secure Shell (SSH) or Windows Terminal Services. Don't forget that your public ports could still be open to danger; others can exploit defects in your web server, such as optimistically configured permissions. One of my clients left an FTP service configured with an anonymous account for more than a year, unnoticed. When we discovered the hole, we found hundreds of obscurely named directories with gigabytes of illegally obtained software. Not only had this hole permitted a group of people to hoard space on our hard drives, but also frequent downloads consumed the bandwidth available for our audience. If my client had read their logs occasionally, as we'll see later in this chapter, they would have seen suspicious activity much earlier.

Assign a member of your team to keep your publishing system up to date on security patches and examine your permissions periodically. I suggest they practice the upgrade on a staged copy of your publishing system before upgrading your site. Even if a major software vendor successfully avoids introducing bugs and viruses in patches, they could change default values that you depend on, like file system permissions.

Any site open to the Internet may be vulnerable to denial of service (DOS) attacks. Instead of malicious users breaking or repurposing your servers, DOS attacks consume all your resources handling requests that look legitimate, preventing your site from responding to your target audience. You could block traffic from offenders at the TCP/IP level but attackers grow more sophisticated, distributing their load across many sources (DDOS attacks) and varying their request patterns. You can purchase third-party monitoring services that examine the pattern of traffic to your site at many layers to diagnose attacks. In addition, you can coordinate with your ISP to block DOS attacks from their side. Remember, even if you can block the attack at the site of your publishing system, it may still harm you by consuming your valuable connection to the Internet.

Operating a Production Environment

Publishing relies on you having a stable system, attended by a team who can keep that system running. Below we'll cover some of the key things to remember about operating your publishing system.

Involve the Publishing Team from the Start

The publishing team operates the content management application in production; educate them early. Depending on your organization, the team could consist of IT staff, web developers, marketers, or dedicated staff. The team needs time to coordinate infrastructure vendors and acquire skills to operate your site. What if you picked a publishing system that crashes your enterprise systems? Your publishing team can catch that too.

Ideally keep servers simple and replaceable. When a server does crash in production, you'll want to recover quickly. By keeping the publishing hardware and software simple, you can focus your attention on solving the unique parts of the production problem. If you can't afford a separate server for each purpose, combine servers with related purposes. As an example, if you have a database, a web server, and a firewall, combine the web server and database, and separate the firewall. Why? You'll want to lock down your firewall as tight as possible, which could make your web server hard to administer if it sits on the same box.

Measure capacity based on vendor recommendations. I suggest you start with worst-case scenarios. If your site handles the worst case, you'll cover everything else. To identify extremes, find places that require the most processing. For example, your home page may carry news summaries, events in a calendar, two layers of navigation, an alert box, and weather syndication. Most users will enter your site through this page, multiplying its impact. This would be a good test candidate for capacity provisioning.

Avoid needless dependencies. Is there any reason not to configure the hardware and network deployment platform in parallel with initial authoring? I've seen hardware vendors take six to eight weeks to deliver servers. That time could come while you assemble the first draft of site content or afterward, delaying production. You use a hosting company? What if your host gets the configuration wrong the first time? Most content management systems seek to eliminate dependencies between content, presentation, and publishing.

After picking a publishing system and making worst-case tests, many of my projects start evaluating hardware configurations. They'll acquire sample servers, perform configuration and capacity tests, and propose adjustments in a tight loop. They keep regressing over the same tests, to measure progress across all configurations.

Test Early, Test Often

Can you over-emphasize testing? Maybe, if you have a fixed budget. Software testers try to minimize the cost, but cover the most defects. On publishing systems, you'll find that the cost to cover correctness is low. Did the page render correctly? You can see it. Expect to spend more time on fault tolerance and capacity issues as described earlier. Although you can grind out numbers for capacity and fault tolerance, you might invest more in tools and determining what your measurements mean. These comments downplay the importance of accessibility testing, but I suspect your template and transformation designers will work more on those issues than your publishing team.

You'll need a test plan. What happens without one? I had a client who picked a different event to end their counting on each time. Did you notice that the JavaScript hierarchic menus completed rendering after the browser said, 'Done'? What were we measuring? Was it the server response time or the browser rendering time? What intervals in the lifetime of a request-response should we focus on? Informal testing has a way of spawning more questions than it answers.

Because of the variety of features to be tested (timeframes, staff, and so forth), no one test plan fits all. We'll mention some approaches to testing later in this book.

Separate Publishing from Your Development Environment

Plan all changes. List the steps ahead of time, and practice on another copy of your production hardware, software, and network if possible. You'll likely find errors that you didn't anticipate or resources you missed. Beware that every difference between your testing and production systems raises prospects for problems in production. For example, if you don't enforce database passwords during practice, you'll miss errors where the software fails to propagate the password.

Define a process to commit changes to production and rollback on errors. Either the whole change occurs, or you restore a backup. During changes, lock out contributors if you'll impact their content. Let's say you wanted to install a new patch to your web server. First, make the change in your test environment web server. Second, test your site. If you discover that parts of your site cease to work and you can't figure out how to fix the problem, then roll back your test environment and contact the manufacturer. You prevented unnecessary downtime on your production servers.

Limit access to qualified personnel. Consider deploying a professional service provider to delegate low-level issues, even if you work in a small organization. Do you want to be responsible for replacing hard drives in RAID arrays in the middle of the night? In larger companies, try rotating developers through publishing to give them first-hand experience of front-line problems.

You might say, "But I'm a web developer, not a hardware maintainer." Most developers I've worked with benefited from hardware and networking knowledge. If someone configures a network adapter card incorrectly, your software may be the first to report the error. Without hardware knowledge, you could spend days searching for this problem in your code, ultimately giving up on that server. All parts of an information system impact your software.

Schedule Routine Operations

How many times have you been frustrated to discover that as your midnight deadline approached, the web site you used went down for a backup? If only you'd known in advance, you could have got the details earlier. Manage audience expectations as early as possible. If you anticipate downtime, advertise it to your users and provide them a route to inquire. Better yet, schedule periodic operations to reduce conflicts from your audience each time.

What kinds of tasks does a publishing system perform periodically?

- Backup

- Re-indexing

- Purging

- Report extracts

- Cache updates

- Upgrades from development

- Patches from vendors

Eliminate Dependence on Specific People or Resources

Bottlenecks will prevent you from solving problems. They come in the form of staff members with unique knowledge, a lack of spare hardware, network connections without redundancy, and so forth. Even by adding capacity to a bottleneck, you haven't removed it from the critical path; you've delayed the bottleneck's replacement and reduced stress on your staff. The bottleneck remains to bite you later.

You can prevent material bottlenecks by design and purchase. How do you cut down on human bottlenecks? Avoid solutions that only one member of your team could understand – you can't transfer the work to others. Document your production configuration and processes. Get more than one source for resources. Train and rotate multiple operators. You get the idea.

Plan for Failure

When do you need a plan? Whenever you have something that's too big to think about all at once, takes several people to complete, or that happens over a long period of time. Failure falls into all three of these categories. When something fails, you may not be aware of how far the situation extends and who's impacted. You may not have considered the publishing system in a long time.

- Brainstorm disaster scenarios. Have fun with this. Tackle trivial scenarios, like pulling the network cable out of your server, and obscure ones, like copy-and-paste errors.

- Test disasters on the development environment and record recovery procedures. How will you diagnose the disaster you just caused?

- Every time you change the production environment, update your recoveries. Otherwise, your plans rot with time and you lose your investment in documentation.

Third-Party Monitoring

Can you reliably test whether your audience can use your application? Most likely, you use the same machines the developers use, and you can't see your application from across the Internet easily. Consider delegating a vendor to remotely monitor the site for downtime. To determine your budget, account for the cost of downtime. Provided you find a reliable vendor, you can fund outsourcing by capping your disaster costs. To go one step further, you can configure a backup production environment off-site at a managed facility. Falling over to another facility could give you more time to solve problems on your primary production system.

Don't forget to test the vendor. Pull the plug yourself on a non-critical machine and see if the vendor responds.

Publish To More Than Just Web Browsers

You invested in your content. Why provide only one way to reach it?

In this section we'll talk about why you might publish to cell phones, print, and Braille browsers in more than one language. We'll also discuss how to apply templates and transformations from Chapter 3 to target accessibility scenarios. Finally, we'll investigate the kinds of services you might provide for your audience and to reach other audiences through syndication.

Scenarios for Content

Knowing your audience is an important aspect of publishing. What proportion uses your site all day long? How many return once a month? What languages do they speak? What browsers will they use? How fast are their connections to the Internet? How does your site benefit them? How do they discover you? If publishing systems distribute your site to your audience, they should meet the needs of your audience.

How do you determine which needs to address? Define what success means for your site. Can you fund your site based on a quantity of readers, or do you need to sell a quantity of products and services? Determine what you have to do to capture enough audience members to succeed. List the size of your audience associated with each barrier separating them from your site. Prioritize the barriers based on return. Compromise on cost-effectiveness. Plot your progress and make someone accountable for it.

What if you can't assess your audience in advance of launching? You can speculate based on a few samples. Many accessibility web sites report on the browsing behaviors of different demographics. You could conduct a focus group of people from your target audience. I once participated in a session with forty people for a local hospital, where we observed how the group used site navigation to find doctors treating an ailment. We discovered that elderly people often lack dexterity to work a mouse, and that most likely they would ask their children to find answers for them. Who should we target? The site's managers chose to attract relatives of the patient.

Here are a few more business cases focusing on accessibility:

Support Enough Browsers To Capture My Audience

Why limit the browsers your web site supports? You may want to cover as much of your target audience as possible, but in making your site cross-browser compatible, you'll lose access to the more advanced custom features of a line of browsers. So, target the most popular browsers in your audience.

Who decides what the most popular browsers are? Your access logs may not accurately reflect your audience because of your site's reputation. As a web professional looking for technical answers, would you surf Microsoft's sites using a competing browser? Even getting to know your audience doesn't guarantee you'll anticipate their browser changes, such as browser settings. What will you do for users who turn off cookies and JavaScript, or who access your site through a firewall or content filter?

What happens if you go the other way? Try limiting your site to adhere to strict W3C standards. Many browsers and devices deviate in their adherence to these standards.

What should you do? Compromise: create pages that degrade well across unsupported browsers outside your target. Stick to structural and semantic markup, and apply styles from cascading style sheets. Don't forget backward compatibility; not everyone surfs with the most current browser. Older browsers vary greatly in how they support CSS versions 1 and 2.

Reverse the Flow of Information By Publishing To Print

In older businesses, you may find that information flows from contributors to print documents, with the web professional gathering content from paper or print layouts. Traditional print documents are hard to maintain and difficult to use in other formats.

One of my clients manufactured thousands of sensors, sold through product data sheets to engineers and purchasing officers. Many data sheets copied the same product specifications. Engineers and purchasing officers liked to identify a line of sensors that could solve their problem, and then compare specs for individual sensors. My client had a hard time keeping everything current. When a spec changed on the product, they had to keep at least half a dozen documents in sync. Now they want to add a product catalog to their web site that produces the same data sheets that engineers and purchasing officers use in print.

Our team proposed to reverse the flow of information, making the web site the most current source of product specs. We produced the print spec sheets by reporting of the managed content. The report templates targeted paper instead of web browsers.

He who controls the publishing process wields power. In some organizations, the web team could threaten those who produced the print. Be sure you recognize the print team's understanding of their audience and the business; they should remain a valuable asset to the web publishing effort.

Delivering Content To Those in the Field

I once worked with a team of light railroad mechanics at the city's airport. Their railroad was the only connection between local city transport and the hub of gates to airplanes. The airport permitted them less than five minutes of downtime per day. If a problem occurred on a rail car, they had to diagnose and repair the car in that time. Did they have time to run into the office and search the web for diagnostics and parts? No. Clearly, they wanted access to that information from palm-top computers. Even more, the web site narrowed documents to those related to the conditions reported by the rail car. Without on-location access, the content would be worthless during those five minutes.

In less controlled environments, you may find that your audience's mobile devices change frequently. Just like cross-browser problems, you may need to target a set of devices and account for software upgrades.

Localize Content

People in other communities speak other languages and understand other cultural conventions. Unless we address their locales, they experience the same barriers that people with the wrong browser suffer from. Localization includes concerns about character set, text direction, conventions (for example, date order and currency), graphics, colors, and semantics. I'm sure you've all heard the stories about how red means go in China, and stop elsewhere. I've heard that orange makes something look "cheap" in Germany, but that yellow backgrounds with black Helvetica lettering has that effect in the United States. Localization is about more than words; it could impact your whole template.

All that said, if you can't deliver your service to a particular locale, should you support it? Imagine that your company cannot ship its product to a given locale, yet your site's audience includes people there. Maybe they speak the same language as those in a region you do support? Consider how frustrated they'd be and how much time your company would waste trying (and failing) to address orders from that locale? Don't support audiences with your publishing system that your organization can't satisfy.

Search Engine Crawlers

If your audience can't find your site, other accessibility concerns pale. Without debating the impact of a search engine listing on referrals to your site, if you don't get indexed, you won't appear among any results. Again, help the crawlers find important information by publishing semantic markup and structure.

Disabled Users

You've already read about the number and influence of users who are disabled; they may comprise a significant portion of your audience. Think about motor-skill impairments. Do your cascading menus require dexterity that your audience can't match, making your site impenetrable? Can users who are color-blind work your navigation scheme? What if green boxes highlight buttons to commit work, while red ones cancel? Users who are visually impaired apply adaptive technologies, like screen readers. These rely on semantic and structural markup, just like search engines and cross-browser applications. If you target users who are disabled, your publishing system must support them.

Compliance

Laws may regulate how you present your content. In the United States, departments and vendors of federal government, and soon state and local governments, must adhere to laws providing access to persons who are disabled, such as the Americans with Disabilities Act and Section 508. Although no case law for these exists in the United States yet, consider erring on the safe side, and accounting for these requirements now.

Not all regulations cover access for persons who are disabled. The Health Insurance Portability and Accountability Act of 1996 (HIPPA) in the United States lays down guidelines for handling patient records on systems such as web sites. To comply, your site must separate and audit access to patient medical and billing records, in an effort to ensure privacy. Your publishing engine must satisfy the business case you operate in.

Templates and Transformations for Publishing

In Chapter 3, you learned about how you can use templates and transformations to present your content. How does your publishing system address all these additional scenarios with them? When an audience member makes a request, your publishing system selects the appropriate template and transformation to satisfy it. How is this different from the sample execution model described earlier? We added accessibility input to requests on the publishing system. Not only does your request tell the publishing system what page you want, it also includes what browser, bandwidth, legal jurisdiction, and language to use when selecting a template and transformation.

Here's a sample Unified Modeling Language (UML) class model of the template and transformation concepts we'll discuss, to illustrate how they relate. For clarity, I simplified many of the details. Most likely, your publishing system improves on this model. For our discussion, all applications run on a single **Page**, the **Browser** represents the entire request context, and I limited **Content** to one kind of document.

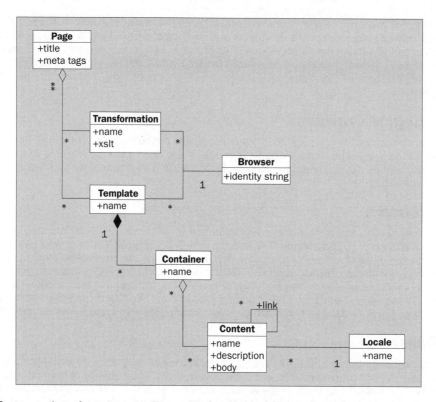

Each Page consists of one or more Templates and Transformations. As before, Templates represent the interactive features and content that could be displayed on the requested Page. Pragmatically, the audience member's Browser might be overwhelmed trying to display all the interactive features and content in the Template. To address this situation, the publishing system picks the template associated with the requesting Browser. The Transformation maps the Content in the Template to the Browser's language.

How does this model handle cross-browser compatibility, print output, and mobile devices? Add Browsers for each class or instance of Browser, like Netscape Navigator 4, Adobe PDF 4, or a Samsung PCS phone. Then build a Template and Transformation to satisfy your output requirements. The Adobe PDF template ignores navigation, while the Samsung PCS phone strips images and breaks the Content body into more pages.

Each Template is made of one or more Containers. A Container gathers specific content to serve a purpose and fill a space in the Page, like the chunks from the last chapter. For Internet Explorer 6, you might make Containers for the Page's left-side navigation, breadcrumb navigation, alert box, site search form, footer, and the body of the page. For a Nokia mobile phone, you might omit breadcrumb navigation and the footer, and provide a compact version of the left-side navigation. The coordinator for the Page selects the content they want to include. Alternatively, the coordinator could provide a query against the content repository to obtain matching content.

Say a search engine crawls your site. The publishing system determines that the Browser is a crawler. The publishing system picks a Template and Transformation that emphasizes your `<meta>` tags and the semantic structure of your Template and Content.

What if I reach this page and I choose to continue in another language, like Korean? The publishing system renders the same Page, but each Container follows the links that map selected Content to their alternatives in the new Locale. As an aside, I've learned that one item of content may turn into many in another locale, and vice versa, so I suggest you avoid making one-to-one maps between content in different locales.

These examples demonstrate how your publishing system handles a variety of devices and audiences without creating countless permutations of your content. This is the value of separating your content from the way you present it. Your publishing system takes care of merging content and presentation so you can handle unique audience requests.

Learn from Publishing

After launching a site, do you know how your audience reacts to it?

You can poll, survey, and conduct focus groups. While you'll get interesting results, be careful: market research books will counsel you to carefully craft the questions you ask. More than likely, you'll get feedback from a portion of your audience. Which portion? You can infer some answers to that from your site access logs that capture everyone. You can collect their use of the site, which could be more telling than their impression.

User needs change over time. By logging the activities on your site as a side-effect of publishing, you'll gather feedback to guide your contributors. Use feedback to shorten the paths to most used content, and use popular paths to advertise less seen content. Adjust site navigation to reduce searching. Adjust applications like searches to return more targeted results. Decide on new areas to populate based on user feedback. You can't do this unless you record activity on your site.

Hard Evidence of Who Uses Your Site

Know your users. Your acquired audience may differ from the one you set out to capture. The hospital site I've mentioned several times routinely attracts students studying cancer. I didn't anticipate students as major users of the site, but they could raise awareness among patients as much as broadcast advertising.

Publishing should match your audience's needs. The hospital has a decision to make. They can enhance the site to encourage more students to visit, or they can concentrate harder on attracting patients. Regardless of which direction the hospital takes, they need to continue testing logged activity to ensure that the content reaches their intended target audiences.

Monitor Use

Now that we've seen why you want to report on your site activity, let's talk about what information you can find, and how to use it to enhance publishing. Your publishing system can archive activity from the following resources. In general, the more detailed the resource is, the more you can learn.

Web Server State (W3C web logs)

Web server state consists of the variables that your web server uses to process requests. Microsoft's Internet Information Services, Apache, and many other web servers output W3C-compliant log files. Third-party tools like WebTrends and LiveStats produce reports from this information. This low-level information tells you details such as who made the request, what request they made, the browser they used, and how long the web server took to fulfill the request. You can read a data dictionary of the W3C log file by browsing the W3C site. By assessing related log entries, web log reporting tools attempt to guess at the click path your audience traverses through the site.

CMS Server State

Your publishing system knows about the path to a page and its locale, and can add these details to logs and reports. Your CMS can apply log information to make index views ordered by popular rank as well. By showing the least-popular features at the top, you can promote your least-visited pages.

What if your publishing system produces unreadable URLs? Can you still use third-party reporting tools? Yes, if you use your publishing system to compensate. See if it will export W3C-compliant log files. If so, your publishing system can rewrite the URLs with more descriptive resource names.

User Profiles

Anyone using third-party reporting tools on sites attracting visitors from the US notices that at least a third of the population lives in the state of Virginia. How can so many people live in one state? Simple. Their ISP registers the IP address that places their traffic on the Internet in Virginia. The web reporting tool performs a reverse-DNS lookup to return the user's fully qualified domain name. Your web reporting tool may use this domain name to look up the location of your ISP's registered InterNIC contacts. Many large corporations and Internet service providers like AOL register their domain contacts in Virginia, skewing the demographics in your reports.

How can you get around this skew in consumer access? You can register users on your site, and authenticate them each time they return. Alternatively, after registration, you could reduce the user's need to authenticate by storing the user's identifier in a cookie. Your publishing engine can then tie their profile directly to logged requests. Later, you can relate any detail in your user profiles to site activity, including sessions, buying habits, and preferences to page views.

Application State

The embedded applications on your site contain state too. By logging the search queries to your web site, you'll find words that users resort to when they can't find your navigation. You'll also discover search words entered for things you could add to your site. You can tune your navigation and tune search results to promote specific areas of your site. Similarly, by logging purchases in your shopping carts, you'll find out all kinds of things about people's buying habits.

Understanding Use

Suppose you're not sure if logging is a good idea. It might expose weaknesses in the site your team put together, and could lead to misunderstanding when others try to use statistics inappropriately. Before committing to a logging and reporting project, I suggest you define the problems you're solving. Can you get that information from the reports you gather? Let's find out.

What Can You learn?

From traditional web logs, you'll learn about the overall browser spread among your audience, their paths through your site, the most and least popular pages on your site, and the time spent on a page. Note that exceptions exist, diminishing the accuracy of this information.

Misleading Logs

Web logs record details from your web server about each request. Web reporting tools infer some things from this data that may mislead you. Here are a few examples.

- Your web reporting tool tells you the duration of time visitors spent on a page. HTTP is a connectionless protocol, meaning that every request establishes and tears down a connection to the web server. How does the web reporting tool know how long you viewed the page? The tool looks for subsequent requests from your IP address. If two people share the same IP address, or you never request a page again in the log, the duration gets skewed.

- You read about repeat visits in your logs. Similar problems arise. Your web site might use cookies to uniquely identify your browser, but many people block them. Some online services make every one of a user's HTTP requests from a different IP. Others hide all their internal computers behind one IP (network address translation).

- We already mentioned the fallacies involved in implying user location from reverse-DNS lookups from your IP address. These often return the InterNIC-registered location of your Internet service provider or corporate gateway, rather than your surfing location.

- When you view lists of popular pages, are they actually dead ends or steps on the way to many goals? Your users may get to a page on your site and leave frequently. Alternatively, your users may traverse through a page on your site to get to many others. Depending on your reporting tool, those bridges and dead-ends may obscure the pages your users really find valuable.

- Some publishing systems use "404" error handlers to interpret rewritten, readable URLs. If your publishing system doesn't configure the error redirection page to return a 200 OK to the web browser, you can clog your web log with error results. These hide real errors on your site.

- Some browsers spoof other browsers, supplying ambiguous browser identity strings or letting you set the string. These browsers subvert the report.

Read your publishing logs with a critical eye, and know the caveats before sharing information with others.

Perspectives: The Myth of the Anonymous Audience

How can I learn about my audience if they're anonymous? I challenge you: how anonymous is your audience when a member raises a problem to your attention? While solving that member's problem, you learn enough about that member's needs to respond. You'll remember that member's need, referring to it when drawing requirements for your next task. You invested the least effort possible to discover that user's needs.

So you learned about one person incidentally. You might say it's impossible to learn about your whole audience, one person at a time. Many polling techniques rely on sampling individuals; the key is to understand how an individual represents others and how to pick samples. If you invest effort, you can gain great insight into your audience's needs. You can start by browsing logs of all the problems your team addressed on the site, and move up to focus groups and user polling coordinated by a marketer.

Technically, you can identify many of your audience members. Through logging, your audience members leave a trail across the Internet. You tally a hit in your web logs, and records at their ISP link their address to their account details. Yes, they can work to cover their trail, obscuring some members. Again, you'll need to invest effort to discover exactly who they are. The law may govern your access to some of these details, too.

Even with the trail, you still don't have their needs. Go back to your logs and outbound sampling. Make sure you identify caveats limiting your assertions.

Summary

Most publishing systems use a combination of dynamic and static rendering. Dynamic rendering responds to your request with a unique query against the content repository. Static rendering caches previous requests and their contexts, returning precomputed results wherever possible. Your system may apply these strategies to different parts of your page template, for example.

Involve your publishing staff from the start. Through repeated deployments and planning they'll grow comfortable with operating your site in a production environment.

A key part of publishing is learning about your audience. They browse your site differently from authors, judging it by factors like responsiveness, availability, scalability, interfaces, fault-tolerance, and security. Your audience may change over time. If they can't get to your site using their preferred method, they won't use your content.

While operating your publishing system, you can gather logs of your audience's activity. Manage your audience's expectations about how you'll use their input. You can capture state from more than just your web server, including your publishing system, user profiles, and embedded application state. Define the problems you want to solve with reporting before deciding which reports you'll produce, learn what data supports a report; otherwise you may draw misleading conclusions.

We've now completed our investigation of the three stages of content management: Asset Management, Transformation, and Publishing. The rest of the book will cover more practical information, starting with a discussion of the things you need to be aware of when buying or building a content management system.

5

- Reasons to Buy a CMS

- The Questions to Ask Vendors

- Licenses and Costs

Author: Dave Addey

Buying a CMS

Now we've covered the nitty-gritty of why we need a CMS and what it entails, we can move on to how we go about getting and using one. There are basically two options for this: buy in a solution from one of the many vendors, or build your own. In this chapter we'll cover the first option, investigating the questions you may want to ask a vendor before making a decision. We'll take a closer look at the second option in Chapter 6.

Why Buy?

The quickest route to CMS acquisition, though not always the cheapest, is to look at the many CMS products available, and buy in a solution. Why would you want to buy?

For Your Own Use

If you manage a large web site or intranet, with many pages and multiple authors, implementing a CMS will involve a sizeable investment of time and money on the part of your organization. Many organizations in this situation will immediately look to the commercial market for a suitable product.

The practice of buying solutions has one very large benefit: **someone else has already done the hard work**. In Chapter 7 we'll look at ways to make sure that implementing their hard work is as easy as possible for you. For now, we need to make sure you choose to buy the right system for your needs.

To Sell To Your Clients

If you work for an agency, you will likely have clients with content management issues similar to those described in earlier chapters. These clients will either be ignorant of the joys of content management as a cure to their pains (which means a potential sales opportunity for you), or will be shopping around for a content management solution themselves.

Of course, as an agency, you could build and sell your own system (and for more information on doing so, see Chapter 6). But it may be better for you to partner with an established CMS tools provider and to offer their product range to complement your existing agency services. Many CMS vendors will offer an ASP (Application Service Provider) version of their product, allowing you to build and sell systems based on their product in return for a license fee.

Increasingly, larger CMS companies are moving towards operating as out-and-out software companies, rather than providing professional services of their own to implement their CMS products. There's a very good reason for this: the profit margin on a license sale is much higher than on a services implementation. This does mean that the market is wide open for agencies and professional service companies to partner with CMS vendors, to offer solutions based on their systems.

But beware: if you choose to partner with a CMS vendor to satisfy your clients' needs, or to build your own systems based on their products, be sure to check that the support they provide meets your requirements and your clients. It also has to be worthwhile for your clients to fill their content management needs with you rather than going direct to the vendor. Be sure that you can add enough value to the process. It has to be worth your while, too – there's little point selling someone else's product if you don't make a profit from the relationship.

The Purchase Process

The process for analyzing and purchasing a CMS will vary depending on the scale of your organization's needs. Similarly, the range of products that you evaluate will vary depending on your content management budget, from top-end systems such as Vignette and Interwoven, to lower-end systems produced by agencies and smaller CMS companies.

Your role, as a web professional, in the purchase process will similarly depend on the scale of the organization's CMS requirements. For a very large purchase, senior management within your IT or Marketing department will most likely own the process. In this situation, your involvement is likely to be as a technical consultant or representative of the CMS implementation team. For a smaller budget or simpler requirements, you may be able to take the lead in a CMS purchase.

There are several stages to the process that are appropriate whatever the scale of your CMS needs.

A Big Document Full of Questions

You can call it an **Invitation to Tender**, or a **Request for Proposal**, or anything else that takes your fancy, but in essence it's a **Big Document Full of Questions** (or a **BDFQ** when you bring it up in meetings). This document summarizes your content management requirements, and asks pertinent questions about the CMS on trial. A list of the kinds of questions you may want to ask can be found later in this chapter.

This document is your chance to consider what features are important to you, and also to allow decision makers within your company to have their say. If your IT department suffers from severe paranoia, now's the opportunity for them to add a few questions to the BDFQ.

CMS companies are used to receiving these documents, and a BDFQ is typically between four and twelve pages long. Be wary of receiving stock answers to your questions – if you feel you've been fobbed off by a sales person who doesn't understand the technical question being asked, then ask again.

As with all software purchases, it's far better to find out the truth about a system's limitations before someone signs the purchase order, especially if you're the one who has to implement the system (and most likely you are). If in doubt, be pedantic and make sure you are happy with the answers you have received.

Show and Tell

You wouldn't buy a car without taking it for a test drive, would you? It might drive like a moose or, even worse, have terrible sound quality on the in-car stereo. So, make sure you see a full demonstration of all assessed systems in action.

Demonstrations should cover all sides of the system, including author interface, template creation interface, administration functionality, and workflow management – anything that your specification process flags up as important for your organization's needs. Make sure representatives of all interested parties (including authors, template developers, and systems administrators) view the system in action, as their reaction to (and buy-in towards) the system is very important.

If you're relatively new to CMS, then the first author interface demo you see from a trained sales guy may well make you go "wow!". A good CMS, when shown off to full effect, can look pretty cool to the untrained eye, so don't forget to keep your naturally cynical viewpoint on life close to hand. However, it doesn't matter one jot what the CMS in question can do for the sales guy if it can't be customized to meet the requirements of your site and your authors.

The CMS vendor may be willing to provide a user- or time-limited demonstration copy of their CMS for your use. The same rules as above apply to this demonstration – it is still just a sample implementation of the CMS.

Don't Think Out of the Box

It's not often you'll get that advice. Let us explain what we mean. Anyone who is trying to sell you a CMS will want you to think that once the license fee is paid, off go your content troubles, wandering into the sunset. You take a figurative CD out of a figurative box, click "*Install*", and the world is a happier place, just by the application of money.

If only it were that simple! Regardless of what the spam in your inbox may tell you, you can't lose weight without a bit of exercise.

You see, the naked truth about content management systems is that if you dig deep underneath all of the marketing information, what you'll find is really a content toolkit: a collection of prewritten bits of code which can be put together in a variety of ways to build different web sites. What you see when a CMS is demonstrated is a good implementation of these tools, customized by the CMS vendor in a demonstration site of their own designing.

What does this mean for you? Well, unless your requirements exactly match the demonstration site you've seen (and they won't), then you're going to have to spend some time and energy customizing the CMS to your requirements.

Remember, you're buying the system to save time building tools you'd otherwise have to create yourself. Try and get a picture in your mind of how the system would work for your site, and if in doubt, ask.

Don't Believe the Hype

There are so many content management systems on the market now that CMS vendors are constantly repositioning their products in the marketplace in an attempt to steal a yard or two over the opposition. If you believe the press, then CMS 'X' is a code management tool, a portal, an e-learning authoring tool, and a calendaring application, all whilst making your lunch and walking the dog.

Truth is, the content toolkit described above means that a CMS can *potentially* be all of these things. In nearly all cases, all of the above are just clever implementations of the same basic system in conjunction with some custom templates. Sure, if a CMS vendor has built a similar application to the one you need, based on their system, then you may save time by reusing their code. But if they claim to have a fully blown portal featuring both whistles *and* bells, then laugh loudly in their faces.

Proving the Concept

It's important to see how easy (or otherwise) it is to customize the CMS in question. Don't sign on the line until you've seen someone create a new template to your requirements using the system's template creation interface.

Ideally, a company which values your business should be willing to create a basic "proof of concept" installation of their system, customized to match your corporate site design. If it takes longer than a day or two to mock up their system in your design as a proof of concept, then think carefully about how long it will take you to modify the system in the future.

If you can obtain a copy of this branded proof of concept site, then do so. Getting buy-in for content management within your company is much easier if you can demonstrate the system internally, especially if it already matches your corporate identity. There's nothing worse than a Marketing Director stating that they love the system in principle, but you can't possibly use it because the company logo needs to sit on the right, not the left.

If there is a specific feature, especially a non-standard one, which you need to integrate with the CMS, then make sure you see this in practice. It's amazingly easy for a salesperson to claim something is magically possible in the run-up to a license sale.

Your Role in the Purchase Process

We saw above that your involvement in the CMS purchase process will vary depending on the ownership of the project and the amount of money involved. But whoever makes the final decision as to which system to buy, chances are it'll then be up to you to implement the system and make it work. You'll find Chapters 7 and 8 on implementation and migration will provide a lot of hard-learned reasons for asking the questions given below, so in order to make your life as easy as possible when it comes to implementation and migration, take as much of a lead on your BDFQ as you can. If anyone quibbles about why you're being so picky, you have our permission to wave Chapter 7, *Implementation*, under their noses.

Questions You Must Ask: The BDFQ

This list may not be totally exhaustive, as some organizations will always have additional specific requirements, but if you cover all of the subject areas opposite, you won't go far wrong. Obviously, the answers to some questions will carry more weight, when making your decision, than others.

We'll split the questions up into three sections relating to the three processes of CMS we covered in previous chapters – asset management, transformation, and publishing. A downloadable version of these questions can be found at www.glasshaus.com.

Asset Management

Authoring Interface

- Does the authoring interface make sense to non-technical users who are familiar with a particular word processor, such as Microsoft Word?

- Does the content interface allow WYSIWYG editing of content?

- How does the CMS cope with HTML code in content?

- Is content previewed using the same template-rendering as the published version?

As we noted in Chapter 2, CMS users will range from those comfortable with HTML to those who struggle with basic word processing software. Assessing the author interface of a CMS is, therefore, about more than just features.

Many systems use a web browser-based interface for content authoring. If this is the case, then apply your knowledge of web usability and design to the admin interface, and think about how your authors will react. Try it out on them if possible. Authors will need training, and the more intuitive they find the interface the better.

The authoring process will be easier if the CMS allows WYSIWYG editing of content. In reality this will probably be a word processor interface for text editing, which should allow users to gain a good idea of how their content will look when transformed for publishing. Ideally, the CMS will preview a page of content using exactly the same transformation templates as the live site, so users can preview exactly how their content will look.

Some authors will be HTML-savvy, and may request the ability to add HTML code within designated parts of your template. Find out how the CMS handles this, and whether different sets of HTML tags can be allowed for different types of authors.

Site Structure

- How does the CMS allow the author to manage the site structure?

- Is a visual hierarchical view of the site structure available for the administration interface?

- Can the CMS render the site tree as a navigation system for your live site?

- Does each point on the site tree correspond to a page as well as a folder?

- Can pages or groups of pages easily be moved from one part of the site structure to another?

- Can pages be copied from one part of the site structure to another?

- Is the site structure available to template creators, allowing the addition of breadcrumbing and site maps to your site?

When you manage the content of a web site, you're not just dealing with its text and graphics. You'll also need to manage the structure of the site and its associated navigation. There are two main approaches to this.

The first is to allow authors to create as many pages as they like, without applying any structure to these pages. Then, using a navigation-building tool, the user builds a structure for their site, linking to some of the pages they have created. The navigation is built manually, with the CMS ensuring it is presented correctly.

The second approach is for the CMS to manage the site structure. This is usually done by presenting the author with a hierarchical tree view of the site and allowing them to add pages to the various branches of the tree. Typically, this takes the form of an expanding tree similar to the Windows file structure, for example that illustrated on the right.

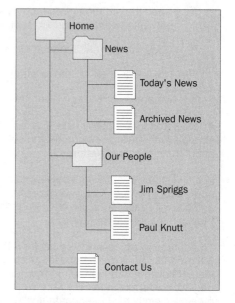

However, the tree metaphor has a problem. Imagine a site structure like that above. Our simple site has two main areas: one containing news, one containing profiles of its staff. It also contains one "anywhere" page – a contact us page.

Now, let's translate this structure into some site navigation. It might look something like that on the right:

It's pretty clear what happens when someone clicks on "*Today's News*", or "*Archived News*" – they get the appropriate page. It's also clear what happens when they click on "*Contact Us*" – they see a page. But what happens if someone clicks on "*News*", or on "*Our People*"? These are areas, not pages.

There are a few ways the CMS might tackle this. One is to build the site so that every point on the site tree is both a page and a potential folder. So, our author would first create a page called "*News*", which would be a general page about the fact that the site contained some news. Then, the author would create two more pages, grouped under the "News" page. These effectively become subpages of a *News* area. Using this technique, everything is a page, and all eventualities are covered.

What if we don't want an introductory news page? Maybe news is an area of the site that doesn't need an introduction – it's just there for grouping purposes. However, users will still expect something to happen when they click on our "*News*" heading. Non-clickable items on navigation are just going to cause confusion.

Another option is for the area names ("*News*", "*Our People*") to link to the first page in that area. For example, clicking on "*News*" would link to the "*Today's News*" page. This has the downside of assuming that the first item in an area will always be an appropriate introduction to that area of the site.

The final option is to render our site navigation as an expanding tree itself – that is, clicking on "*News*" would expand the navigation to reveal "*Today's News*" and "*Archived News*". Clicking again would hide the *News* sub-areas.

A CMS should not restrict the way in which you structure your site. Some site areas will warrant an introductory page, some will not. It's partly a question of how you want to design your navigation system. But the reason for the question is this: make sure the CMS doesn't limit what you can do with your navigation. All systems will have tackled this page / folder issue in their own way, and you need to make sure your chosen system doesn't force you to build your site in a particular way.

The design translation of your site should not be limited by a CMS, either. If you've built some good navigation code already, then all your CMS needs to do is to fill in the gaps – translating the site structure at any given time into your choice of navigation code. Make sure you are not limited in how you do this. For example, some CMS insist on using a Java applet to present the navigation in your live site. A system like this will severely limit how closely you can match your own navigation needs. And we don't want that, do we?

Link Management

- How does the system allow authors to create and edit links to other pages within their site and external URLs?

- What happens if an internal link is broken, for example if a page is deleted or expires?

- Will the system check for the availability of external links, and if so, how does it notify the user of these broken links and their location in the site?

- How does the CMS allow the linking of files (for example Word documents, Powerpoint presentations, PDFs) to the site?

- Can images be links?

- Does the CMS provide an interface for creating image maps?

As discussed above, your CMS should make managing the site structure as easy and as foolproof as possible. So creating a link between pages should be as simple as choosing a page from a tree view of the site structure.

Where things get interesting is when pages are moved or deleted, and links need updating or removing. Any CMS worth its salt should automatically update links to moved pages. If pages are deleted from the site, then a CMS should automatically remove links to these deleted pages. Chances are these links will be something like "*Why not find out about our new range of sausages*?" If the sausage page goes, a CMS should remove the link, but leave the text of the link on the page (otherwise, the sentence above would be chopped in half). The content author for our linking page should then be notified that sausages are off the menu, so they can update their page accordingly.

This has some implications for baking and frying (see Chapter 1 if you are unsure about our use of these culinary terms). If your CMS is frying your pages – that is, rendering them each time they are viewed – then it should be able to check the current site structure as it renders the page, and find out whether links in the page are still valid or not. If your site is baked and then published, then all pages with sausage links will have to be tracked down by the CMS, re-baked and re-published when the sausage page is removed. Moral: sausages are better fried.

Authors may need to link to non-HTML documents such as PDF files, Word documents, and Powerpoint presentations. Find out how your CMS will approach this. Are these files uploaded to a central repository, and then selected by the author from a list? Or are documents uploaded and associated with a particular page or paragraph, whose template will generate an automatic link? Both approaches are equally valid, but one may be more appropriate for your needs.

Some systems may come with a fancy tool to allow non-HTML-savvy users to create image maps on images. This is a nice trick. The more tools like this your CMS provides, the fewer times you'll get pestered by content authors to "just create a quick image map".

Accessing the System

- Does the system require custom software to be installed on an author's or template developer's PC?

- If the system is browser-based, what browsers and operating systems does it support?

- Will authors be able to access the CMS remotely?

The big advantage to a browser-based admin system is that there is no need to roll out any software installation – assuming your authors have a supported browser, and a network connection to the CMS server. If a CMS requires a custom-made application for content editing, this will need installing on to authors' PCs, with associated IT rollout hassle.

There are very few things that can't be done via a browser interface, so be wary of these non-browser-based applications. Remember that we want authors to see their content previewed in a web browser anyway, presented using the same templates as the live site.

It may be the case that your content authors are not all connected to a nice fast corporate LAN. If your staff are spread out all over the country or the world, content authors may be creating and changing pages via dial-up connections. If the CMS makes heavy bandwidth demands, then life will become even slower for the already-frustrated remote worker.

That said, page previewing should not cause a bandwidth problem. Why? Because you should be previewing pages using the same transformation templates as your live site. If pages created with your live templates don't match the bandwidth limits of your users, then you haven't done a very good design job at all.

Workflow

- What does the interface for workflow creation look like?

- Can authors create their own workflows?

- Can authors make changes to content and save their changes without the need to submit the content to the next stage of the workflow?

- Can comments be attached to a particular stage of the workflow?

- Does the workflow allow documents to be sent back a stage if not approved?

- Can workflow members be notified by email / SMS / other appropriate methods when documents are waiting for their approval?

- Can time limits be put on the different stages of the workflow, with notification sent to administrators to flag late documents?

- What information is available about the user's workflow performance?

- Can groups of pages be passed through the workflow as a grouped package?

The larger your organization or site, the more important workflow becomes. As we saw in Chapter 2, workflow defines the processes your content must follow from creation to publication. Your CMS should provide an interface for authors to create workflows, ideally with a visualization of the workflow as a whole.

Workflow links closely with user and role administration – the CMS should allow workflow stages to be assigned to users, groups of users, or users with a specific role. For example, a legal signoff stage could be assigned to a pool of lawyers, any of whom would have permission to read and sign off documents in the workflow.

Some Content Management Systems have an internal inbox for each user, containing any tasks that are currently assigned to them. It is useful if the system can alert users to the fact that their input is required to the document workflow process for a given document, typically via e-mail, as users may not check the CMS regularly to see if their input is required.

If your organization has an intranet with personalized content for each user, it may be useful to add a user's workflow inbox to their personalized view of the intranet. If you intend to do this, make sure that your CMS allows external access to its workflow system.

The workflow creation and management process should allow you to be as flexible as possible with your workflows. Will the system support parallel workflow, where a document needs approval by several users in any order before it progresses to the next stage?

Depending on how you feel about control, you may want to monitor how your workflow members are performing. Are they approving documents in time, or is one particularly slow user adding a day to the publish time of every page? It may help if the CMS allows you to add a time limit to each stage of the workflow, and notify a monitoring user if the workflow stage is not completed in that time limit. Think about who within your company will play the role of the workflow police.

Users and Their Rights

- Can you create multiple users, with different access rights?

- Can roles be created and assigned to users to aid the workflow management process?

- How are users and roles managed?

- Can users be grouped?

- Can access rights to create / modify / delete pages in different areas of the site tree be limited by user / role?

- Can access to templates be limited by user / role?

- Will the CMS user access system link with your existing LDAP (Lightweight Directory Access Protocol) or other directory servers?

- Does the CMS provide any information on authors' performance and content editing history?

- Is there a limit on the number of users the system will support?

- Can users create other users? If so, can their user creation rights be limited and controlled?

Don't just think of your CMS users as authors – you will most likely have users fulfilling many more roles than just that of content creator. Your CMS needs to be flexible enough to define users, and groups of users, with different permissions.

Some users may take a "superuser" role, with permissions to create, modify, and delete other users' permissions. In a large site with many users, it is useful to be able to structure your user permissions to spread the administration workload.

Ideally, your CMS should support a full user / role access control system, allowing access to be limited by user, by site area, and / or by template. Creating roles and assigning permissions to these roles allows similar tasks to be easily assigned to many users.

You may well have an existing directory server of PC users within your company. Think about how this will link in to your CMS. Will users have to log on to their PC, and also to the CMS admin interface? Can their user settings be stored in (for example) an LDAP server? Bear in mind that your company's user management needs will grow in the future, so the more flexible the user management system is, the better.

There is no real reason (other than licensing) why a CMS should place limits on the number of authors and roles you can create. However, depending on the user management interface, dealing with large numbers of users may be hard. If you have a test installation of the CMS, try creating a large number of users and see how the interface copes. Even better, create users and roles which match your current workflow requirements, and use these to create the workflow processes you will require.

Multilingual Content

- Can the CMS cope with content authoring in multiple languages?

- What approaches are available to multiple languages?

- Does the CMS support non-western character sets / unicode editing?

Of course, it's possible that this is of no relevance to your company. Think again. With the possible exception of one-country intranets (and even then I'd argue), every web site will one day need to tackle the issue of multilingual content. Even if you don't need to deal with it now, your investment in a CMS is an investment that you will work with for several years, so do find out how the CMS tackles multilingual sites.

CMS or not, there are two main approaches to multilingual content.

- Build a completely separate version of a site for each language.

- Build one site, with one structure, with each page having multiple copies, one for each language.

There is a difference between these approaches, and your decision as to which approach to take should be based on your reasons for having a multilingual site.

If you have to publish in several languages because of a need to communicate to several different territories, then it may be worth building a site for each territory. This is especially true if each location will have a different content structure. If you have one set of content for all users regardless of their location, then one multilingual site would be more appropriate.

For example, a car manufacturer that sells its cars in many countries may have different ranges and sales processes, and therefore different site structures, for each country. In this case, multiple sites (one for each location) would be appropriate.

Conversely, a Swiss news site aiming at a Swiss audience (with three native languages – German, French, and English) would be best placed to produce one site with one structure, and translate each page into three languages. In this case, the CMS needs to be able to handle multiple copies of the content on one page in the site structure, and publish the appropriate version to three separate copies of that page.

Of course, if you sell your cars in Switzerland (or in Belgium, or the US, or any other country with more than one native language) then you'll need a combination of both. And if you don't sell your products to more than one location yet, bear in mind that you may well do so in the future.

Version Control

- Does the CMS store previous versions of pages?

- Are there any limits as to how many versions of content are stored?

- Can versions of pages be compared?

- Are deleted pages stored for rollback?

- Does the CMS provide versioning and rollback for non-text assets (images, PDFs etc.)?

- Can the audit history of the site be viewed?

- Can a snapshot of the entire site be taken and used for rollback in the future?

Version control is important, especially when you have more than one author working on your site. Even the best authors make mistakes. More importantly, so do workflow reviewers. Your CMS should allow you to roll back to earlier versions of pages quickly and easily.

There may be more pressing legal reasons to keep previous versions of your site. Some financial companies have to be able to provide a copy of how their site looked on any given day. This can be achieved by taking a daily snapshot version of your site, if your CMS allows. If not, a third-party spidering application may be necessary to grab a copy of the site via more traditional means.

Metadata

- What metadata can be stored at a page level – keywords, description, live / expiry dates?

- How is the entry of metadata presented to users on the authoring interface?

- Can metadata be made mandatory for a given page?

Rolling out a CMS is the perfect opportunity to reassess your content, and assign appropriate metadata for pages. Even better, with a CMS you can (if your system allows) force authors to add metadata to their pages before allowing the page to be published.

Some systems allow the assignment of automatic live / expiry dates for pages. This can be very useful if sensitive content is embargoed until a set time. Especially if that time is 3am, and the alternative is for the trusty web professional (that is, you) to come in early and throw the switch.

A similar method can be useful to automatically archive or remove content after a given time, either by assigning an expiry date to a page, or by defining a time-to-live for content within a particular area of the site.

Transformation

Authoring with Templates

- How does the CMS present a choice of large numbers of templates to an author?

- Are visual previews of templates provided to the author?

- How does the CMS deal with paragraph templates within a page?

- Does the CMS place any limits on the number of paragraph styles on a page, or their positioning on a page?

When a site has many templates for content creation, it can be hard for the average content author to know which is the appropriate one to use. This is true of both page and paragraph templates. Some CMS can provide authors with a preview or small image of each template, together with a full description of its purpose.

Template selection may become quite complex for authors. You may have different page templates for each section of a site, for different types of content, or even for different registered site users. Likewise, in a multi-column page layout, your page may require a selection of paragraph templates for each column.

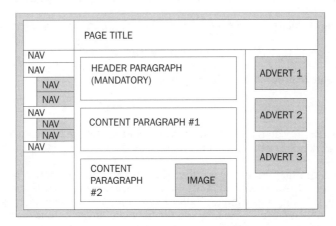

Imagine we are trying to create the page layout shown in the figure above. Here we have navigation down the left-hand side of the page. The navigation will appear by default, generated by the system.

Along the top of our page is a page title. The page title is a property of the page template, as it is a page-level attribute. If this page template is selected, we need to ask authors to enter a mandatory page title for their page.

Our header paragraph is also mandatory, and so we do not require the user to choose a paragraph style for this paragraph. However, our author must ensure that this paragraph is completed before the page is submitted for approval.

The remaining content paragraphs in the central column will make up the main content of the page. We may have several different possible templates for these paragraphs – for example, text left and image right, all text, a styled table, text right and image left. The author needs to be presented with a list of appropriate paragraph templates with which to build their page. We can make the author's decision process easier by creating thumbnails of each template in action.

More complex functionality may require specialist paragraph styles. For example, we may create a paragraph template that draws a graph based on values entered by the author. We may want to offer bar chart, pie chart, and scatter graph options.

Our right-hand column contains three adverts, each of which is based on an "*advert*" paragraph template. We wish to make sure that only adverts can be added to this column, so the author would be presented with no choice as to which paragraph style can be used when adding new paragraphs to this column.

Of course, this is only one design, and each specific requirement will be different. But make sure that your CMS doesn't limit the layout and paragraph options you can create and offer to your authors, and that it makes it easy for authors to choose the right templates to create their content.

Template Creation

- What languages can be used for template creation?

- Do the skills required for template creation match those within your company?

- What is the template creation interface / IDE (Integrated Development Environment)?

- What debugging features does the template IDE provide?

- Can you use your own IDE to develop templates?

- Can several template creators work on the templates?

- Does the IDE provide template check-in and check-out to manage multiple template creators working on templates at the same time?

Each CMS will place certain limitations as to what languages can be used to create templates and customize the system. For example, Vignette craftily allows users to create templates using either JSP or ASP, neatly allowing it to integrate with existing systems within most major corporations. Other systems are not so flexible, and may require template developers to learn arcane scripting languages or CMS-specific syntax. Either way, be sure that the skills within your team either match or are complementary to those needed to customize the system. Whatever system you choose, you'll have to learn its idiosyncrasies, even if you've been using the same language for years.

Developing templates is not as simple as just creating sample HTML pages. It involves scripting (dare I say it? programming?) the functionality and interaction of the templates as well. For a typical CMS implementation, this may be a job for several template developers, and it is possible that this team will be a mix of your colleagues and developers from the CMS vendor. Using the vendor's developers ensures that the combined team has a good knowledge of the product, but will incur additional costs. There will be additional costs of training your own developers in the CMS, although working alongside developers with experience in the system may eventually prove more valuable for knowledge transfer than your developers' original CMS training.

As a result, the IDE for template development is very important. Some systems provide a full custom application for template development and debugging. Others allow you to use your own choice of IDE, or a text editor if you prefer.

If a development environment of some form is provided, it should allow several template developers to work on the same group of templates at the same time. CMS implementation is a large-scale software project, and if the IDE can offer version control, check-in / check-out, and remote editing functionality, then the development process will be greatly aided, especially if not all developers are in the same location.

Graphics and Multimedia

- Can uploaded images, or images in media libraries, be manipulated and resized without the need for authors to use graphics editing tools, such as Photoshop?

- Will the CMS generate graphical title and navigation images in web formats (GIF or JPEG)?

- Can a range of fonts be used to create these images, to match your corporate style?

- Does the CMS make provision for a shared library of media items?

- How does the CMS deal with Flash movies created by authors and designers?

- Can the CMS update content within Flash movie templates?

How many of your content authors are experts in Adobe Photoshop? Would you trust them to create navigation images to your exacting corporate style guidelines? In fact, do they even know what Photoshop is?

If your CMS has graphics manipulation capabilities, it can save an awful lot of training time and graphics software licensing. It can also make sure that your users don't go away and create a page with green-on-brown navigation items featuring 2.7Mb JPEG images.

Let's assume we have a template that allows for a text-left, image-right paragraph layout, with a fixed image width of 150 pixels to ensure all images on the page align neatly. We certainly don't want users uploading images direct from their shiny new digital camera, as our 150-pixel-wide column will be forced off the page and into another country.

Wouldn't it be great if our CMS could take any image they upload, shrink or crop it to our corporate size, and then output a JPEG with 60% image quality time after time? Suddenly image manipulation springs to the top of our feature list. Some CMS do this, some don't. Find out which your potential choice is.

Ideally, the uploaded image should be stored in its original bloated form, and scaled and rendered for the Web as specified in our templates. This way, the web version of the image can be re-rendered should the corporate design requirements change in the future – to require all photos to be 200 pixels wide and embossed with a smiley face, for example. Rolling out new templates should require no reviewing of content, graphics included.

The same principles apply to navigation images. Let's assume you have a navigation system constructed from a number of GIFs, each with the corporate font beautifully anti-aliased and pixel-perfect. Each time a new section or page is added to the site, you have to open Photoshop, and manually create a matching pixel-perfect image. A CMS with font rendering capabilities can generate hundreds of these navigation graphics for you. Automatically. As soon as a new page is added. It has a certain appeal, doesn't it?

Once you have a CMS with a basic set of image generation and manipulation tools, all kinds of possibilities become available. Font rendering + drawing circles = pie charts, automatically generated based on the author's own data. Image scaling + font rendering = beautiful home page images. Your page titles can be perfectly realized in the corporate font with a curvy swish in the background, if curvy swishes are your thing. The possibilities are endless, and more importantly, the style is consistent.

Find out how the CMS in question deals with reuse of content assets. Your press officer might own a brand new digital camera, but that doesn't make him or her a great photographer. If you can provide a library of pre-approved stock photography for authors to include on their pages, you can enforce a level of image quality whilst enabling users to brighten up their pages for free.

Wouldn't it be nice to include Macromedia Flash movies in your site, but let authors change the movie content? Well, you could install a movie generation product such as Flash Generator, but there is an easier solution. As of Flash 4, you can pass parameters into a Flash .swf movie from a text file when the movie is loaded into a web browser. So, if you define certain parts of your Flash movie to be filled at load time, you can feed these values into the movie from a text file generated by your CMS. When an author changes the content, our CMS regenerates the parameters file in the correct format, updating the content of the movie when next viewed. As long as your CMS is able to create text files from author-maintained content (and it should, as HTML files are text files at heart) then this option should be available. That said, this is a pretty neat trick, so it's very possible that the CMS sales guy may not have thought of it before.

Modules

- Are there any pre-existing template modules? For example:

  - Discussion forum

  - Chat

  - Graph generation

  - Form creation

  - Auctioning

  - Shopping carts

Any CMS company that has been through a number of implementations of their system will invariably have found the same functionality requests coming up time and time again. The list above is a typical example of regularly requested features that may be offered as part of the core system, or as add-on modules that can be easily slotted in to your site. Usually, a **module** is just a collection of custom templates providing the kind of functionality described above, craftily branded as a "module".

Another caveat: some modules will be more easily integrated than others. A prewritten discussion forum may save development time, but may not work quite as you require. Check you are clear as to your requirements for these additional modules, and that any prewritten code contains all the functionality you need. If it doesn't, ask for a quote for the work needed to add in your requirements.

Some modules, such as auctioning and shopping baskets, are particularly susceptible to this. Any CMS vendor who sells their own e-commerce system is probably selling a system they have developed for the specific needs of another client. As a result, it may need extensive changes to meet your own needs. If anything, paying for an e-commerce module for a CMS is usually buying the right to implement e-commerce with that system, rather than a complete system itself.

Publishing

Publishing Process

- How does the CMS transfer content from the author environment to the live environment?

- Can content be published from one author environment to multiple live environments?

Different Content Management Systems tackle the publishing process in different ways. However, most make the distinction between an author server, where content authoring takes place, and the live server that hosts the actual web site, as in the diagram below.

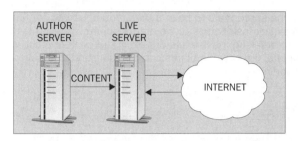

These different "servers" don't have to be on different machines – they may all live on the same physical server. The important distinction is that they are separate instances of the site, with the author instance containing as-yet-unpublished content.

Even if your server requirements are this simple at the moment, they may expand and become more complex in the future. In the set-up in the next diagram, we have three different live servers – one hosted in the US, one in Europe, and one hosted internally. The CMS needs to be able to publish content to all three servers with their different hosting circumstances. The publishing process should still be the same for an author or a content approver – clicking one "*publish*" button – with the CMS automatically updating all live servers.

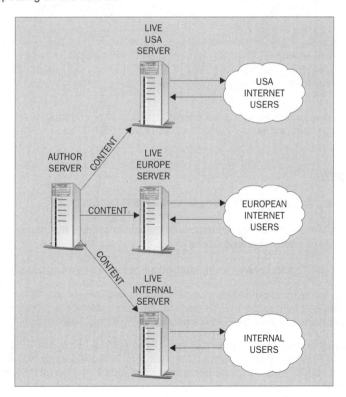

Find out how the CMS handles publishing content from the author environment to the live environment. If the live server is hosted externally, it may be necessary for content publication to be made via a secure SSL connection.

In some cases it may be appropriate to have a third type of server, for template development. This server would have a similar installation as the author server, allowing template developers to try out new templates without breaking the live site or holding up content authors. Once template development is complete, the new templates can be published to the production environments, as shown in the next diagram:

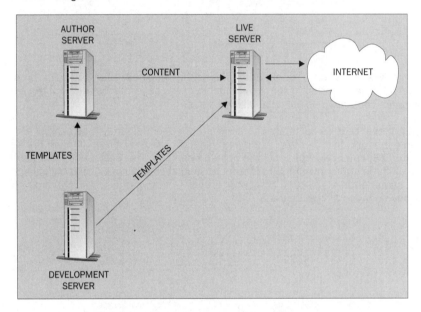

Not all Content Management Systems will provide the flexibility you may require now and in the future. Present your intended server set-up as part of your BDFQ, and find out how the CMS would achieve this.

Multiple Targets

- Can content be published to multiple devices and targets?

- Can the CMS create different versions of the same content (for example, a print version or a version for visually impaired users)?

- Does the CMS allow content to be flagged as being appropriate for particular targets?

If you require the flexibility to publish to multiple devices and targets, make sure your CMS doesn't limit which devices and languages can be used for content publication. (Ask yourself whether you need this: don't feature it in your BDFQ as a priority if you'll only ever be publishing HTML pages.)

All CMS will publish HTML. They should also be able to publish to any text-based format (for example, XML, RTF, WML). For all of these formats, the CMS is essentially taking a template, that is a sample piece of HTML, XML etc., and filling specified gaps in the template with content assets from its database.

Life gets more interesting when we have to deal with binary data. Publishing binary content (images, sounds, movies) to text-based publication methods (most notably XML) will require some form of encoding, and it is worth checking if this is supported natively by your CMS. Some target platforms may require images to be generated in a specific format, for example, WBMP (Wireless Bitmap) format for a WAP page.

It may be necessary to publish to more complex formats too. The most obvious example is the creation of PDF files. PDF generation requires content translation and compression, and you will need to find out if the CMS supports this natively or by integrating with existing PDF generation software (with the latter being more likely). In the case of PDFs, a previous project in which the CMS vendor successfully generated PDFs for a specific application would be a good reference, especially if the server technology used is similar to your own.

Your CMS should allow a page of content to be published in several different ways. The most common form of this "one-to-many" publishing is to have a "printable version" link on each page of your site, linking to the same page rendered with a printer-friendly layout. A CMS should be able to generate these multiple versions of pages from the same page content for you (subject to the creation of appropriate templates).

There are other situations where multiple versions of your content may be appropriate. You may wish to display content differently for visually impaired users, or provide a graphics-light version of your site for remote workers.

The logical extension of one-to-many publishing is to publish the same content to different devices as well as different sites. In an ideal world, one page would update your Internet, intranet, WAP site, and PDA site. But each has their own limitations – such as 1Kb of text on a WML page – so check if the CMS allows for content to be flagged as appropriate for some or all targets.

Integration

- What experience does the CMS company have of integrating their system with the other software and hardware in use in your company? Can they provide examples of successful integrations?

- If they have no experience of integrating with your software, what is their suggested solution to the integration?

- What access does the CMS give to its content storage database?

A great CMS isn't worth peanuts if it won't integrate with your existing software and systems. Buying a CMS should not require you to rewrite any web applications you've created or bought in the past.

In a world with content management, your CMS will be providing global page elements (navigation, style formatting, titles, metadata). If you want these elements to appear on web pages generated by other systems, then look carefully at how the CMS brings together page elements from different sources to build an amalgamated page.

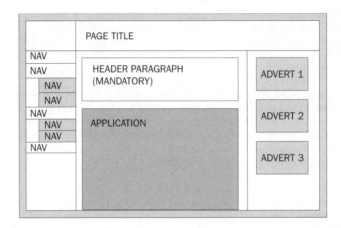

Consider the layout in the diagram above. Here, most of our page elements come from the CMS, but the main page content area is a web application (maybe a timesheet system, or a project-tracking system). Applications like these, which generate custom pages based on user input, need to be fried – that is, generated each time they are viewed. Your CMS needs to be able to bring together these different page elements and provide a presentation layer of navigation and other elements around the application.

If (for example) your CMS is JSP-based, and your existing applications are written in ASP, think carefully about how the two page elements will be brought together on one web page.

One approach is for the CMS to handle all HTTP web requests and pass any form postings to the application's web server, receive a generated web page in return, and embed this within the completed page. This has the advantage of keeping all HTTP requests on one CMS-based server. The downside to embedding the application in this way is that each page requires two web accesses to be made – one from your browser to the CMS server, and one from the CMS server to the application server to retrieve the application's page. If the application server requires a session to be active for each user, then the CMS will need to replicate this session relationship with the user's browser.

There is an alternative. If your application is just too plain different to play nicely behind the CMS presentation layer, then maybe the CMS can make its page elements available to your existing system instead. In this scenario, the application grabs a copy of the navigation and other necessary page elements, and wraps these elements around itself. If these elements remain the same whilst using the application (for example, the navigation and page title do not change), then the CMS could bake the page elements, effectively creating some header and footer HTML code for the application to wrap around itself. This reduces the need for two HTTP requests to be made, as the wrapping process is then a file include rather than a page access.

Your CMS may also need to talk to systems that are not web-enabled. There are a whole range of databases, systems, and mainframes that you may want to integrate with your web presence now or in the future. If you use specific databases or legacy systems within your organization, check if the CMS vendor has previous experience of integrating with those systems. If connector code has not already been written, then you could end up paying for a new connector to be created. If this is to the CMS vendor's benefit (that is, if they can resell it), then make sure this development cost is shared.

Servers

- Has the CMS company any experience of implementing their system on the same server / platform / database combination as your company will use? Can they prove it?

- Can the CMS server coexist with your company's other systems? Again, is there any previous experience of this?

- Can the CMS vendor provide performance statistics for their CMS from a live, high-load implementation?

- Are they able to make guarantees as to the performance of their system under a given load?

- Can the CMS run on multiple servers to spread the load?

- Is the CMS multithreaded, and does it support multiprocessors? What IT support skills will be needed within your organization to support the CMS?

- Can the system be remotely monitored to alert and action any system problems?

This is where your IT department can give the CMS vendors a hard time. A perfect CMS implementation is useless if it runs like a sloth, or if it takes down your servers every few hours. Look for examples of installations of the CMS using the same hardware and software combinations as your own company. If you can, get client references to gain an unbiased view of the CMS in action.

It is notoriously hard to tie down a guarantee of server performance, as there are many variables that are unknown until the implementation has been completed. Seeing the system cope with a high load elsewhere is a good way to increase confidence, and avoid embarrassing performance in the future.

Make sure the system is scalable via the addition of more servers and processors in the future to cope with increasing load. Ideally, the only limit on server and processor scalability should be how much you are willing to pay for the license.

Licensing and Implementation Costs

I've saved the worst bit till last. You're going to have to pay for all of this. Well, *someone* is going to have to pay for all of this, and so you need to be aware of the licensing and implementation cost issues on their behalf.

License vs. Implementation

A CMS vendor will charge you a license to use their software, and they will probably make a hefty profit margin on this license. What they may not do is give you a complete idea of the costs involved with actually implementing the CMS. As we shall see in Chapter 7, implementation is a major task.

As a rule of thumb, the implementation of your CMS should cost roughly the same as the license. Many people would find that ratio highly contentious, and I guarantee that for most companies who are budgeting for CMS, the budget split is nothing like 50/50. Why? Well, the impression a CMS salesman will want to give is that their CMS requires little or no implementation cost.

This is understandable – if a CMS can magically cure all your ills without the need to spend lots of money on implementation, then you can afford to spend lots of money on that high-margin license. Buying a license to some wonder software is a much sexier purchase than budgeting for six months of hard graft implementing a system.

The biggest mistake that companies make time and time again is to buy an all-encompassing license for a big-name CMS without having any idea what they are going to do with it, or how it will be implemented. Even with the best will in the world, it will take some time to install, customize, and migrate to a CMS, and there's no point in paying $2 million for an all-singing, all-dancing enterprise edition of a CMS if your first twelve months of implementation will only use a fraction of its functionality. You can always come back and buy more features later on. I know of companies who have gone back to their CMS vendor after twelve months with a request to buy more functionality, only to find that they've been paying for exactly that feature all along as part of their license. Read Chapter 7, *Implementation*, before you're done, and remember to be realistic.

How Long Is a Piece of String?

Ok, so I'm being a little harsh on the poor old CMS sales guys. They've got to earn a living. Maybe they do want to sell you a license and run, but let's assume that they genuinely want to help you budget for a successful implementation, making you a happy client who will evangelize on behalf of their system.

The problem is, it's very hard for a salesman to put a realistic cost on the implementation phase of a CMS installation. Most people who are buying a CMS are nowhere near as prepared as you, dear reader. They may think they know exactly what they want – that is, *everything*. And even with a realistic idea of your immediate CMS requirements, there are many unknowns that only become clear through detailed specification, as discussed in the *Concept Phase* section of Chapter 7.

That's why I advocate the 50/50 rule again. If the license proportion is very high, then either you're being ripped off, buying more than you need, or not appreciating the implementation costs.

Remember, the sales guy will only be quoting for the products and services his company provides. The actual implementation costs will include budgeting for your time, the time of your in-house development team, and the cost of any external consultants you may involve to help with your implementation. 50/50 is a good proportion for the total implementation costs, and it may be appropriate to buy a few days of professional services from the vendor. Don't forget to factor in the **internal resource costs** of implementation.

Implementing a CMS takes time and money. Don't forget this. I'll keep saying it till it sticks.

Sharing the Knowledge

As we discovered at the start of the chapter, there is one big advantage to buying a CMS – somebody else writes it. But there is a downside – somebody else wrote it. Which means you didn't. Which means that anyone who will be implementing the system will need to learn how the system works in order to customize it, now and in the future.

Ideally, your CMS vendor will provide developer training, either on-site or at their own facilities, to educate your developers about their system and its idiosyncrasies. There will probably be a cost incurred by this, so find out what training programs the vendor can provide.

One of the best ways to learn the details of a CMS is to implement it alongside the vendor's own developers. They should have built many sites with the system before, and will be able to pass on shortcuts and learnt lessons to your own developers.

Different systems will come with different amounts of supporting documentation, both technical and practical. One advantage of working with vendors who have a supporting partner network is that they may have a good documentation database in place to support system implementers. If this exists in the form of a support web site or extranet, ask to see the site.

Don't forget that authors need training too. We'll look at author training in more detail in Chapter 8, but for now, find out what author training programs the vendor can provide.

Think About the Future

If you're spending a large amount of money on a CMS, the license may well include an ongoing yearly charge. Make sure you know what this ongoing charge is, because you're going to be paying it for a while. Make sure you know what it covers, too. Ongoing license fees provide CMS companies with guaranteed revenue, and it's your job to make sure it's not easy money for them. To put it another way – get your money's worth.

- Does the ongoing license cover version upgrades? Does this cover both major and minor point releases of the software?

- What is the CMS vendor's product roadmap for the system?

- Are there opportunities for your organization to influence future development of the system?

If you're paying a hefty chunk of cash every year to continue using a system, and then the vendor chooses to release a new major point release (say, because of a new market positioning), then you don't want to be stung for yet more money. There will be some costs involved with upgrading to a new version of a CMS anyway – remember, your site didn't come out of a box, and upgrading the core system may involve modifying the way your customized system is implemented.

Many CMS companies have gone from a services background to a software background. I bet at some point during this book you've thought, "I could write something to do that". Well, that's where most systems have come from – agencies or developers producing a CMS for their own needs or a client's needs, and then realizing they're on to a good thing and packaging their CMS as a product. But agencies aren't software houses, and don't all work to the same high level of software planning and development as you might be used to with desktop applications. This can make upgrading an interesting process.

Insist upon seeing the system's product roadmap. If it's not looking at least a year into the future, then neither is the vendor.

- Does your ongoing license cover support? If so, what is supported?

This comes back to the "core system" vs. "custom installation" argument. It's relatively easy for the CMS vendor to support the core system – after all, they wrote it. It's much harder, maybe even impossible, for the vendor to support your custom implementation of the system, especially if the vendor had little or no involvement in the implementation. Be very clear on what your support hours cover. If you receive telephone support, do the people at the end of the phone know anything about your particular site? Can support be provided on-site, or is it just by e-mail?

Make sure you get a good idea of the vendor company's financial situation. If they aren't going to be around in six months time, then neither is your support. And if they haven't implemented their system for anyone else, then run for the hills.

CMS Service Partnerships

There is a growing trend for CMS vendors to team up with partners to provide implementation services for their software. You may be reading this chapter with the aim of being a partner yourself.

If you do receive services from a partner rather than directly from the vendor, your license support agreement must be very clear as to where the support responsibility lies for the different aspects of the project. Who supports the core software? Who supports the implementation? If you do not have much technical involvement with the implementation of your CMS, and outsource this to a CMS vendor or their partner, then there may be a time period after which any bugs or problems with the system will not be fixed as part of the support agreement.

Find out what support resource is available in your country or area. Technical support is only useful if both parties are awake at the same time and speak the same language. And that means speaking the same technical language too.

Just like a cute little puppy, a CMS is for life, not just for Christmas. You will be using your CMS for many years to come. You really can't put a value on having a genuinely supportive relationship with the vendor or partner.

Summary

In this chapter, we have seen that there are distinct advantages to buying an established content management system and gained an overview of the purchase process. The first rule of buying a CMS is to ask as many questions as possible and we have covered all of the important questions in detail. We've also looked at the licensing issues with a CMS purchase. Finally, we have emphasized the point that budgeting for implementation costs is **very important indeed**.

In the next chapter we will look at the alternative route to a content-managed utopia – building your own system.

6

- Reasons to Build a CMS
- Making Sure You Are Prepared
- Choosing the Right Technology

Author: Dave Addey and Inigo Surguy

Building a CMS

In the previous chapter we discussed the process of choosing a commercial CMS solution. We now turn to the alternative route you might take: building your own. In this chapter, we will discuss when and why to build, and the approaches you can take to creating your own CMS.

Why Build?

There really is only one way to make sure your CMS matches your exact requirements, and that is to write it yourself. Which isn't to say that creating your own CMS is the easiest or cheapest way to meet your needs. It all comes down to a question of how much control you need and whether existing software matches your needs.

So, why would you want to build?

For Your Own Use

Your site may have relatively simple needs, and not require complex CMS functionality such as workflow or version control. Alternatively, your needs may be very specific, and not well matched by any commercially available CMS. In either of these situations it may be inappropriate to buy an expensive, multi-featured CMS, especially if you have web application developers within your company. If this describes your situation, building a system that exactly matches your requirements may be a better investment.

Think carefully about how your CMS needs will grow in the future. If your site will grow in terms of pages, authors, and functionality then you need to be sure you have the skills and the foresight to develop a scalable system. If your initial CMS build is a success then other sites within your organization may be clamoring to take advantage of your system.

You may need to implement a CMS as a solution to a larger content problem, or as a system to be rolled out many times within a large organization. As we saw in the previous chapter, software system purchase appeals to larger organizations in this situation. There are drawbacks to purchasing rather than building, and one in particular stands out – knowledge transfer. Unless you build a system yourself, you will not know everything there is to know about the system, and this can be seen as an unnecessary risk by some organizations. Your decision should be based in part on your company's attitude to internally developed systems, and the internal support that can be provided for such systems.

To Sell To Your Clients

Money and profit, these are two very good reasons to build a CMS. Many companies and agencies are jumping on the content management bandwagon and creating all kinds of systems to enable their clients to manage their content, in return for some nice money. It seems that in the past few years every agency in the world has created, or has thought of creating, its own CMS to sell. Equally, everyone from Oracle to Microsoft to IBM has created their own CMS solution. As you might imagine, these systems vary widely in terms of scale, quality, and price. The market is pretty crowded. Don't try selling your own system to your clients unless it can offer something different or you are aiming at a niche market. There are enough free open source systems available for companies to avoid buying one at all if they wish.

If you are thinking of developing a CMS as a product to sell, do yourself (and your clients) a favor. Imagine for a minute that you are a potential buyer of your system. Read Chapter 5 from a buyer's viewpoint. Imagine that they have also got their hands on a copy of this book and are wise to the world of CMS purchasing. Your system doesn't need to answer all of the questions in Chapter 5 with a resounding "yes", but bear in mind that you need to convince your clients (current and potential) to use your CM solution over everyone else's, and they'll be asking the same questions you would.

It's a Question of Time

Whatever your reasons for content management, the choice of buying vs. building will be in large part decided by your time scales. Whether you buy or build, you will need time to implement your CMS. If you choose to build, you will have an initial software development project of maybe several months before you can even begin implementing the system for an actual site.

The time required to develop a system needs to be weighed against the time that can be saved by designing your own system with a clear picture of your needs in mind. Any purchased CMS should have been designed to be as generic as possible, and will require a reasonable time investment to customize for your specific requirements. The same ideal of a generic system should be true of a homegrown CMS too, but if time is tight for CMS implementation then the build and implementation stages will become blurred, with the system being built as a specific site (or set of sites) rather than a generic system.

If at all possible, avoid blurring the "build" and "implementation" stages. It may mean that your first CMS-based site can be put live quicker, but building your second site will require the core CMS system to be unpicked from the first site before being implemented for the second, costing more time in the long run and making it harder to support the core CMS. If you ensure that your CMS build is a separate project from your implementation, this won't cause you a problem.

It's a Question of Control

We have established that the main reason to build your own system is to gain complete control over how it works and how it develops. If you choose to build, make the most of this freedom. It is all too easy to claim freedom of development as the main reason to build your own system and then ignore your users and authors during the system specification, ending up with a system that is as far from your actual needs as any you could have purchased.

If your needs are specific – maybe you need to integrate with legacy systems, or output your content in a proprietary format – then building will give you more flexibility to meet your requirements. If you do have fairly generic needs, or need a system that has the potential to be completely flexible in the future, then buying may be a better option.

We're not just talking about control of development. Building your own system gives you ownership of the system without needing to pay a license to anyone else, ever. You can also sell the system with a license of your own if you wish.

However, control has a number of disadvantages. If you have complete control over a system, then you have complete responsibility when it fails. Make sure you can cope with (and are prepared for) the inevitable breakages and support requests. Selling your system may require licenses, service-level agreements, user and technical documentation and commitments to support, all of which come with costs to your company. And although it's great that you have the system's developers in-house, this benefit is pretty soon negated if they choose to leave your company.

Are You Prepared?

Before you start to develop your CMS solution, what do you need to think about? In this section we'll cover some of the issues you will encounter when preparing to build your own CMS.

Picking the Right Team

So you've decided to develop your own system. Developing a CMS is a fully blown software development project. As such, it requires specification and design, project management, technical leadership, database and server administration, development programming, documentation, user acceptance, quality assurance, and user training. If anything on that list makes you nervous then look around your organization and make sure you have the skills (and time commitments) available to fulfill each role, or can acquire the skills if not.

The choice of who develops the system will be decided in part by your company's approach to internal systems development. If you organization has an in-house systems development department, it may be company policy that this department should develop any and all systems used by your organization. It is likely that this department will be tasked with the production of your CMS, or will start to ask tricky questions if they are not.

If you (and those who manage the web sites) are not part of the development department then your relationship will be that of a client and supplier. The internal development team will have other project responsibilities and time constraints, and may have other priorities to developing your system on time and on budget, especially if they have other pressing projects as well. That said, your internal development department should have all the processes in place to develop a system fitting in with your organization's infrastructure. Taking this official route will help with management buy-in and budgeting.

You could get an external agency to do the development work for you. Their core business will be software development, whereas your organization's probably isn't. As a result, they are more likely to have all of the skills listed above. They also have the incentive of building a successful long-term relationship with your company to generate more business in the future. That said, their involvement is likely to cost more than internal development, and may be harder to justify for budget sign-off.

With an external agency, it's very tempting for you to write a specification for your CMS, hand this to the agency, and wait 6 months for the completed system to be delivered. The external nature of the relationship coupled with the physical journey necessary to visit your agency may make regular meetings and prototyping difficult. Conversely, with an internal department you should find it easier to have regular project meetings, and they should have a better understanding of your business.

Whoever develops your CMS, it is very important that you are diligent about knowledge transfer and documentation. This is easy to forget when developing a system internally, as the developers will still be around once the system is complete. But even your favorite developers may move on to another company one day. Be diligent about documentation, and avoid the knowledge of your shiny new CMS leaving the company when its creators do.

The situation is different if you are an agency developing a CMS to sell. The list of roles above is still valid. However, a web or Professional Services agency will be more familiar with the project management and technical development of web software, and these roles may fit more naturally into your existing team.

Remember that any resource assigned to software development will be out of action for some months, and won't be earning revenue for you in this time. You will need to calculate in advance whether the return on this investment will be large enough, and soon enough, to justify this. Chances are you'll want your best developers working on the CMS. Invariably these are the same people who know most about your other clients and systems, and others will have to cover for their day jobs whilst they are developing the CMS.

Whatever your company situation, there is a classic system development situation that you should avoid at all costs: the one developer syndrome. You could take your best developer, lock them in a dark room with only an Internet connection for company, and let their creative juices simmer until a beautiful CMS is cooked. Web developers with software development aspirations find this opportunity tremendously appealing, as it is a chance to swap the drudgery of site updates and menial changes for some "proper" software development. But ask yourself this. Do they have a history of software development, with the appropriate level of self-discipline, project management, and system testing knowledge? Can they fulfill all of the roles listed above and still write the thing? Are they willing to approach system development with a user's needs in mind? And, if they can do all of these things, why aren't they being paid more?

Developers love writing great features, but they're not necessarily great features that anyone needs. If you ask a developer to create a workflow system without specifying what it needs to do, don't be surprised if they come back in six months time with a beautiful workflow creation GUI that is used once to define your workflows and then never used again.

It's okay to get your best developer (or developers) on the CMS case, as long as the development team keep in touch with the end-users of the system, and provide prototypes during development for user comments and feedback. This client feedback will be harder to gather if you are developing your system to sell, but this client-focused view of the system is essential if you are to avoid spending six months developing a system which no longer matches users' requirements.

Choosing the Right Technology

For the purposes of this chapter we will assume that your CMS interface will be based in a web browser, as this invariably gives the quickest and easiest route to CMS creation and deployment. As a result, our CMS needs to be written in an environment that is web-focused and able to integrate with databases and file systems. There are a number of approaches you could take, using a variety of platforms and technologies; we'll take a look at each of them in turn.

ASP

If you work for a large company, I'd wager I could find a Windows server somewhere in your organization. It's a safe bet that pretty much any company will use Microsoft servers for some of their applications and hosting setup. If they do, they will have a version of ASP (Active Server Pages) installed. Any machine running IIS (Internet Information Server) on Windows (and that includes any server from NT upwards) comes with ASP installed, making it an easy choice for companies to use for their web systems.

As with many web scripting environments, ASP works by embedding code within web pages. When a browser calls the web page, the ASP engine runs the embedded code and performs actions (for example, database queries or form processing), generating appropriate HTML as a result. Someone browsing your site sees only a page of HTML; it's just that this HTML is generated specifically for them in each case.

The simplest approach to ASP development is to include various sections of ASP code embedded within your page. A more advanced approach is to use ASP scripts within page code as a presentation layer for COM (Component Object Model) objects. COM is Microsoft's specification for building modular, object-oriented software components. These may be objects you have written or bought, back-office systems being viewed via their COM interface, or applications such as Word being scripted via COM

ASP is a platform, not a language. You can write your ASP scripts in either VBScript or Jscript, with the ASP server handling script processing. You can also use other languages, such as PerlScript from ActiveState (*http://www.activestate.com*) within ASP.

ASP has the advantage of integrating well with Microsoft technologies, and as such is easy to deploy alongside other Microsoft systems such as Microsoft SQL Server. It is easy to use for developers with experience of other Microsoft technologies such as VBA (Visual Basic for Applications). As a commercial product, ASP comes with good documentation and support from Microsoft. There are plenty of add-ons for ASP but, unlike PHP and Java, many of these cost money.

However, ASP is not well-supported on non-Microsoft platforms. There are ASP engines for other platforms, but they are not as reliable or as fast as the cross-platform alternatives such as PHP and Java. Besides, one of the main benefits of ASP is its COM integration, and this is of little use when running on a Unix platform.

ASP.NET

ASP is at an interesting stage of its development, as "classic" ASP is now being phased out in favor of ASP.NET. Like ASP, ASP.NET is a framework for running other languages. The languages it supports are all .NET languages – VB.NET (the updated version of Visual Basic), JScript.NET, C# (Microsoft's new Java-like .NET language), and a number of other more obscure languages such as Eiffel.

Compared to classic ASP, ASP.NET has two main advantages:

- It is much faster. Microsoft claims a speed increase of 3- to 5-fold.

- It has a large standard library, although this benefit is offset by the availability of few third-party components until .NET becomes more established. For example, ASP.NET comes with XML controls, regular expressions, image generation, and mail libraries by default. These features are also available for classic ASP, but require additional installations and cost money.

At the time of writing, ASP.NET is in its infancy, and has yet to prove itself as a development platform. However, as Microsoft's heavily promoted web future, it is a safe bet that it will become a well-supported, and much used, platform before too long.

Java

Another option for developing your CMS is Java (*java.sun.com*), from Sun Microsystems. Java is cross-platform, well-established and well-supported. If you need the flexibility of using either a Windows or Unix server for your CMS, or need to integrate with non-Microsoft applications and systems, then Java may be the right choice for you.

The design approach of Java lends itself to an MVC (Model, View, Controller) software model, allowing you to separate your data model from its appearance and from its business logic – for example, EJB (Enterprise Java Beans) for the data model, JSP (Java Server Pages, similar to ASP) providing the presentation layer, and Java Servlets handling the logic. This separation of design from content is one of the primary benefits of a CMS, and Java is ideally suited for systems where repurposing of content is a requirement. For a simple CMS, you may choose to just use JSP for all of the functionality described above.

Choosing Java will give you access to a variety of existing open source content management tools. For example, Apache Velocity (*jakarta.apache.org/velocity*) is a major open source templating engine based on Java servlets. Cocoon (*xml.apache.org/cocoon*) is a Java-based XML web publishing / content presentation framework. There are many other commercial and open source Java libraries available, and chances are if there's a major piece of functionality you need, someone out there has already written it in Java. Many of these libraries are related to XML, XSL, and other web technologies, and are therefore potentially very useful for CMS creation. Importantly, many are free and open source.

There are a few downsides to choosing Java as your development language. Java is a more complicated and more verbose language than either ASP or PHP. Although this has benefits for large projects, it can be over-complicated for web system development. Fewer organizations have existing Java server installations than either Apache / PHP or IIS / ASP installations. Likewise, if you're looking to buy hosting for your CMS, it is generally harder to get hold of Java-based hosting services.

If your development team will need to learn a web scripting language in order to develop your CMS, then they will find Java to have a much steeper learning curve than either ASP or PHP. Take a look at the existing skills in your team, and be aware that your choice of language may require you to recruit more developers in the future.

The final downside to Java is simple – it's not made by Microsoft. It all depends on your company's (or potential client's) infrastructure – if integrating with all things Microsoft is essential, then ASP may be the safest choice.

PHP

PHP (*http://www.php.net*), short for PHP Hypertext Preprocessor, is a widely used general-purpose scripting language well-suited for web site development. Like ASP and JSP it can be embedded into your HTML pages.

PHP is an advanced, fully featured web scripting language. Its three main selling points as a choice for CMS development are:

- It is free

- It is cross-platform

- It has many, many useful features built in by default (take a look at the function list at *http://www.php.net/manual/en/funcref.php*, and be wowed by the sheer scale of the list)

PHP fits most naturally alongside the Apache web server, as well as other web servers such as IIS. It is well-established and well-supported on Unix, Linux and Windows. Its open source nature means that new web features are quickly integrated into PHP, and most add-ons to the core product are free.

The only main downside to PHP is its level of acceptance within large enterprise-scale clients. This is changing as PHP becomes more acceptable and more recognized, but some large companies have little or no experience with or trust of PHP in-house, and may feel that PHP does not come with the same guarantee of future availability and support as a commercial product. That said, the skills required to work with PHP are very similar to those of an ASP / JSP programmer, and can be easily picked up by someone with these skills.

Other Possibilities

There are other options for CMS development. For example, if your organization uses Lotus Notes, consider Notes as a platform for content management. Notes has very powerful document management and workflow management functionality built in by default. If you have many existing Notes databases, these will need integrating with your CMS, and this will be vastly simplified if your CMS is Notes-based also. Notes replication can benefit a CMS, allowing offline content authoring and easily distributed content publishing. However, a CMS based on Notes may be best advised to use the Notes client application rather than a web browser for its author interface, so this approach will not be covered in detail in this chapter.

ColdFusion, from Macromedia (*www.macromedia.com/software/coldfusion/*), is a web site development toolkit that runs on Windows, Linux, and Unix. It is based around a system of HTML-like tags that provide an easy-to-use and flexible language for developing web-based applications. ColdFusion MX, the latest incarnation, is Java-based, and integrated well with Java systems and Microsoft COM. ColdFusion is not free, but is well supported by Macromedia.

You might want to use Perl (*www.perl.com*) – a widely used language that (whilst not specifically created for the web) is good for text processing and web page generation. Perl is available for all major platforms, and will integrate with IIS, Apache, and other web server software. One huge benefit of Perl is the CPAN Perl module archive (*www.cpan.org*), which contains a prewritten module for pretty much any functionality you can imagine. Perl has excellent support for text manipulation, especially relating to regular expressions. Perl is free, open source, and well-supported.

You could choose to write your CMS in Python (*www.python.org*). Like Perl, Python isn't specifically aimed at the Web, but is a competitor to Perl that is rapidly growing in popularity. Python is free, open source, and runs on all major platforms. Compared to Perl, Python has a clearer syntax, making for more easily readable programs. Python is intended to be easy to learn, and is the basis for Zope, a major open source CMS.

Open Source?

You don't necessarily need to start your CMS development from scratch, even if you don't use a commercial system such as Lotus Notes or ColdFusion. Adapting an existing open source CMS is kind of a halfway house between buying and building. It won't match your exact needs, but (being open source) you can customize it to your heart's content, and as a free starting point it may save you a lot of time.

The main benefits to building upon an open source CMS are:

- You get a large amount of prewritten functionality for free

- The base CMS will be in use by other developers, and a community may well exist to help with customization

- You have control over everything, and can fix all of the bugs without depending on a CMS vendor to do it for you

- You will have no commercial vendor tie-in

And the downsides:

- Because you didn't write the system yourself from scratch, you will need to learn its idiosyncrasies

- The system won't exactly fit your needs, and may need extensive adaptation

- An open source CMS may be harder to sell internally (senior management may have a "free software is only worth what you pay for it" attitude)

- You may have to fix bugs yourself, and cannot rely on a vendor to do so

- Documentation is often poor compared to that of commercial systems

If you are using all or part of an open source system, you need to be aware of the license that comes with that system. For example, the GPL (Gnu General Public License, *www.gnu.org/licenses/licenses.html*) – a license that covers many open source products – requires you to make your sourcecode available if you distribute a system based on GPL-protected code.

Starting with an open source CMS can potentially save you a lot of time. Whether you eventually choose to use an open source CMS or not, they can all be evaluated for free, and are worth looking at even if you are developing your own system from scratch, as they contain many useful ideas and references.

Defining a Product Roadmap

You might think that you want your homegrown CMS to have every possible feature you can think of. Unfortunately for you, new features are dreamed up every day. Besides, some typical CMS features (such as workflow and versioning) take a lot of development work. If you don't need all of these features now (and chances are you don't), decide which features are most important and which can wait until a future version. If you do need all of these features immediately then consider buying a CMS instead.

In this section, we'll work through possible solutions for each of the main areas of functionality of a CMS, and give advice as to how important this functionality is likely to be at different stages of your CMS's development life cycle.

Asset Management:

Authoring Interface

When developing your own system, keep interface usability in mind. Develop the system with authors, rather than for authors. Show prototypes as you develop, and be prepared to revise your interface based on author feedback on these prototypes.

Your author interface should ideally not require, or allow, authors to use HTML. It is better to limit the author's control over layout than to allow them to break a site horribly from incorrect HTML inclusion. Although content authors who know a little bit of HTML may complain about this, when you come to re-purpose the content so it can be published as a PDF, or for a WAP phone or PDA, HTML will become a major hindrance. Your content should not contain presentation code – it should be stored and edited completely separately from its final presentation style. If you do have to allow HTML code inclusion, think very carefully about which HTML tags you allow, and how their inclusion may limit content reuse.

Providing a WYSIWYG (what you see is what you get) editor may be the most familiar interface for your users, but don't be tempted to give authors too much flexibility over design. It is much better to allow your authors to assign named styles (such as "Subheading" or "Section title") to their text rather than to give them complete control over how their text will look. If your content is marked up using styles, changing your page design in the future will be a matter of defining new translations for those styles. It becomes impossible to enforce a corporate design, and change this design in the future, if your authors can assign their own choices of colors and fonts to their text.

Perspectives: Shortcuts to WYSIWYG Editing

You don't have to develop your own WYSIWYG editor if you don't have the time or skills. You could integrate with a prewritten solution such as the XS DHTML Editor from www.laneve.com.

Another way to provide rich text editing is to use the Internet Explorer contentEditable *attribute. This is a feature in IE 5.5+ that provides a simple content editing interface for free. Adding code such as* <div contentEditable="true">Edit me!</div> *to your page will give an example of this in action. Clipboard integration and keyboard-shortcut support are provided by default. However, this option does require you to insist upon all authors having IE 5.5+ installed, which may not be possible for larger organizations with standard software rollouts.*

We don't want content authors to be able to edit every single element on a page. Rather, we would like to allow them to fill one or more content areas on a page with paragraphs of content. To think about this generically, base your page structure around a page template with one or more content areas, each of which can have one or more paragraphs added to it by the author. Each content area will have a list of available paragraph templates upon which paragraphs can be based.

Make sure your authors can preview their page whilst adding paragraphs and editing content. This preview should be generated in exactly the same way as the live version of the page. If you are generating content for several different targets (for example, an HTML version and a WML version), it should be possible to view a preview of each different version of the page.

Authors need to be able to add metadata to the page. This will include information such as the page title, page description, and keywords. It should be possible to make these fields mandatory. Although this may annoy your content authors, it's the only way you can be sure that they will add this information to a page. You will be eternally grateful for your stubbornness should you subsequently wish to search for information on your site.

The author's details should always be connected with the page, as should the content owner's details. Note that this isn't always the same person. If possible, store their job title as well as their name and contact details. People's jobs change within a company, and this makes it much easier to track down the new content owner if the original author has moved on. Whilst you're there, store a created (and last modified) date for the page too. It's bound to come in useful later.

You may want your CMS to include spell checking, especially if content is to be published to a live web site. One way to do this in a Microsoft environment is to script Microsoft Word from a web page and use Word's spell checker to flag misspellings back to the browser (*www.pcnineoneone.com/tweaks/scripts8.html*). If you prefer, content can be posted to the server for server-side spell checking. See *aspell.sourceforge.net* for a free, open source server spell-checking tool for PHP and Perl. Alternatively, there are a variety of commercial spell checking solutions available.

Site Structure

There are several different approaches to site structure management for you to consider. We'll take a look at a number of these approaches in this section. The approach you choose will define how you store and structure pages within your CMS. Think carefully about your requirements to avoid limiting your system if you need to add more flexibility in the future.

The simplest approach to site structure management is to split your site into several predefined sections. In each section, allow the author to build a list of pages, and decide how those pages should be ordered in a one-level index.

This approach is ideally suited to news areas and archive sections, or any other content area where a large number of documents need to be created and managed based on some ordering criteria (date published, alphabetical, etc.). You may wish to allow authors to create many pages, each of which has a page property (such as date published) and dynamically generate the section index based on this property.

Alternatively, you may want to allow authors to manage and change the index order of pages themselves. This can be best achieved by asking the author to select the page they want to move, then select a point on the index for this page to be inserted, typically "before the document entitled xxxx". If the final item on the list of insertion points is "At the end of the list" then a page can be moved to any point in the index, as illustrated below.

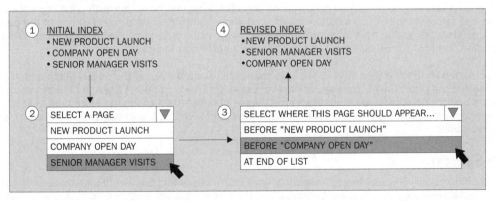

This method of re-ordering a list is equally useful for changing the order of paragraphs on a page. If you have several paragraphs in a column, and want to move (for example) the last paragraph to the top of the list, use the same method to select the paragraph to move, followed by its new destination.

The downside to an index-based approach to site structuring is that it does not give authors complete flexibility as to how they build the wider structure of the site – they are limited to creating content within certain predefined site areas. The next level of flexibility comes from giving authors a navigation-building tool, allowing them to create a pool of pages and then build a multi-level navigation system with links to various pages in the pool.

Creating a navigation-building tool is not as easy as it might sound. You need to give authors the ability to build a tree structure in any way they see fit. As we saw in Chapter 5, this comes with certain issues to which there are several possible approaches. It is up to you to decide which approach is best for your system.

The final (and most complex) method of dealing with site structure is for the tree hierarchy and the site structure to be one and the same, rather than building a tree from a pool of content pages. The issues with this approach are explained in Chapter 5 and this is the approach taken by some enterprise-level systems. Building your system in this way will give the most flexibility in the future.

> **Perspectives: Shortcuts to Hierarchy Management.**
>
> *If you want to include full hierarchy management in your system but do not have the skills or time to develop a hierarchy manager, consider using an existing tool instead. If you have chosen Java as your development language, you could use the Java Outline Editor (outliner.sourceforge.net), a Swing-based hierarchy outliner tool.*
>
> *If you are using Zope (see Other Possibilities above) as a basis for your CMS, then hierarchy management is provided "for free" within Zope. If hierarchy management is an essential for your CMS, take a look at Zope as a possible starting point for your CMS creation.*

Link Management

Your authors will need to add links to their pages. The simplest way to add this functionality to your CMS is to allow authors to add "hotspots" to sections of text on their pages, with the hotspot being a complete URL link. In this way the author can link to an external site or browse their own site, find the URL of a page, and add this as a link in the same way.

This has the distinct disadvantage of requiring authors to know the URLs for pages in their site in order to create in-site links. A much better solution is to present the author with a list of pages in the site and ask them to select a page to link to. You should store this link as a reference to the page's unique identifier, rather than its current URL. This way, when a page is (inevitably) moved to a new location, the link can be regenerated based on the page's new location.

If you are baking the pages in your site, you may want to store a list of the pages that link to a page alongside the page itself. This way, when your page is moved, you don't need to search through your entire site to find other pages that link to the page – you just run through the stored list of links and re-bake them accordingly. If you have relatively few pages, searching through the site may be an easier option.

Site Search

Searching your site is an essential feature if your users are to find content. It's also one of the most overlooked features of web sites. Do consider how important a site search is to your users – on a small, well-categorized site, you may be able to do without it. You can implement a search at a later date without any real impact, as long as you have planned with search functionality in mind.

The most basic and most important form of searching is searching the content your authors have added to the CMS. If you have insisted on authors adding `<meta>` tags to their pages then the search can include these fields as well as the content on the page. All of these elements to be searched are simply text, stored in our content repository.

To search this content we could use a tool that indexes the generated HTML of the site, such as:

- Swish-E (*www.swish-e.org*)

- Ht://Dig (*www.htdig.org*)

- Lucene (*jakarta.apache.org/lucene/docs*).

These tools work by building an index of the site every so often as specified in a schedule. This provides speed benefits, as the search is performed over an optimized index rather than every page of content. The downside to this approach is that a search is only as up-to-date as the latest index. Since the search tools listed above are separate applications from your CMS, they will need to be called by your CMS and have their results formatted in a way that is appropriate to your site.

Alternatively, you could search your content repository directly. How you choose to do this is entirely dependent on the method of content storage you choose. If you are using a file-based repository, you may still be able to use one of the tools listed above to search the non-HTML text elements in your repository. If your textual content is stored in an SQL database, you can use an SQL SELECT statement to search for keywords within the content.

The next level of searching you will require is the ability to search file attachments (for example, PDFs and Word documents). If you are using a Microsoft server environment and want to index and search Microsoft Office documents, consider using the Microsoft Indexing Service (which will also index HTML). Otherwise, the best approach is to use a text extractor program to suck the text from your documents, and then index them via the tools mentioned above. XPDF (*www.foolabs.com/xpdf*) or Acroread (*www.adobe.com*) will extract text from PDF files, whereas Wvware (*www.wvware.com*) extracts text from Word documents.

Don't forget you may also need to search back-end systems that are linked to your CMS. In this case, the content of these systems won't be stored within your own content repository. How you search these systems will be entirely dependent upon the system in question. However, combining the search results from your back-end search with the local file and content search will not be easy, especially if you are using a different tool for the back-end search. It may be better to present results from different systems as separate groups of results instead.

Users and Their Rights

If you are developing a small system, or if you have a small number of content authors, you may want to avoid developing a complex user management system. We say this from bitter experience, having written a fantastic XML-based user and role management system for a client in the past. The client in question seemed rather nonplussed by our programming achievements, and set up one super-user account for one author to make all subsequent content changes.

Even if your CMS doesn't need to stretch to full user rights and security management, you need some form of user system, if only to identify authors as different people and track who has authored what. You should implement this in all but the simplest of CMS. For these requirements a cookie-based system is an easy way to track an author's identity without the need for server-side authentication.

If you are creating a CMS for internal use, you will probably already have some form of user / password authentication system in your company. Since you are writing the CMS yourself, and the main benefit of this is to make it appropriate for you and your business, all you need to do in this case is to integrate with your existing system. If you need to store information about authors, store this information in the existing user directory as well. This may allow you to use an author's PC or intranet logon process for your CMS and avoid multiple logins for different systems. In short: don't write a user management system if you can just tie into your existing one.

If you do choose to develop a system with user access control, don't assign these access rights to individual users. Instead, assign access rights to a variety of roles, and then assign these roles to users. This gives a much more flexible approach to user access management. This approach ties in nicely with workflow processes, allowing a role rather than a list of users to be assigned to a workflow stage.

You will need to store a user's e-mail address with their details, so you can contact users when they have actions to fulfill at various stages of a workflow. However, e-mail addresses change, so don't use this as a user's unique identifier in your system.

Before you create an all-singing, all-dancing user management system, think carefully about who will use it. The list of users may only need updating once every six months by a developer editing an SQL table. In this case, creating a beautiful Java Swing interface is probably a little excessive.

Workflow

Chapter 5 lists a variety of features that you may (or may not) require from a workflow system. If you need most or all of these features you should seriously consider buying a commercial CMS. Developing a fully featured workflow system is a major programming project in its own right, and it may not be cost-effective to create this yourself.

The simplest instance of workflow is to pass a document through several discrete stages of editing and approval on its way from creation to publication. You don't have to store multiple versions of a document to achieve this (but if you want to, see the *Versioning* section below). This form of workflow can be achieved by storing a field with the page document indicating which workflow is assigned to the page, and storing an indicator of which stage of that workflow the page is currently at.

Users with workflow responsibilities need to be prompted to make content changes and pass the document forwards or backwards in the workflow. We would suggest that the interface for passing a document from one stage of a workflow to another enables the approver to add comments describing their involvement and changes. As well as being stored with the document, these comments (together with a call to action) can then be e-mailed to all users who have the roles assigned to the next stage in the workflow, alerting these users that their involvement is now required.

Do your users need to be able to create their own workflows? As with user management, if the workflow is not going to change frequently, don't bother building a beautiful GUI for workflow creation.

Multilingual Content

Your CMS may need to manage content in several languages. It is not possible to cover all of the issues relating to multilingual content here, but if you are dealing with international text and character sets, consider using Java or ASP.NET as your language of choice, as both use Unicode (*www.unicode.org*) exclusively. PHP is not as Unicode-savvy at this time, nor is classic ASP. If you only require support for Western European languages you should not have any character set problems in any of these languages.

If you store copies of a page in multiple languages, consider using automatic browser language detection to decide which version of the page to serve to a user. Most browsers support the `accept-language` HTTP header (*www.w3.org/Protocols/rfc2616/rfc2616-sec14.html*) to let you discover a user's preferred choice of language. However, even if you do have clever language detection, always make sure that users can easily switch to view the other versions of the page. Multilingual users may (for example) prefer to read the English version of a page in preference to their native language, especially if their native version is not well translated.

Versioning

Simple page versioning can be added to your CMS by storing a new copy of an edited page in your content repository each time an edit is made. You may, for example, want to store a new version of a page each time the page moves to a different stage of a workflow. Don't store a version number with each new copy – store the full date and time of the edit instead. All versions of a page should have a common identifier to identify them as being the same page.

Storing a new version of a page may not just mean storing a new block of text. Pages will contain non-text elements such as images and PDFs and you will need to store new versions of these page elements too. Logically, we are creating a new version of a page, but practically this may mean creating new versions of several page elements in order to do so.

For binary files, this can cause your content repository to become very big very quickly. Don't just cheerily store a new copy of an image or an attachment every time the containing page is changed. Instead, you should check whether the image or attachment itself has changed, and if not, don't create another copy – make a reference to the same attachment as before. Trust us, you will save yourself gigabytes of disk space if you are prudent with avoiding asset duplication.

If a page is "deleted" (removed from the live site), you should store some sort of date- and time-stamped deletion marker. You should also store who performed the deletion, and possibly why. With all of these versions and deletion markers in place, it is possible to generate a view of your entire site as it was at a particular point in time. Assuming your server's clock is set to the right time, that is.

You don't just need to store versions of your pages and their elements. If your templates change, you will need a copy of the old templates in order to be able to roll back to a view of your site at a particular point in time. You should be able to use the same mechanism for template versioning as you have used for your pages.

If you want a more sophisticated versioning system, tracking just the differences between versions and therefore using less disk space, you might want to look at integrating with RCS (*www.gnu.org/software/rcs/rcs.html*). RCS is the GNU Revision Control System for managing multiple revisions of files. RCS is free, and versions of RCS are available for all major platforms.

If you already have a version control system (and if you are developing a CMS, you really should have a version control system for your system code), it may be more appropriate to integrate with this instead. If you don't have a version control system, there are several open source and commercial systems available, such as CVS (*www.cvshome.org*), SourceSafe (*msdn.microsoft.com/ssafe/*), ClearCase (*www.rational.com*), and Perforce (*www.perforce.com*). For more information see *www.c2.com/cgi/wiki?VersionControl*.

There may be very pressing reasons to be able to roll back to snapshots of your site. For example, one of the clients we have worked with in the past has to take a snapshot of their site at 12pm every day for legal reasons, and the rollback functionality mentioned above enables this.

Transformation:

Template Creation

We established the benefits of templates in Chapter 3, specifically their ability to separate the content and structure of pages from the design of those pages. There are several different approaches to template implementation for your CMS, and the choice of approach you make should be based on your specific CMS requirements.

HTML and CSS

The simplest way to use templates to separate design and content is by using HTML and CSS. In this method, your CMS generates simple HTML and then design styling is applied to this HTML by using a CSS (short for Cascading Style Sheet – see *www.w3.org/Style/CSS*). If your design changes in the future, a replacement CSS is introduced to reflect the new design. You don't need any particular tools or skills to write CSS, just be a reasonably knowledgeable web professional. CSS 1 covers text and document layout styling. CSS 2 allows even more control over document styling than CSS 1, including media-specific stylesheets and automatic numbering. Unfortunately, almost all browsers only partially support CSS 1 and 2, and as a result only simple design changes can currently be made with CSS in these browsers.

For more information on CSS, see: *Cascading Style Sheets – Separating Content From Presentation*, published by glasshaus, ISBN 1904151043.

HTML Templates

There is one major thing that CSS (in its currently supported state) cannot do. You can't add additional content to your pages with CSS 1, such as including standard images, and boilerplate headers and footers. To include these additional site-wide content elements, you will need to make use of templates.

One approach is to create sample HTML templates, and dynamically replace sections of these templates with user-edited content. For example, a page header template might be:

```
<html>
<head><title>%%TITLE%%</title></head>
```

When the page is displayed, our CMS would replace the %%TITLE%% code with the title text for the current page. This approach is valid with slight changes in syntax in JSP, ASP, ASP.NET, or PHP. %% is just an identifying code – you can use whatever you like (but make sure it doesn't appear anywhere else in your page).

This approach is good if you would like your template development to be done by HTML authors who don't have any experience with a scripting language. This approach works for multilingual sites, and for targets other than HTML (for example WML), if you provide some way for the author to choose which template is applied for a given page.

Custom Tags

So far, we have seen how to control the layout of content, and add standard content elements using templates. However, we have not yet considered how to add functionality and conditional content generation to our pages.

A standard approach to adding this kind of functionality is the creation of custom tags. For example, you may wish to create a %%CURRENTDATE%% code for template developers to add to their templates. Rather than being replaced with a simple author-edited text field, this would be replaced automatically by the current date every time the page is generated.

Beware! Once you start adding a few custom tags like this, your template creators will demand more and more and before you know it, you will have invented your own miniature scripting language, complete with loops, database lookups, file access, and kitchen sinks. This is the route that a lot of the early commercial CMS products took, and many ended up with their own proprietary reinventions of the wheel as a result.

A tag-based approach is well supported by JSP, ASP.NET, and ColdFusion. JSP calls its tags 'Taglibs', ASP.NET calls them 'Custom Controls', but whatever the name, they are as a standard way for you to create your own custom tags (similar to HTML tags) for template creators to include in their code. These tags are placeholders for reusable bits of functionality, and can be customized in each instance via parameters in a similar way to HTML tags. These tags make it easy to provide reusable functionality without the need for extensive code to be embedded within your HTML templates.

For JSP, you might want to start tag creation by using the JSP Standard Tag Library (*jakarta.apache.org/taglibs/*) and developing your own tags as necessary. ColdFusion comes with a large number of tags as standard, and many more are available from *devex.macromedia.com/Developer/Gallery/CustomTags.cfm* (although many of these cost money). The most recent version of ColdFusion also supports JSP Taglibs.

Embedding Code

Rather than using your own tags to include common scripting language functionality, you could just use a scripting language itself. ASP, ASP.NET, PHP, JSP, and ColdFusion can all be embedded within your HTML templates to perform actions (such as database access) and generate custom HTML based on the results of these actions.

Embedding code is an attractive approach, particularly to developers, as it gives complete freedom to embed any functionality at any point of any template. However, this means that you will need the involvement of a developer with scripting skills in order to change your templates, or at the very least someone who is comfortable with making even simple design changes to a template full of scripting code without breaking that code.

If you need a mixture of common functionality and some custom functionality then a combination of common Taglibs and custom embedded code may be the best solution. Both are valid approaches, and there is nothing wrong with using a combination of the two if this meets your needs.

XML / XSLT

A combination of XML and XSLT (Extensible Stylesheet Language for Transformations – see *www.w3.org/TR/xslt*) provides the most elegant method of content transformation. However, it may be too complex an approach for your requirements, so don't take this route unless you already have good XML skills in your development team. The following description of the XML / XSLT process is quite technical, so if you're easily daunted, look away now. Perhaps make a cup of coffee instead.

Still here? Here goes. If your content repository stores content as XML, or if you have some way of pulling your content from its repository as an XML representation, then XSLT may be the best way for you to apply design to your content. XSLT is essentially a way of transforming XML documents into other XML documents. And, when it comes down to it, HTML web pages (likewise WML pages) are essentially just XML documents.

This is where our previous comments about getting authors to mark up their content in terms of styles rather than "red font, bold" come in useful. You can define an XSLT transformation for each of your content styles, and apply these transformations to your design-free XML to generate design-specific HTML. If the design changes in the future, simply create replacement XSLT files to transform your XML into the new design format.

Perspectives: XHTML

Strictly speaking, you would use XSLT to transform your XML documents into XHTML, not plain old HTML. Why the extra X? Well, the HTML you know and love is very like XML – it's made up of tags with parameters, and these tags have opening and closing formats (such as `<td></td>`). But "normal" HTML isn't quite tidy enough to qualify as "proper" XML.

XHTML is the name for HTML that complies with the rules of properly formed XML. XHTML mandates a level of strictness that was optional in earlier versions of HTML, such as putting quotes around all parameter values. XHTML is "well formed". For example, our pages cannot include just a `<br>` tag on its own – the element needs to be closed (in this case the correct XML-compliant format would be `<br />`, since the element is "self closing"). Likewise, XHTML insists that you close your `<p>` tags with an `</p>`.
XHTML is compatible with all browsers that support the less-strict forms of HTML. And besides, it's being generated for you by your XSLT, so it doesn't require you to unlearn all those bad HTML habits you've picked up over the years.

XSLT gives you complete flexibility over the designs that can be implemented for your content. Furthermore, it allows you to define rules that not only change the design of the content, but also change and remove elements of the content if appropriate. So if you want the WAP version of your page to only include the first content paragraph, your WML XSLT can automatically strip out the rest of the content for you.

There are two approaches to applying XSLT to your XML content. You can perform these XSLT transformations on your web server, and serve up the resultant HTML. Alternatively, with IE5+ for Windows and Netscape 6+, you can send both the raw XML document and the XSLT document to the browser, and these browsers will apply the XSLT transformation for you. This has the advantage of saving processor time on your server. Additionally, sending XML and XSLT files reduces bandwidth usage, as a reused common XSLT file will only be sent to the browser once, rather than the styling information being sent in every single page in the form of transformed HTML.

In order to perform these transformations server-side, you use an XSLT processor, such as Xalan (*xml.apache.org/xalan-j/extensions.html*) for Java or MSXML (*msdn.microsoft.com/library/en-us/xmlsdk30/htm/xmconxsldevelopersguide.asp*) for Microsoft environments. PHP integrates well with Sablotron (*www.gingerall.com/charlie/ga/xml/p_sab.xml*) for XSLT transformation.

There is a downside to the XSLT approach. Using XSLT on its own doesn't give you the same abilities to embed functionality within your pages. Some things that are really simple in a scripting language, such as inserting the current time, aren't yet possible in XSLT.

To combine the benefits of scripting and XSLT, most XSLT processors have the capability of "extension functions". For example, MSXML lets you add JScript into the transformation process. Xalan provides similar functionality for its supported languages, including Java and JavaScript. This allows the template creator to get the best of both worlds – scripting *and* transformation. Of course, once you add a specific scripting language into the mix, you may lose the platform portability of the XSLT process.

It might be useful to stagger your design transformations across several XSLT files. Apache's Cocoon (*xml.apache.org/cocoon*) can apply a pipeline of XSLT pages, one after another. You can achieve the same result using other XSLT processors, by performing one transformation, saving the result, and then performing a new transformation on this result. Since the output of an XSLT is another XML file, we can continue to apply as many XSLTs as we wish. If a site design uses standard headers and footers for the entire site, but a different design for different site subsections, then we can apply one XSLT for the standard additions and follow it by another for the specific site subsection.

XSLT really does allow you to create anything from XML. For example, we have successfully used XSLT to generate RTF files from XML documents for Word integration. There is an accompanying technology known as XSL:FO (XSL Formatting Objects) that has been used to create other file formats such as PDFs from XML, using tools such as FOP (*xml.apache.org/fop*). For more information on XSL:FO, see *www.w3.org/Style/XSL*.

It's not hard to create an XSLT document, but it is a specialized skill, and is certainly harder than using a basic scripting approach. XSLT is not at all like CSS, even though both acronyms share the word "stylesheet". XSLT is essentially a programming language, but it's not a top-down scripting approach like PHP or ASP. In short: don't take this approach unless you are confident with your XML skills.

Graphics and Multimedia

We saw in Chapter 5 how image manipulation can be a very useful feature of a CMS. But how should you go about adding it to your own system? Thankfully, there are a range of prewritten solutions for image creation and manipulation that can be easily integrated into your own system.

ImageMagick (*www.imagemagick.org*) is a flexible, free, cross-platform image generation tool that can be called from a command-line interface, and therefore used by a variety of scripting languages. ImageMagick can convert, resize, rotate, and sharpen images, as well as drawing shapes and fonts on top of images.

If you are developing for an ASP platform, you might want to use a COM-based tool, such as ASPImage (*www.serverobjects.com/comp/Aspimage.htm*), a commercial COM object for image generation and manipulation. Alternatively, ASP.NET comes with built-in image functionality as part of its standard libraries.

Java comes with its own standard Java 2D libraries for generating images. Alternatively, Gimp (*www.gimp.org*) for Unix is a free,full-featured graphics manipulation package, which (like ImageMagick) can be called from the command line.

PHP and Perl both support the GD libraries (*www.boutell.com/gd/*) for image generation and manipulation. CX_GIFGD (*http://www.geocities.com/SiliconValley/Way/4282/*) is a similar library for ColdFusion. The latest version of ColdFusion, being Java-based, supports the same image generation methods as Java.

Whichever graphics tool you use, check out its support for any fonts you will need to use for image generation. If you only have a Windows version of your corporate font, you may not be able to use this font on a Unix platform for font-based image generation.

Another option for image generation and manipulation is SVG ("Scalable Vector Graphics"). SVG is an image format for representing images as vectors in a similar style to Macromedia Flash. SVG is actually a form of XML – defining graphics as XML-based vector drawing instructions. As such, it is relatively easy to convert XML-based data into SVG images using XSLT. This can be very useful for creating charts and graphs from numeric data stored in XML format, for example.

In order for a browser to view SVG images, it needs to have the SVG plug-in (available from *www.adobe.com/svg*) installed. The SVG plug-in supports animation and scripting as well as images, all defined in XML. Very few users currently have the SVG plug-in (certainly far fewer than have the Flash plug-in), and so this is not a viable means of graphics generation for sites where the plug-in cannot be guaranteed.

However, there is another way to use the XML conveniences of SVG for image generation. It is possible to generate your SVG XML code on your server and then convert this to a standard web format (GIF, JPEG) using a server-side tool such as Batik (*xml.apache.org/batik*). This standard image file can then be served to a browser as normal. There are still relatively few tools supporting SVG, but the backing of Adobe means this is likely to change in the future.

In Chapter 5, we discussed an easy way to customize the content of a Flash movie by passing parameters into a template movie file. But what if we want to actually generate a custom Flash movie based on the content in our CMS? ColdFusion, as a Macromedia product, integrates well with Flash for movie generation. PHP supports Flash generation using the libswf module (*www.php.net/manual/en/ref.swf.php*). JGenerator (*www.jzox.com*) is a Java-based Flash Movie generation tool that has a free "Community" edition. Bukoo (*bukoo.sourceforge.net*) is a relatively new project to generate Flash movies from ASP or ASP.NET.

With the new client-side content customization features in newer versions of Flash, consider whether you need to use a full generation tool for your Flash customization needs.

Publishing:

Publishing Process

The simplest form of publishing setup is to have only one server, with a password-protected administration area. In this situation, all pages are stored on the same machine, and a page's published state is managed by a "live / not live" flag within the content repository. This setup is easy to create and tidy to maintain, and may well be appropriate for many CMS needs, but it does have two disadvantages.

Firstly, it requires a hosting and security environment in which we are happy for content authors and viewers of the live site to view content on the same web server. This may not be possible for security reasons. If there is a technical issue with the authoring environment this may put the production environment at risk. Secondly, this solution is not scalable. It provides no way to add load balancing or multiple live site servers to the hosting arrangements.

A more scalable solution is to have separate authoring and live servers. All content authoring takes place on the authoring server (which may sit behind a corporate firewall), and when pages are put live, the page data is copied to the live server or servers. This may take place via FTP or some other appropriate means, and needs to be verified as having completed successfully in order to avoid publishing or network issues making the live site out of sync with the author instance of the site. Note that it is not just content that needs to be transferred to the live server – any changes to templates will also need to be put live, with the same checking in place.

This setup is much more flexible, but it does have its disadvantages. If content is created on the publishing server by site users (for example, in a live discussion forum), the system needs to have some way to replicate this content with the other live servers and / or back to the author environment if appropriate (if backups are taken from the author environment, or if forum moderation needs to take place). The only real solution to this is proper two-way replication between all servers, but this is a very complex piece of functionality to create. If you really need two-way content replication, consider a commercial CMS instead. Even then, not all commercial CMS products will offer this feature.

A further complication is added if content is authored in more than one location. If this is the case, consider Lotus Notes as a development platform for your CMS. Notes supports flexible two-way replication for content creation and editing, and is well equipped to deal with content replication conflicts. If you need to tackle replication on a Windows platform, Robocopy (part of the Windows NT / Windows 2000 Resource Kits) provides two-way replication for files and folders, as does Rsync (*www.rsync.org*) on Unix.

Multiple Targets

We may want our CMS to publish multiple versions of a page for different targets or purposes, such as a printer-friendly version of a page, or an optimized version for PDA or WAP. Earlier in this chapter we discussed ways of generating PDFs using XSLT. PDFLIB (*www.pdflib.com*) is a commercial PDF generation tool that gives an alternative route for PDF generation, allowing existing PDFs to be edited and new documents to be created. PDFLIB integrates with Java, Perl, PHP, Python and COM.

> ### Perspectives: Printable version for free
>
> *One of the most common reasons to generate multiple versions of a page is to create a "printable version" of a page, reformatted to be printer-friendly. If we can assume your site users are using the latest browsers, you can generate a print version of your web pages "for free". Rather than having to generate print-friendly code, these browsers allow a different CSS file to be specified for different media. Add the media parameter to a stylesheet link tag, for example* `<LINK rel="stylesheet" type="text/css" href="print.css" media="print">`, *and* `print.css` *will be used whenever the page is sent to a printer.*
>
> *You can easily remove elements such as navigation and adverts from the print version of your page by setting their display property to none in the* `print.css` *file. If a printable version of the page was your only reason for implementing multiple templates, and you can guarantee that your users will have the latest browsers, then you don't need multiple templates.*

You might want to publish your content to PDAs, too. You can do this via AvantGo (*www.avantgo.com*), but AvantGo charge for making your content available to users. Alternatively, there are plenty of HTML viewers for Palm and PocketPC platforms, assuming we can produce cut-down HTML for a PDA. We can use alternative templates to produce simpler HTML for a PDA, but we may also need to reduce the amount of content on a page. XSLT transformation, which allows content to be removed as well as transformed, would be ideal for this.

Performance

Depending on how you build your CMS it may require a lot of page generation, which may in turn put a lot of load on your CMS servers. There are several ways to reduce the impact of this and improve the performance of your system.

One of the simplest ways to make your system faster is to encourage caching of pages. There are various levels of caching that can be implemented. For example, it is good practice to ensure that a browser does not return to your site and ask for a new copy of a page unless the page itself indicates that a new copy is required. In order to avoid this, your pages need to contain all of the required HTTP cache headers supported by standard browsers, see *www.w3.org/Protocols/rfc2616/rfc2616-sec13.html#sec13* for more information about which headers should be sent, and how.

If you can, include page caching for your CMS as well, to avoid pages being re-generated for each user if it is not necessary. An even better form of caching for a CMS is to cache separate page fragments rather than the entire page. On dynamic pages, it may be that only a small part of the page will change regularly, and regenerating all other page fragments is not necessary. However, if your site's load will be low, this isn't necessarily worth the development effort.

If your publishing setup allows publishing to more than one live server (see previously), then you may want to implement load balancing between several identical live servers to distribute page requests (and therefore server load) across more than one machine. If you anticipate very heavy load, consider buying a commercial CMS instead. Its commercial development doesn't guarantee excellent performance, but it is more likely to have been used and tested in high-load situations before.

Summary

In this chapter we've covered why and how to build your own CMS. We've learned that building gives you the control to create a system that matches your requirements better than any system you could buy, but that building comes with responsibility. We have provided practical solutions to the most common CMS features, and covered the various technologies you can use.

Now you've developed your perfect CMS, it's time to look at the most important stage of all – implementing the system.

7

- Roles and Responsibilities
- The Concept Phase
- The Production Phase

Author: Dave Addey

Implementation

OK. We're doing well. Whether you've bought it or built it, you now have a shiny new content management system all ready and raring to go. But there's something not quite right. Why doesn't it produce web pages that look anything like your own site? Why doesn't it have your own workflows and functionality built in? Why, in short, isn't it already exactly what you need?

We saw in Chapters 5 and 6 that, regardless of whether you buy or build, the resultant CMS is essentially a content toolkit, comprising all of the functionality necessary to manage the assets in your site. This toolkit now needs customizing to your requirements – a process often called **implementation** – in a way that allows a specific set of authors to manage the content of a specific site. For each site, we need to go through a rigorous CMS implementation process. This chapter will show you how.

It's a Game of Two Halves

You may think you know what your site is going to look like, and how it is going to work, but I guarantee that I could ask you at least fifty questions about specific details, and all fifty would require some thinking or research or consultation with colleagues. (Recall the difficulties you may have had in Chapter 2, answering questions about your *existing* site.) Moreover, even when all fifty questions had been answered, you'd need to remember the answers on top of everything else in your already hectic life. It's absolutely vital that the requirements of your specific implementation are researched and written down in a clear and detailed way. This document will become the specification for your system, the delivery document for your implementation team, and the test sheet for your QA (Quality Assurance) team.

If you're producing a document in conjunction with colleagues and clients, you need an easy way to refer to it. It's time for a TLA (Three Letter Acronym). You can call this document whatever you like, in words appropriate to your organization, but for the purposes of this chapter we'll call it a **System Implementation Specification** (**SIS**) document. According to *http://www.acronymfinder.com*, SIS also stands for Simple Internet Solutions, but don't tell anyone that – they might get confused and think that CMS implementation is easy.

There's no point making this document up as you go along. The SIS needs to be signed off by all parties before production begins. Your CMS implementation needs two discrete phases – an initial *Concept Phase* (resulting in a SIS), and a subsequent *Production Phase*. We'll run through both of these phases later in the chapter. First, let's recap as to why we're here, and who will be involved in the project.

Reasons for CMS Implementation

If you are embarking on a CMS implementation, you will probably be in one of the following three situations:

Bought to Use

You have bought a CMS for your own organization's use.

In this case, it is likely that the CMS vendor will offer implementation services as part of their sales pitch. Quite how implementation work is split between yourself and the vendor will depend on how you wish to manage your CMS rollout. Some companies look to buy a CMS and manage all subsequent implementation themselves, in which case the vendor would have little or no involvement, other than to provide support and training. Other companies look to buy a system and rely entirely on the vendor for its implementation.

The work split will be driven by the skills available within your organization to manage the implementation yourselves. If you have never implemented a CMS before, or are unfamiliar with the CMS you have bought, you should budget for some involvement from the CMS vendor, regardless of the skills within your company. Whether the vendor leads the implementation process described below is up to you.

Built to Use

You have built a CMS for your own organization's use.

If you are implementing your own CMS for your own organization, the complete responsibility for the CMS implementation will lie within the organization. Although the relationship is entirely internal, there is still a client – just an internal one. These can sometimes be the most demanding clients of all.

Bought or Built to Sell

You have either licensed or built a CMS to sell to your clients.

If you are selling a CMS to your clients, you will probably be offering implementation services to those clients (unless they want to do the implementation themselves, in which case you will inevitably end up getting involved when they have problems). In this case, the reverse of the *Bought to Use* scenario is true. The project management of the implementation will probably lie within your own company, with the client role filled by the budget holder within your customer's organization.

Roles and Responsibilities

Wherever the responsibility for CMS integration lies, the same roles need to be filled in order for the project to progress smoothly. In this chapter we will refer to these roles generically, without drawing too much attention to whether these people work for the CMS creators or the company for whom the CMS is being implemented. The implementation process should be the same either way.

Those roles in full are:

- Project Manager

- Technical Lead Developer

- Designer

- Developers

- Client

- Users

Project Manager

The project manager is arguably the most important member of the CMS implementation team. This person has responsibility for the delivery of the project on time, on budget, and to specification. The project manager will be the central point of contact between the project's end-users, the implementation team, and the CMS vendor or development team.

If you have purchased a CMS, it is typical for both the vendor and your organization to have a project management resource assigned to the CMS implementation. The vendor will have more experience of implementing their CMS, and may prefer to take the lead on SIS creation with your organization's involvement. If the vendor is providing developers and other implementation resources, they should be keen to ensure the SIS is realistic and deliverable, as it will cost them time and money to complete the implementation otherwise.

If your organization is not developing the SIS, your project manager's role will be one of liaison and ensuring your organization's best interests are represented in the SIS and subsequent production phase.

The project manager takes responsibility for assigning and managing the development resource for the project, and creating and updating the project timeline plan accordingly. It is the project manager's unenviable task to make sure that any issues that may cause project delivery problems are noticed and flagged as early as possible.

Where changes to the implementation requirements do occur, the project manager is responsible for managing these changes and updating the project plan. We'll take a look at change management processes later in the chapter. If an external company is implementing your CMS, bear in mind that requesting changes may well incur additional costs. The project manager will need to ensure the successful completion of these changes and their inclusion in the cost process.

Your project manager(s) should have previous experience of running web application projects, and ideally come from a trained project management background.

Technical Lead Developer

The technical lead takes responsibility for the technical aspects of project delivery. Working for the project manager, the technical lead may also organize the time and efforts of your implementation team. The technical lead is responsible for ensuring code quality and consistency during template creation and code authoring.

As lead developer, the technical lead has an additional responsibility to notify the project manager of any technical issues that will affect the delivery of the project, and to suggest alternative approaches to minimize the impact of these issues.

Designer

The designer will be primarily involved in the *Concept Phase*, to create visual representations of the site design and layout. This may involve designing the "look and feel" of the site from scratch, or alternatively taking an existing design and adapting it for the CMS.

The primary reason for the designer's involvement is to help the client to express his or her design and functionality needs in a way that can be visualized and understood by everyone involved with the project.

Developers

Developers are the technical experts, the programmers who transform a generic CMS into a beautifully crafted installation. The team of developers may be a mixture of people from the CMS vendor and the client's organization, but either way, they'll be doing the bulk of the implementation work. As such they are to be respected and valued.

Client

One person your project can't be without is a client. Clients are as constant (but not as easy) as pi.

If you have bought or built a CMS for your own company's needs, and are implementing the system internally, then the client will be the internal budget holder or site owner. If you are implementing a CMS for an external company, then the client is the main contact and decision-maker within that company. In either case, the client may be a group of people rather than just one individual – it doesn't matter, as long as one member of the group has the authority to write a check. There are three easy ways to spot the client:

- They are the one with the money

- They are the decision-maker

- They are the one whose needs you must satisfy

The client will be involved in the SIS creation process, giving their input and explaining their needs. They will sign off this document when (and only when) they are happy that the implementation it describes can meet these needs.

The client will hopefully have a pretty good idea of what their CMS needs are, though they may not yet know how these needs translate into a fully functioning web system. It is the project manager's role (with the help of the rest of the implementation team) to translate these needs into a CMS implementation that fulfills the client's requirements.

CMS Users

Although the project manager was the most important person on the implementation team, the CMS users (or "users" for short) are the most important people who will actually work with it on a regular basis. Their involvement in your implementation project may only be intermittent and consultative, but it is absolutely essential that they *are* consulted regularly. Otherwise there is no way to know whether the system you are developing is usable and amenable to their needs until it is too late.

I've deliberately avoided calling these people "authors", although a lot of users may fall into that category. "Users" covers anyone – authors, administrators, editors, approvers, and content reviewers, even lawyers – who will use the system for its prime purpose, the management of content assets.

Concept Phase

Now you've gathered your team, we move into the first of our two phases: the concept phase.

This is your chance to define exactly what will be delivered and when. Its one overriding mission is the banishment of all doubt as to what the finished implementation will be like.

Typically, the concept phase should take between two and four weeks, depending on the scale of the initial CMS implementation and the number of people involved. This phase is led by the project manager, and results in the creation of a System Implementation Specification (SIS) document.

If four weeks sounds like a long time to spend just planning the implementation, think again. The time taken to specify the project in advance will be saved many times over later on in the project. The single most common failure for a CMS implementation is a lack of understanding of the project deliverables (and of commitment to those deliverables) by all parties involved. I'll say it a few times till it sticks: don't ever skimp on this stage.

You could argue that it is impossible to specify *everything* in advance. You'd be right. Part of the purpose of the concept phase is to put in place a plan for dealing with changes and unknowns, and to catch them as soon as they occur. We'll deal with this later in the chapter.

Budgeting

There's one other reason to undertake a concept phase. No matter how skilled the estimator or how clear the initial project requirements, it is impossible to accurately estimate how long the production phase of your project will take (and therefore how much it will cost) without specifying the deliverables in detail. Until the concept phase is completed, the best you can get is a guessed estimate as to how much the production phase will cost.

What you *can* do is specify how much it will cost to run a two-week (or four-week) concept phase, and agree to define the production phase budget on the basis of the SIS document. This document will specify exactly what is to be delivered, and from this specification it *is* possible to give an accurate cost for the production phase. If the estimate was good, this shouldn't differ too much. If the estimate was bad, it is much better to realize this before the production phase begins, and revise the cost estimate accordingly. If the revised costs are too high, reduce the requirements.

If you are implementing a CMS for another company, and you have trouble convincing the client of the value of a concept phase, sell it in this way: if they don't like the revised costs you have to offer, then they will still have an excellent description of their requirements that can be taken to another CMS company (as appropriate). And if they don't want to spend the time getting the project right first time, get off the implementation team as soon as you can.

Concept Phase Timeline

The diagram overleaf shows the various stages of a concept phase. We'll run through each of them in detail overleaf.

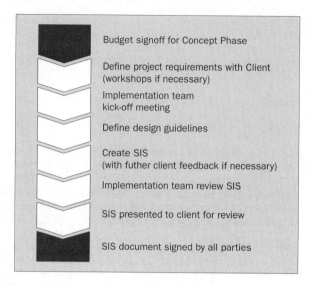

Budget signoff for Concept Phase

Define project requirements with Client (workshops if necessary)

Implementation team kick-off meeting

Define design guidelines

Create SIS (with futher client feedback if necessary)

Implementation team review SIS

SIS presented to client for review

SIS document signed by all parties

Budget Signoff

This is a quickie, but worth saying anyway – before you begin the concept phase, make sure everyone is clear how long it will take and that a budget has been signed off for it.

Define Project Requirements with the Client

The client may have already created a document detailing their purported requirements. Beware of the difference between "wants" and "needs". Translating one into the other is the work of a prudent and tactful project manager. Whatever exists will form the basis of your SIS.

These project requirements will not contain all of the information required to write the SIS. Plan to spend some time with the client to ask questions and help formulate their thoughts. Running workshops with the client and a selection of users is a very good way to achieve this. Don't be afraid to ask lots of questions, as it is your job to produce a SIS that is achievable, but be sympathetic to the client's day job. Be constructive and suggest options wherever there are gaps in the client's definition of requirements. Part of this stage will be educating the client as to what is and isn't possible with the CMS (and more generally on the Web).

Implementation Team Kick-off Meeting

Having gathered as many requirements as possible, the implementation team should meet to kick off the concept phase. This is the project manager's opportunity to brief the team on the initial scope of the project, and present the project requirements to the team, ready for them to go away and work on the complete SIS document.

Define Design Guidelines

The project specification shouldn't just cover the technical requirements of how the CMS will be implemented. It also needs to cover how the CMS-generated site will look and function in the browsers you choose to support. The designers need to work with the project manager and the client to define the "look and feel" of the site in detail.

This stage may involve some creative design or adaptation of existing designs for CMS use (or a bit of both). These designs need to show how the site will look, but should also be exacting in their description of how the site will expand and adapt to varying forms and quantities of content.

Providing pixel sizes and paragraph-level descriptions of the designs will help them be translated into code when the design is converted to actual templates. These design specifications will form part of the SIS document and their inclusion avoids any doubt as to how the designs will be realized.

Create the SIS

Chances are the client will not be technically minded. This will make the project manager's job one of tact and explanation, but does have its benefits. The primary aim of the specification is to avoid any doubt. Explaining something technical to a non-technical client requires the subject to be broken down into clear, easy-to-understand chunks. The project manager will need to make sure that the SIS is written in a way that is understandable and agreeable to both the client and the developers who will work on the project.

If further issues arise as the SIS is being written, keep going back to the client for clarification. The client can't be expected to have thought of everything, and will no doubt be grateful for your on-going involvement.

A sample outline of a SIS and the subjects it should cover can be found later in this chapter.

Implementation Team Review SIS

Before the SIS is submitted for approval by your team, it should be thoroughly checked and approved by the implementation team. These are the people who have to make it all happen, and if anything in the SIS is unclear or even downright impossible to them, now is the time to change it.

SIS Presented to Client for Review

The SIS should not contain any shocks for the client if they have been consulted throughout its creation, except maybe for a revised estimate of the project costs. However, it will need to be reviewed by the client before they are happy to sign it off, and this may result in the need for further document revision.

SIS Document Signed By All Parties

Your SIS will be the final list of deliverables for the project. It will also contain the final costs for the project delivery. As a result, it is very important that both the client and a representative of the implementing team sign a final copy of the document.

This signoff process is especially important if the two parties are not from the same company. If you are implementing for someone else, or someone else is implementing for you, then this document will define the delivery from one company to another. If things turn nasty in the future and the client is not happy with the implementation, then the SIS document should resolve any arguments as to what was promised.

The SIS Document

In this section, we'll look at the various subjects you should cover within your SIS. Not every project will require detailed coverage of all of these subjects, but any that are appropriate should be covered in detail to avoid any doubt as to what will be delivered.

Audience

At the beginning of your document, specify its intended audience. Bearing in mind that the purpose of the SIS is avoidance of doubt, this section should detail the name of the site in question, and the involved parties. These will take two sides – technical members of the implementation team, and non-technical people within the client's requirements team. Each team will read the SIS with a different need, but the document should be comprehensible to both.

Executive Summary

OK, so I said it should be comprehensible to non-technical people. That doesn't mean that all of them will want to read it. Your client may need to get budget signoff from their managers for the production phase of the CMS implementation. Provide an executive summary at the beginning of your SIS to give an overview of the solution and its proposed business benefits, and you will do your client a favor when they come to sell the project themselves.

Hosting Setup

This section is an opportunity to clarify exactly where and on what systems the CMS site will be hosted. It should detail the hardware and software setup of the hosting environment to enable the implementation team to create a development environment (if appropriate) that closely matches the system's real environment. As well as covering the hosting environment, this section should detail any aspects of the surrounding network that may have an impact upon the implementation, such as routers, firewalls, and connectivity speeds.

Be sure to detail the responsibility for system backup and support. This should include defining the responsibilities for the hardware on which the site will be installed. It is very easy for a client to assume, for instance, that the implementation team will be backing up their system on a daily basis unless it is made clear where this responsibility actually lies. Detail what will be backed up, how, when, and by whom.

Detail any databases that will integrate with the CMS implementation, and provide an overview of their system setup and connection details. This is especially relevant if the databases are hosted separately from the CMS system and connection issues need to be resolved. You shouldn't start the production phase without knowing how the various parts of the system will be connected.

If the site will be hosted via an SSL (Secure Sockets Layer) connection for data encryption, then you will need to purchase a secure certificate for the site. This will take several days to apply for, purchase, and install, and should be specified in advance within this section also. The same goes for any domain names that will need to be either bought and set up, or moved, in order for the site to go live.

User Roles

The CMS in question may or may not have a full user and role administration interface. Either way, the client should be clear exactly what roles they require and with what permissions, so the implementation can be customized with these roles in place from day one.

Ask the client to consider these roles in advance. This forces them to work out exactly what their publishing and workflow needs will be for the site. For each role, detail the role name, responsibilities, and permissions, together with a brief description of that role's purpose.

Site Structure

This section will depend in part on how your CMS approaches site structure management. But whatever approach it takes, chances are the site will have some predefined areas (such as "*News*" or "*Company Information*"), and some site-wide areas (such as "*Contact Us*") that will exist by default. Even if the site authors will be allowed to modify the site structure to their hearts' content, an initial site structure should be defined to ensure all parties are clear as to how the site will be built.

If the CMS is being used to build a replacement for an existing site, then this site map may well match the structure of that site. However, the structure should still be considered and specified to ensure it is achievable and appropriate for the new CMS.

Templates and Design

The design and template structure of your site are closely linked, and this extensive section needs to detail exactly how the site will look and work. It is best to think of a page within your site as several different rectangular areas, each of which will be of one of the four following types:

- Global branding (header, footer, logo)

- Navigation

- Global functionality (functionality that appears on every page, such as a search box)

- Content area (to be filled with paragraphs)

Global Branding

Certain elements of the site design will be consistent across the entire site. These design elements (which may include page titles, page footers, and company logos) exist to ensure the site branding is consistent throughout the entire site.

Create design mock-ups for these areas, and include the design mock-up screen grabs within your SIS. Specify exactly how the branding will be represented and give pixel values where appropriate. For example:

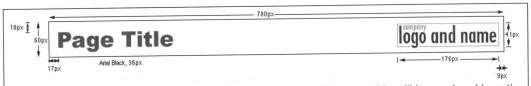

The page header will be 780 pixels wide by 60 pixels high. The page title will be rendered in anti-aliased Arial Black using the web color #993333 on a white background at 36 pixels high and output as a 16-color GIF image. This GIF will be inset 17 pixels from the left and 18 pixels from the top of the page header area. If the page title GIF, when rendered, is longer than the 578 pixels available, it will be cropped to 578 pixels.

The company logo will be aligned to the right of the page header area and will be a GIF image 176 pixels wide by 41 pixels high to be provided by the client. This image will be inset by 9 pixels from the right-hand edge of the page header area, and aligned in the vertical center within the page header area.

Always be as specific as possible with your design description and illustration. Remember, the purpose of the SIS is to avoid any vagueness and doubt as to what will be delivered. It may take some hard work to get design signoff to this level of detail from the client, but this is better than the design being vaguely specified and then changing every few days during the production phase.

Consider what will happen if an author creates content that is too long for the design. For example, when text is rendered as an image, if the text is too long, will the text automatically wrap onto two rows (or three, or four) or will it be cropped?

Global Page Properties

There may be some page properties that are global to all pages, and these should be specified in the SIS. They may include the page title, and metadata such as keywords, descriptions, and page live / archive dates.

Explain how these properties will be entered and stored, and whether or not each property will be mandatory.

Navigation

Navigation is a special case of global branding, and needs to be defined separately. If there is already a navigation system that matches the client's design, this may not require complete specification. Otherwise, the navigation system needs specifying too.

Remember, the client is not likely to be familiar with every last nuance of web technologies. We're not just writing a specification, we're educating the client as to what is and is not possible within their site. This is nowhere more important than with navigation. The client needs to be clear as to what will happen when the navigation is built.

There are many books available to help you design a useable navigation system. For example, see *Usable Web Menus* (glasshaus, ISBN 1904151027). Whatever approach you take, this section of the SIS should answer the following questions:

- What size space will the navigation system fill?

- How many levels of navigation should be displayed?

- Is there a limit as to how many navigation items will be displayed at a given level? If so, how do users access pages further down the site tree than this limit?

- What happens if a navigation item's text is longer than the navigation area's width?

- How will each level of the navigation be rendered (with a design mock-up)? Does the navigation expand when clicked, or pop out, or does clicking cause a new page to be loaded which then features the expanded navigation?

In short, this section needs to cover all of the design issues that would normally arise with a navigation system, with the added consideration of how these elements adapt as the navigation content expands.

Page Templates

Depending on how your CMS is constructed, there may be sections of the site in which authors can select from a list of page templates when creating a new page. Each of these page templates must be defined in detail with a graphical representation of the page and its layout.

The page templates define the different content areas of the page, and how these fit with the branding, navigation, and other global features described above. The diagrams below give examples of two different page layouts that share the same global page areas.

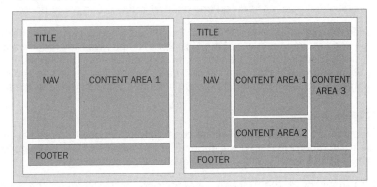

Both of these designs share the same page header, footer, and navigation template, but provide different page layout options for a page of content. You may wish to give authors a choice of two such templates for a particular site area. In this case, both templates need defining within your SIS document, as shown below for the second design.

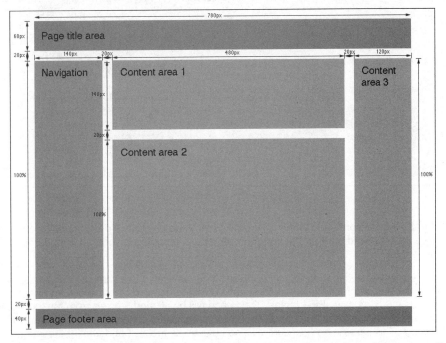

In this example, pixel measurements are used to illustrate that these areas of the page will conform to size, regardless of what content is added, by using word wrap to ensure a fixed width. Note that it is harder (some would say impossible) to guarantee a fixed height for a content area if the content area contains text, as the height will be affected by a site viewer's browser settings. The CMS can cut text to a certain number of words or characters, but this may not guarantee a fixed pixel height. However, in content areas that contain only images this is possible.

In the diagram above, "100%" is used to indicate that certain areas of the page will expand to whatever size is available to them (sometimes called a **liquid design**). In this example, whichever of the three columns is the longest will define the point at which the page footer begins. These expansion issues must be clearly answered and defined in the SIS to avoid doubt.

As well as defining the available page templates, the SIS also needs to define which of these page templates can be used for various parts of the site. For example, we may require a press release page template, with a custom content area for press contact details. It may be that this page template should only be available within a specific news subsection of the site and nowhere else. All of these page template requirements must be clearly defined with reference to the site map.

Paragraph Templates

Each of the content areas defined above will be constructed from one or more paragraphs of content. Quite how these paragraphs are edited will depend on your choice of CMS. Whatever the method, you should create a layout specification for each available paragraph style.

This specification should cover the exact layout of the paragraph, and detail the various different paragraph elements that need to be supplied by the Author. Let's take an example of a simple paragraph style, as illustrated and described below.

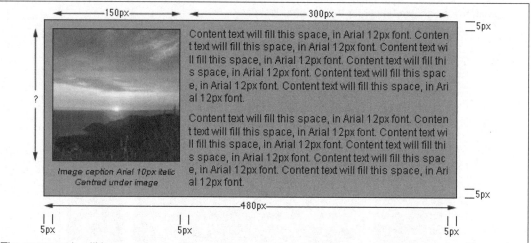

The paragraph will be contained within a 480 pixel wide table with a 1 pixel black border. The author will supply some text and an optional image. If an image is supplied, then an image caption must also be supplied.

If an image is supplied and is wider than 150 pixels, it will be scaled to a width of 150 pixels, with its height being scaled proportionally by the same ratio. Whether resized or not, the image will be rendered by the CMS as a 60% quality JPEG image. The image will be aligned 5 pixels from the top and left of the paragraph border as illustrated. The image caption will be presented underneath the image in Arial 10 pixels italic font. This same image caption will also be used as the `alt` attribute for the image.

If no image is supplied, a blank image will be used to maintain a 150-pixel column where an image would have been placed.

The supplied text will be left-aligned in a 300-pixel wide column to the right of the image, with a 5-pixel border between the image and the text. There will be a 5-pixel border around the other three sides of the text as illustrated. The text will be presented in Arial 12 pixels regular font.

As with page templates, your SIS should specify which paragraph templates can be added to each content area on a page. For example, the paragraph template described above would be appropriate to be added to "Content Area 2", but not "Content Area 3" on our sample page.

Your paragraph requirements will obviously be different to those above, but the same approach is valid for any paragraph style you may require.

Special Page Templates

There will be some parts of your site that will contain special functionality and require custom templates. It may be that these templates do not require author input at all. A good example of this would be a site search. This will require a special page template to generate and format search results.

Specifying the search will require creating a similar page and paragraph layout template as above to illustrate how the search results will be formatted. Your SIS should also specify how the search would operate to avoid any confusion. In addition to formatting information, you will need to answer the following questions:

- Which sections of the site will be searched?

- What items of page content will be searched?

- Will attached documents be searched?

- If an indexing tool is used by the CMS for searching, how often will the index be updated?

- How will search results be displayed and ordered?

- What will happen if no results are found?

There may be other special page templates within your site, such as a site map template (automatically creating a site map based on your current site structure) or a form template (allowing users to create custom response forms). These special templates will depend on the CMS you are using and your site-specific needs.

Your Particular CMS

It's possible that your CMS doesn't make the page / paragraph distinction described above, or structures its content in a slightly different way. It may not have multiple content areas or paragraph styles. However, the principles remain the same – define the page and content layout in as much detail as possible, to avoid any doubt.

At the implementation team review stage of your *Concept Phase*, the team should read the SIS document and think of any questions that are not clearly answered by the document. If you have added enough detail, there should not be anything left open to interpretation.

Modules

Different CMS vendors will offer different prewritten modules, such as chat, forum, or shopping modules. These are usually just custom templates bundled as a 'module' with some specific functionality. In the case of a forum module, for example, it may contain prewritten functionality to manage and moderate a discussion forum. However, the prewritten module may not lay out the forum threads in a way that is sympathetic or appropriate to your site design. It may not manage the discussion threads in a way that exactly matches your forum requirements. You might need to add in a file upload feature if one doesn't exist, or link the module into a custom user database. This section of the SIS should specify how each module would need to be customized and laid out in this specific site implementation.

Unresolved Requirements

Try as you might, there will inevitably be some detail or other that just cannot be resolved before the end of the concept phase. This nearly always happens, and it is best to acknowledge this fact and have a plan in place to cater for it.

This section of the SIS should detail *all* known outstanding information, and make the very clear statement that all time scales and budgets are conditional on these unresolved requirements being met quickly, with no major setbacks. It should only contain references to information that will have no major impact on the project, but cannot yet be finalized. If you find comments like "The hosting environment is still to be specified", then wait until you have an answer.

Change Management Procedure

Even if the "*Unresolved Requirements*" section is empty, some things will need to change once the SIS has been officially signed off. Hosting specifications may change, the client may change their mind about some functionality, or an organizational restructure may require the site map to be reworked. Whatever the reasons for change, this is much easier to manage if you have a change management procedure in place and clearly explained to all parties before the project begins.

Your change management procedure should require a **Change Request Form** to be completed for every change to the SIS. Include this Change Request Form as an appendix to the SIS. A sample form is shown below.

<u>Change Request Form</u>

Change request submitted by:

Name: _____ Job Title: _____

Contact Details: _____

Change Request number _____

Date Submitted: _____

Description of change: _____

Benefit of proposed change: _____

(Project Mgr) Impact on project: _____

(Project Mgr) Cost implication: _____

Authorised by Implementation team:

Name: _____ Job Title _____

Authorised by Client:

Name: _____ Job Title: _____

A Change Request Form should be completed by the request instigator, and passed to the project manager for an estimate of the project impact and cost of the proposed change. The completed form should then be passed on to the client for approval and signoff. Written approval must always be received before a change request is implemented.

The introduction of changes requires a certain amount of diplomacy on the part of the project manager to keep the client happy without making too many changes for the sake of change. If the client is ever getting too frustrating, remember their three defining characteristics:

- They are the one with the money

- They are the decision-maker

- They are the one whose needs you must satisfy

Training and Documentation

Your SIS should specify the training and documentation to be provided, and who this will be provided by. Don't let the client assume they will be receiving a 100-page manual for the custom implementation – detail everything to be delivered.

We'll look at user training in more detail in the next chapter, *Migration*. This section should specify that (for example) "three days of training will be provided for Authors in the form of workshops held at the client's site".

Where the responsibility for training falls will depend on the client relationship (internal or external). It may be that, for an internal project, a separate training department will handle all training. Just make sure that this section specifies where the responsibility lies.

Documentation falls into two main groups – user documentation (for content authors and other CMS users) and technical documentation (for the system support team who will look after the CMS in the future). Both types of document require a specific set of writing skills, and these may not be found within the implementation team. Besides, the implementation team will be busy implementing. Consider bringing someone on board from outside the team to create this documentation. As an outsider to the team they will be able to approach the system with a fresh pair of eyes and give an unbiased view in their writing.

Testing

The SIS should contain the full testing plan for the implementation project. There are several forms of testing this should cover.

Browser Testing

This section of the SIS should specify exactly which browsers will be supported by the CMS implementation, both for the author environment and the live site. The audience of the site will have a great bearing on this, and in the case of an intranet (with a standard browser rollout) it may be an easy choice. For a general web site, the client may need to be advised on which browsers should be supported. If a site already exists, analyze its log files to get a profile of the browsers that are currently used by your site users.

The proportion of users of each major browser changes gradually over time, with the majority of users having one of about four browser/version combinations. That said, in an ideal world your site would "support" (to a greater or lesser extent) *all* browsers. But if the site contains functionality that will only work in a certain browser version, these versions *must* be specified.

The HTML of your site must be tested thoroughly against these browser specifications. The client should be made very aware that changing this browser specification in the future might have serious implications on the time scales of the project.

"Browser testing" may need to take into account more than just standard web browsers. If you are outputting versions of your site for PDA, or WAP, or some other form of digital output, then a testing plan also needs to be created for these platforms.

Code Testing

Your template and customization code needs to be thoroughly checked before the site is put live. The developer who has created a template should check any custom template code against the SIS requirements before passing the code to the technical lead for approval. The technical lead, who has ultimate responsibility for the code quality and integrity within the site, should then revisit the code to confirm that the developer has met the documented requirements.

If your SIS document is as detailed as it should be, this testing process should require no further information in order to validate the code.

User Testing

When it is ready for delivery, the entire system must be tested in a normal usage situation. This testing will come up with two distinct types of errors:

- Coding bugs within the system

- Perfectly working code that users cannot use or do not understand how to use

Your approach to user testing will depend on your views on iterative testing and the ongoing availability of real users for prototyping trials. We are trying to define our exact CMS requirements in the SIS, but if user testing shows that these requirements don't actually meet the needs of users, it is obviously better to discover this *before* the site goes live, so that appropriate changes can be made via the change management procedure.

A good approach to user testing is to run a "simulated" user test first, with members of the implementation team using the CMS interface to manage dummy content. This should mean that any obvious interface bugs are discovered before the system is tested by real-life users. It would be even better if these simulated users were non-technical colleagues outside of the implementation team. Non-technical people are generally more likely to find whatever's broken. Pick the most awkward people you know, and they'll make ideal simulated users.

Once your system has passed the simulated user test, try it out on a group of real users. See how they get on. If the system is bug-free but users struggle to use a particular part of it, reassess the interface for that area.

Users tend to regard "I can't get it to work" and "It doesn't work" as one and the same thing. To an extent they are right – it doesn't matter what great functionality a system has if it cannot be used by its target group of users. If the problem stems from the usability of the underlying CMS, then it might be time to revisit Chapter 5 or 6.

The end result of this stage of testing should be that no part of the user experience is unclear, contains coding bugs, or allows users to horribly break the system by clicking on suspicious red buttons. Unfortunately, some user problems may be caused by inexperience of the system and resistance to change rather than genuine usability errors. It can be hard to distinguish the political and personal user acceptance of a new system from genuine design issues.

Systems and Integration Testing

If your development environment does not exactly match the eventual live server environment, a further code test should be performed once the site is installed in its final home. This should verify that the customized CMS installation operates as required within the live environment. Any application and systems integration code should be rigorously checked at this stage. It is likely that integration work cannot be properly tested in a development environment, and care needs to be taken – especially where the integration is being tested with existing live systems.

Load Testing

No matter what the CMS creators tell you, you can only gauge the performance of a system once it is installed. Besides, your custom CMS implementation will contain all kinds of custom templates and code that might adversely affect the normally supercharged performance of your CMS. If the load on your site is going to be "high" (especially if your pages are fried), then perform a load test before going live.

This load test *must* use the final finished version of the CMS implementation, running on the live hardware. If you are not set up to load test a system, get someone in to do it for you. This author has seen beautiful implementations dissolve into arguments between departments, client, and CMS supplier simply because the load performance of the site was not tested in advance.

The biggest problem with load testing may well come from the servers, not the CMS implementation. If the system is well written, and the site receives much usage, then the simplest way to scale the load capabilities is to install more servers and balance the load over these multiple servers. Implementing the CMS to cope with load balancing may require recoding, so your testing should discover if this is the case in advance.

It is useful to find any bottlenecks in your system setup by increasing load until a 'maximum' throughput is reached. At this point, it should be clear which element of the system is causing the most strain (perhaps a database, or connectivity bandwidth). Even if these issues do not need addressing immediately when the site goes live, this will give some idea in advance as to what part of the installation will need upgrading or recoding when load increases.

Project Plan

On completion of the specification part of the SIS, the project manager will be able to create a project plan for the implementation. This project plan (usually created in a project planning application, such as Microsoft Project) should be included with the SIS as an attachment or appendix.

Try and set several milestones throughout the project plan. Clients like to see partial deliverables as a project progresses. If you can promise certain deliverables, prototypes, or demonstrations on your terms in advance, and you know they are coming, you should be able to satisfy a client's desire to see progress without impinging on the project time scales.

Whatever final deadline is set in the SIS project plan, the implementation team should aim to work to project completion at least a week before that deadline, and the project plan should be structured such that this is possible. If this means that the project is delivered a week early, the team will all be heroes. If it means that (as is much more likely) the extra week is spent dealing with small issues and fine details, then the project still ends up on time.

On a more general project managerial note, don't forget that developers need holidays too. You may not yet have assigned specific developers to the project, but if you have some in mind, check for any holidays they have booked in advance. This should not affect the number of man-days needed to complete the project, but it may affect the end date. Any statutory holidays that will fall during the lifetime of the project should also be accounted for.

Costs

On the basis of the project plan (which should show exactly how long each resource on the team will spend on the project) the project manager can submit final costs for the implementation project. How these costs are calculated and presented will depend on the client relationship, and will certainly be different for an internal and an external client.

There are two costs that are hard to assign from the project plan, namely project management and testing costs. It is possible for an internal CMS implementation that the project manager will be assigned full-time to the project. If the project manager has other responsibilities in either internal or external implementations, then you will need to budget for their time even though they do not actually produce any templates or code.

As a rule of thumb, you should add on between 20 and 25% of the project cost for project management time. This number may not be exact in every case, but it is a good indication of the level of project management involvement in a project relative to the amount of development taking place. This covers such tasks as attending meetings, making phone calls, and answering e-mails from the client.

Testing occurs both during and at the end of the project, and it is useful to have a similar rule of thumb to relate typical testing times to code development duration. Your project plan will detail the time needed to develop templates and code, and you should add on approximately 33% of the total number of production days for testing throughout the production process. This may sound high, but it is a good example of the level of testing required to ensure a successful delivery. Forget to factor this into your delivery plan and costs, and the project will either be delivered late, or won't work.

Additional project-specific testing, such as load testing and complex systems integration, should be costed for separately from this 33% rule.

There is no need to present the costs as an hour-by hour breakdown for each task. In fact, if you are presenting implementation costs for an external organization, this just gives the client a chance to quibble over details of the project costs that should not be open to quibbling. Present a cost for each section of the development – for example, "Creation of global branding templates: 7 days".

Make sure your costs include all of the appropriate sections mentioned in the SIS. For example, don't forget to include the creation of documentation. Similarly, your project costs must include the time needed to install your CMS implementation on the live servers.

Approval

The final section of your SIS document should provide space for the client and a representative of the implementation team (typically the project manager) to sign their approval of the SIS as a complete specification of the project requirements. Don't forget this section – it comes in very useful if the project goes awry.

Production Phase

The concept phase is complete. The SIS is signed. Now it is time to build your custom CMS implementation: the production phase.

Pre-Production

We'll begin by taking a look at a few things that need to be in place first.

Development Environment Setup

A development CMS environment will need to be acquired, installed, and customized before production can begin. If the CMS is not being developed on the eventual live servers, this development environment should mirror the live environment as closely as possible. For example, even if you are using a cross-platform Java-based CMS, don't develop on a Unix server if the eventual hosting environment is Windows 2000. If budgets allow, your development servers should have the same number of processors and amount of memory as the live servers to give an idea of performance whilst developing.

The same goes for SQL databases, network connections, and security settings. The closer you can get to the live environment, the easier your live installation will be. If necessity dictates that your development environment cannot match the live one, increase the time assigned to live installation in your SIS.

This stage of pre-production does not necessarily have to wait for SIS signoff, although it should certainly wait until the client has given a clear and definite indication as to what the hosting environment will be.

Resource Allocation

The project manager and technical lead should take the agreed SIS project plan and assign developers to the various roles and tasks within the plan. Where the implementation is split between a CMS vendor and your own organization, this should be planned jointly by the project managers from both organizations, clearly stating which organization will take responsibility for each task.

Production Briefing

Having assigned resources to the project tasks and therefore defined the full implementation team, the team should get together for a kick-off meeting to ensure everyone has a common mental image of the project. Any issues or questions can be raised, and developers who have not been involved in the SIS creation can be introduced to the project and the client.

This meeting is a good opportunity for the lead developer to introduce any code standards that the implementation team should conform to. All being well, any arguments can be resolved before coding begins.

If you're running this meeting, get some pizza in. If you're a developer, argue for pizza. Developers always work better when they have pizza!

Production

The production stage runs from the end of pre-production through to the final installation on the client's live servers. Developers will write and test code according to the test plan in your SIS (see above). Given the level of detail and specification in the SIS document, the actual production stage of your implementation will run perfectly smoothly, and therefore requires no further description.

Oh, if only that were true…

Production Problems

Something is *bound* to go wrong, no matter how great your SIS document is. The project manager and technical lead will need to maintain a list of any issues that crop up, and ensure that resolutions are found for these issues, and that these resolutions are documented.

The implementation team should meet regularly to ensure a common vision of the project development is maintained (more pizza), and flag up any new or outstanding issues. This is a perfect opportunity for the project manager and technical lead to update their issues list, and inform the team of any developments and change requests. The issues list should be made available to the project team together with details as to who within the team is responsible for finding a solution to each issue.

Maybe your issues list should be managed using a Content Management System? Apparently they're great for allowing several authors to contribute content (that is, problems) to a common data repository. If not, I find a spreadsheet program does an admirable job instead. Each issue on the list must have an owner, an estimate of the effort involved, and a test procedure. Resolutions to tricky issues need testing more than anything else.

Depending on the time scales of the project, it may be appropriate to hold these meetings daily. It is more likely that they can occur weekly, and should never be less frequent than this. Towards the end of the project, when testing and bug fixing is underway, daily meetings first thing in the morning are appropriate to go over bugs found the day before, which can be fixed during the day, ready for that evening's testing run.

Is Monday morning a good time for catch-up meetings? The jury is out on this one. Meeting on Monday morning ensures that the whole team starts the week with a common view and standpoint. It also means they forget any outstanding issues over the weekend. If the project is running smoothly, I prefer Wednesdays. Something always happens by Wednesday.

Installation

Once the CMS implementation is installed and live, the client *must* sign a document to confirm that they are happy that the system delivered matches their understanding of the SIS document. This is the point at which all that time being specific will pay off.

Post-Production

Once the system is installed and working, you can take a long well deserved holiday. Right? Wrong. You might be able to sneak a *short* well-deserved holiday. If your system is a success, then before long the client will want more functionality added. If it is not a success (and, if so, you clearly haven't been paying enough attention) then there will be bugs to fix and changes to make.

New Functionality

Any major new feature request should be treated as a separate project, with its own SIS document (although maybe not as detailed a document as the initial SIS). Beware of requests to "just add one more thing" – *any* changes or new features must be either an official change request for the original project, or a new project in their own right.

System Support

If you are implementing for an external client, you may have a contract period for which the implementation will be supported (the dreaded "90 days", or whatever your license needs to specify). In this time, if the client finds any further bugs or functionality that conflict with the SIS document, then you will probably have to fix them "for free".

For an internal implementation, you can't just call up the implementing agency and say "Hey!". Your organization will need to assign someone or some team to the position of ongoing support for the CMS implementation. Some companies have such a "Technical Support" department. If this responsibility does not stay with the implementation team, then the support department will need training and educating in the system and its idiosyncrasies in order to support it successfully.

Be sure to note the difference between bugs in the CMS and bugs in the implementation. This can often be a very gray area, but can make a big difference as to who should provide support or a fix. This is especially true if you are an agency that implements someone else's CMS for your own clients – if the underlying system contains bugs and causes grief for your clients, will you receive any support yourselves?

Project Review

Once the project is finished, order some more pizza, and get the team together to talk about how the implementation went. Discuss what went well, and what could be improved next time. Pat each other on the back. Eat the pizza – you've earned it.

Content Migration and User Training

Whoa there! There's a whole chapter coming up about migrating your web sites into a CMS. For now, let's take stock and be very smug about a successful implementation.

Summary

This chapter has introduced a process for CMS implementation. We have seen that whatever your role and whatever your choice of CMS, it is essential to plan and specify the implementation as completely as possible before beginning production. The specification document detailed in this chapter provides a good template for doing so.

In the next chapter, we will take a look at how to migrate your existing content into the newly-implemented CMS and make sure your sites never, ever get into such a mess again.

8

- Issues with Content Migration

- Defining a Process for Migration

- Training and Testing

Author: Dave Addey and Alyson Fielding

Migration

So, we've installed the System, and understood the Management. What about the Content? There's a reason why the C in CMS comes first. The whole point of this exercise is to put a system in place to make content maintenance simple, accessible, and consistent, and up until now we haven't put any actual content into our system at all.

In this chapter, we'll look at how to migrate content from that horrible untidy mess known as "Your Old Site" into a beautiful new site, and make sure the site stays beautiful in the future.

The Problem with Migration

Way back in Chapter 2 you sat down and counted how many pages exist in your current site. It's been quite an effort to put a system in place to manage all of those pages, so it's a good job you can now just click a button and copy them all into your new system. Oh, if only it were that simple...

The problem with trying to automatically copy content from your old site to your new site is that the old content isn't just "content" – it's a mixture of HTML, scripts, databases, and goodness knows what else. These various sources are often an unstructured mix of layout information, useful content, formatted images, and table definitions... in short, they're not pretty.

In theory, it should be possible to come up with a script or application capable of scanning through an HTML page and drawing out the content from this page. But how does the script know what is useful content and what is useless? Scripts aren't renowned for their intelligence.

In order for this to work, your existing content would need to conform to certain strict rules. For example, if every HTML page had a correct, unique title within the `<title>` HTML element, then a script could parse a given HTML page and track down this title. (Do all of your pages have unique titles? Thought not.) The same process is much harder for a mass of content on a page, even if the layout of this content is consistent on every single one of your pages. (Is your layout consistent for every page in your site? Thought not.)

Even if it were possible to automate the transfer of content from HTML into the CMS, an automatic process cannot make subjective judgments about the quality and relevance of your content. A script will not know the difference between an out-of-date press release from 1998 and a recent well-authored page. Truth is, migrating is a manual process, and a long one at that.

Don't be disheartened by this. It's a good thing. Recall all of the times you've thought, "I really wish we could take the time to tidy this site up once and for all". Migrating to a CMS is probably the only chance you'll get to take stock and re-assess your site from the ground up. And you've got management buy-in to take the time out from site maintenance to do it! I can't stress enough that it's a lot of time, work, and effort. But believe me, it's worth it.

Before You Start

Remember, you don't necessarily have to do all of the work yourself. In this section we'll make sure we are properly prepared for the migration process, by constructing a **Content Review Document** (CRD), and sharing the task of migration between as many people as possible. We'll also make sure that the style of the new site is consistent by creating a **Site Style Guide**.

Take Stock of What You Have

As we saw in Chapter 2, if your old site has been around for a few years, several people will have been in charge of the content already. In fact, I'd lay money on the current web team being considerably different from the one that implemented the first web site for your company. In the years since that time, the team has probably grown, and now includes authors who specialize in producing content online. Some of the original authors may now be in different roles or no longer be with the company.

As a result, chances are no one person has an overview of all of the content in your site. (If you're lucky enough to have someone who *does* have this overview, make them team leader and first point of contact for questions and queries.) If you're going to begin migrating, you certainly need such an overview. If you spend time assessing and reviewing your content *before* you begin migrating it across to your new site, the time spent will be saved many times over later in the project.

This stage of the project is an ideal time for the migration team to review old content and ensure that all content migrated to the new site is:

- Up-to-date

- Relevant

- In keeping with the company's brand and mission statement

Taking time out to review and assess your content will alert you to any problems you're likely to face in the migration process. These problems can include 'gaps' in content on the new site, or out-of-date text on the corporate information page that your sharp-eyed CEO just happens to spot on the first day the site goes live. To avoid egg-on-face scenarios, take stock of the content you have and the content you're likely to need before you even think about migrating.

So how do you approach this seemingly impenetrable task without needing to lie down in a darkened room for several hours beforehand? Let's create a Content Review Document.

Content Review Document

A **Content Review Document** (**CRD**) will help you:

- Plan your content migration in advance

- Have an overview of the current content on the site

- Highlight any content that needs to be altered before migration

- Detail any new content that needs to be created

- Set deadlines for migration tasks

- Assign responsibility for creating or assessing content

- Ensure all members of the content migration team – including content authors – have a shared mental picture

In short, it's your passport to an easier life.

Unlike the SIS document mentioned in Chapter 7, this document reviews in detail the specific content needs of the new site and what needs to be carried across from the old site. This enables you to flag up gaps in your content strategy – where you don't have enough relevant content from your old site to expand into the planned sections of the new site.

This document needs an owner from the outset – ideally someone who already has an overview of the existing content. If no one has this knowledge, now is a good opportunity to assign someone this responsibility for the future. Many people will contribute to the document, and you need to ensure the owner has an understanding of the whole process and draws it all together. If this document becomes too big to be managed by one person, chances are you are trying to migrate too much content in one go. Consider splitting your site into smaller sections and treating each as a separate migration project. (See *It's All Just Too Much!* later in this chapter.)

How Do I Do This?

Start your CRD by assessing your old web site section by section. You may already have an overview document for your old site (for example, as created in Chapter 2) – if not, you'll have to create one now. Detail each section of content that needs to be transferred, and work out where it will sit on the new site. This is also an ideal time to prune content that is old or outdated and spot duplication.

Previous content authors may have been inexperienced in writing for an online environment. By making sure content owners review all information on the site before it is migrated, you will be able to adapt old content into the new house style, ensuring a perfect fit when migration is complete.

Now's the ideal time to get your PR and Marketing departments on board to give a makeover to that tired-looking corporate information page. We want to ensure that your sharp-eyed CEO has nothing but praise for the new site when he jumps straight to that page on the day you go live. (After all, many CEOs will head straight for this section to check their name, picture, and bio are correct as soon as the new site is live – regardless of how much work your team has put into the new News section or Search facility.)

A spreadsheet package is a good choice of application for building the CRD document. Start by creating a new worksheet for each section of the site. Assign each section to an appropriate department within the company, and detail the pages and subsections within each section on the appropriate worksheet.

For each site section or page, fill in the details shown in the sample worksheet below.

Section: News							
Page / subsection name	Current location	New location	Existing / New?	Comments	Content owner	Deadline	Completed
News home page	news/index.htm	news/	Existing	Re-write in house style	John Smith	10-Oct-02	9-Sep-02
Current press releases	news/pressreleases/	news/pressreleases/	Existing	Needs updating	Bill Bailey	10-Oct-02	12-Sep-02
1999 Press release archive	news/archive/1999/	news/archive/1999/	Existing	Needs migrating	Bill Bailey	10-Oct-02	14-Sep-02
2000 Press release archive	news/archive/2000/	news/archive/2000/	Existing	Needs migrating	Bill Bailey	10-Oct-02	16-Sep-02
2001 Press release archive	news/archive/2001/	news/archive/2001/	Existing	Needs migrating	Bill Bailey	10-Oct-02	20-Sep-02
2002 Press release archive	-	news/archive/2002/	New	Needs creating	Bill Bailey	10-Oct-02	10-Oct-02

News / Corporate / Jobs /

You don't need to detail every single page in your site if there are areas of the site that can be grouped and assigned en masse. In the example above, the archive sections can be assigned as a group without the need to detail all fifty press releases in each section. If your site is smaller, or if you have the time, you can go into as much detail as you like.

If your site is large, with content being managed by many departments across multiple locations, you may prefer to create a web-based version of the above document. This would ensure everyone has access to the CRD and is able to notify the CRD owner when their content is complete and ready for approval. In a smaller company with fewer authors, a spreadsheet should suffice. It really doesn't matter, as long as you have one common version of the CRD, with a responsible owner.

Once the document is complete, it must be circulated to all members of the migration team for agreement and signoff. This will ensure that the migration team has a common mental image of the project before migration begins. The CRD then becomes the central point for documenting all completed tasks and migrated content.

Mind the Content Gap!

When you lay down the specifications for your new site, you're likely to re-evaluate your content, re-organize what you've got in the old site, or create new sections which require new content to be created. All these scenarios can lead to 'content gaps', where you need to create new content that doesn't currently exist.

How do you ensure content authors fill these gaps? Here's where the CRD proves invaluable once again. (Did I mention just how useful this document is?) In your CRD document, as well as listing all of the content from the old site, add in details of any content that needs to be created from scratch. In the example above, a 2002 Press Release Archive has been spotted as a content gap to be created for the new site. This new content area should be assigned an owner and a deadline, just like any other content.

Keeping the Style Consistent

Great. You've found out what needs to be migrated, and who owns the content. It probably involves quite a few people. How do you ensure that one rogue content owner doesn't suddenly start creating a new page style all of their own? How do you make sure that future content has the same style and tone as the rest of the site?

Picture the scene: your new site has gone live. A few days later, you find out that an employee (perhaps used to applying their own interpretation of your company's brand way back in the dark ages near the beginning of your online presence) has just started using a larger font. In a different font style. In green, rather than the corporate colors you've spent months specifying and signing off. And this has taken place because " I didn't know there was a new style: no-one told me". Or even worse: "I've always done it that way in the past. Why should I change now?"

You can pre-empt these issues now, by creating a document that specifies exactly how content should be laid out on the page in line with your corporate brand. This document will be separate from the CRD, and will become a style bible for your CMS users. We'll call it a **Site Style Guide**.

Creating a Site Style Guide

Your Site Style Guide is essential. Ensuring the design of your site is consistent when authors may be sat in different offices, or even different countries, is not easy. Setting up a best practice procedure for content will ensure everyone is clear and in agreement about the brand and style of the site from the outset. It means that when a rogue employee decides to format an entire press release as bold text, you can wave the Site Style Guide under their nose, and tactfully suggest the employee re-acquaints themselves with the document they originally signed up to – cue red faces and apologies.

It's important to remember that any existing offline style guides for print media may work extremely well in print, but are unlikely to be suitable for online communications. Simply cutting and pasting text from printed publications to the online world just doesn't work. For example, paragraph breaks are too few in the print world to translate well in an online environment. Also, the formal style and tone used for your company's print communications may feel out of place with the less formal, conversational style of the Web.

Besides, your company style isn't just about design. It covers everything that sums up your organization's brand. This includes tone and language used in communications, the company focus and mission statement, and how this focus is communicated. In short, it's everything to do with the language and style your company uses when communicating both internally and to customers.

Consider this example. Do you want to create a personalized style with a focus on your customers ("Are you looking for a great night out? Here are ten reasons why you should visit Moe's Bar!"), or are you looking for a company-focused style ("We are one of the best drinking establishments in the area and have won several awards for our beers")? Which one would make your customers visit Moe's Bar? Style matters when you're talking to your customers.

Depending on how much control your CMS gives to authors, the Site Style Guide may need to cover design constants such as font size, color, and link styling to ensure that the visual style remains consistent regardless of whoever works on the site in the future. It can't be stressed enough how important this document is to your company.

Include, Don't Exclude...

Bear in mind that the authors who currently update your site may have previously had a lot of freedom in designing the site and adding content. This will no longer be the case. You will need to use your best political skills to inform them they can no longer have as much freedom. After all, these changes will make the new site clearer and more consistent for your customers, which is ultimately of benefit to the whole organization. This will help CMS users realize you're not just trying to be awkward – there is a valid reason for enforcing these new rules.

To achieve this, you should definitely involve your authors in the Site Style Guide development. It's by far the best way to avoid the authors feeling limited. After all, if they have had complete control over what they write and how it looks, they will not take it too kindly if you flounce into their office and slap a copy of the Site Style Guide on their desk. You won't make friends and keep your authors on your side if you tell them that everything they're used to doing is wrong and they must stick by your rules from now on. You can guarantee they'll feel resentful and will probably try hard to resist your changes.

Besides, these authors may have great ideas that need to be included in the Site Style Guide. They may previously have created a style that is entirely appropriate to your new design and brand. The Site Style Guide owner should meet with a selection of content authors to explain the plan and ask them to contribute their ideas. These can then be drawn together with more than a liberal sprinkling of 'best web practice' from the Site Style Guide owner.

Handing people some ownership of the project and incorporating their experience into the Site Style Guide will make it easier for all parties to stick to one online style in the future. A bit of listening and reasoning now will go a long way to ensuring the spread of good feeling carries on once the new site is live.

Style Guide Considerations

Here are some things you might like to consider for your Site Style Guide:

Tone

Is it We / Us, or You? Remember, web style tends to be less formal than traditional offline publications. You may appeal more to your potential customers if you use a 'looser', more personal approach within a defined structure.

Try using 'We' rather than your company's name for a more humanized approach in your corporate communications. Address your reader – try to use 'you' in your communications, to make it more 'reader-centric'.

Capital Letters

Don't Overuse Capitals When Writing For The Web. Capital letters slow down the reader's eye, making your content much more difficult for the user to read. AND DON'T SHOUT – there are better ways to get people to hear your message than resorting to capitalization.

Formatting

Leaving a line break between all paragraphs will make your text much easier to read than if you copy and paste in large blocks of text.

Copy Style

As mentioned above, writing for the Web is very different from writing print material. You have only a split second to entice the user to read on before they move to another site. Make sure your copy is punchy and lively to create the best chance of grabbing their attention. Your Site Style Guide needs to include hints and tips for effective online copywriting.

Links

Encourage authors to include "calls to action" where follow-up information is available for a subject, such as '*Click here to find out more*'. For anchor links, it may be clearer (and certainly more accessible) to create a link directly from the online copy to the subject you are referring to – for example: '*While on the subject of soft drinks, we recommend Moe's Bar for their excellent Iced Teas.*'

Define a common language style for internal and external links, and make sure that external links launch a new browser window, to avoid losing site users.

Style Guide Signoff

Once the Site Style Guide's owner has collated all suggestions and pruned them into an efficient guide, it's time to get approval from all the people who will be using it. By getting agreement from each author, you not only confer ownership ("I helped create the document"), but also make your life easier when confronting the rogue employee about their creative additions to your otherwise beautifully designed site.

Once you have this document, distribute it to all authors within the company. Consider e-mailing the document to them – they're more likely to read and digest the document if it is supplied to them direct than if they are just sent a link. Link to the document from the content creation interface too. Just to be sure, make some photocopies of the document and hand it to them in person. That way, there will be no excuses.

If you need to reach a large number of authors, consider creating an online version of the Site Style Guide as a central reference point. This can contain updates and changes to the guide, as well as the latest offline version of the guide document for download. The site must, of course, conform to the Site Style Guide rules itself.

The idea of a Site Style Guide site is attractive, but may not be the most appropriate method of communication for all of your authors. If your authors are struggling with the concept of browser-based CMS authoring, they may prefer to have their trusty Site Style Guide printed out on good old-fashioned paper. Use whatever combination of distribution methods is appropriate.

Think Global, Act Local

As has been mentioned earlier in this book, moving from a single language or culture to a multi-cultural environment is quite a feat, but a CMS can take much of the hard work out of this for you.

Because your CMS interface is likely to be browser-based, your remote authors can (in theory) now use the same central tools to author content as everyone else. This makes it much easier to ensure a consistent visual style even though authors may be anywhere in the world.

Introducing a CMS (and therefore redesigning your site) is also an ideal opportunity to develop multiple versions of your site. When your web site was originally put together in the Dark Ages, it's more than likely nobody thought of using any other languages than English. Now, overseas markets are becoming increasingly attractive as a way of generating revenue growth. More than half of the web users in the world speak a language other than English, so you're potentially cutting yourself off from millions of customers (unless your product is really localized). Your company might operate in countries where English isn't the predominant language, and cultural differences mean you need to talk to your customers in a way that is more appropriate to them. After all, wouldn't you rather buy online from a company that communicated with you in your mother tongue?

Producing content for multiple locations is not just a question of language translation. (See Chapter 5 for more on the possible routes you could take.) There are a number of cultural differences too, and your content needs to reflect the language, cultural, and national differences on a local scale. Even where countries speak the same language, cultural and linguistic differences still exist. There's a very good reason why you can buy an Australian-English dictionary, and anyone who says otherwise is clearly either a "galah" or a "drongo". (For more information, see *http://www.macquariedictionary.com.au/*.)

Beware of exercising *too* much control over site style globally. Let your local content authors have a little freedom to find the best way to communicate with your customers within the boundaries of the Site Style Guide. If your authors find it easier to connect with customers at a local level by using a different style to your own, let them. Trust your local authors to know the best way to communicate with their customers. As long as they don't step outside the Site Style Guide, their application of local knowledge will do wonders in endearing your global corporation to customers at a local level.

About the Author

So who are these "authors"? These are the people who will take over the day-to-day task of ensuring the new site content is updated in line with the style guide and design. They're as important as the designers and developers who originally set out the guidelines for the site. Without them, the web site is in danger of slipping back into the days of out-dated content and broken links.

See Chapter 2 for more details on your authors.

Giving ownership of the content to your authors is absolutely vital. If you can't give people ownership, how do you expect them to feel part of the web site and get excited by it? Chances are there's so much content on the site that it needs many people across the company to take charge of different sections, to ensure the site is updated often and with the correct content. If you can hand over sections of the site to departments around the company, there's a greater chance they'll begin to understand the whole web site process, be more sympathetic to your aims, and understand how important the site is as part of your marketing / communications strategy.

If a person or department owns a process within your organization, then they should manage the content within your CMS that relates to that process. They may not be the right person to put that content live, but they should certainly be able to add content to the CMS at the start of the publishing workflow.

For example, maybe your HR Department should take ownership of your *Jobs* section, to ensure all vacancies are updated regularly, and match what's being advertised elsewhere. Your PR or Internal Communications Department may be the best people to ensure that your corporate pages are up to date and the latest edition of the Annual Review or Company Brochure is available online to users.

When assigning responsibility to these departments, remember that they have day jobs too. If at all possible, their additional responsibilities should be incorporated into their job description to ensure they are officially recognized.

That said, who knows – once these departments have the knowledge to transfer information from offline publications to online, they may even begin to integrate the Web into their daily work routine. For example, their offline press releases might begin to have a link to an online version of the press release, or links to related articles on the web site. The ideas are endless and all help contribute to a more efficient company structure. You'll be amazed at the good ideas your non-technical authors will come up with once they have the power and ability to publish to the Web.

With your CMS in place, more than ever before, your content authors can be people with little or no experience of HTML programming. They may only have a basic perception of the Internet. This is the beauty of implementing a CMS – anyone can become an author without having to have years of training in design and development. Which leaves developers to do the *really* fun stuff.

Training for Authors

Your author training needs will be very specific to your company, your CMS, and your workflow process. If you've chosen to buy a system, the CMS vendor may offer author training. You may want the vendor to teach the key Trainers in your organization, and have these internal Trainers pass on their knowledge to the wider author audience.

However you approach it, your CMS training should cover:

- Introduction to the CMS and general guidelines to using the system

- Your Site Style Guide

- Outline of tasks the content author needs to perform as part of the site update

- Outline of the workflow process involved in publishing content to the live site. Ensure each content author has a clear idea of their role and responsibilities in the workflow chain

- A 'how to' guide for adding each section of content (specific to that author's responsibilities), including editing and posting to the home page where appropriate

- Workflow for informing an appropriate person if text needs updating outside the author's remit

- Workflow system for reporting mistakes, errors, and improvements to the CMS

- Where to go if they need help or a 'reminder' about how to use the CMS

Depending on your CMS, you might also like to consider guides for:

- Editing text (bold, underline, bullets)

- Adding hyperlinks

- Images – adding images, image specifications, and accessing a picture library

Migrating the Content

OK. We've taken stock of existing content, and documented this in a CRD. We've specified exactly how content will look using the Site Style Guide, and started to train our authors. Now this preparatory work is complete, we can begin the content migration process proper.

When Can I Start?

By now, you'll be raring to go with content migration, and shouting, "When can I start? When can I start?" It may be you can start sooner than you might imagine. You should certainly start work on your CRD as soon as possible, whilst (and even before) the CMS implementation is taking place. Your CRD should be complete and ready to go by the time the system implementation is complete.

If you complete your CRD whilst the CMS is still undergoing testing, you may be able to start the content migration proper before the system is finally signed off. That comment might not go down well with the implementation team, so I'll explain why this is a good idea. The last stage of the CMS implementation is to test, test, and test again. What better way to complete the final stage of system testing than by asking real users to migrate real content?

This has a downside. A system that is being tested may (okay, will) still have bugs. This might have little impact on your content migration, or it might result in everything breaking horribly. Have a haggle with the implementation team to decide the right time to tentatively start migration. The implementation team needs to be happy that the system is relatively bug-free before allowing users to start entering content. And don't forget to make regular backups.

What Happens If I Press This Button?

There is an additional benefit to getting users involved whilst the CMS implementation is still being tested. No matter how good the specification, there will be some interface quirks or user annoyances that will only come to light when users start to enter content into the CMS. The solution may involve creating easier ways to skip between sections, or renaming the "*User Interface Facilitation*" button to say "*Help*". Whatever irks your users can lead to system improvements of benefit to all.

Create a CMS feedback mechanism for users to make comments and suggest improvements – maybe an online feedback form, or (if more appropriate) a paper-based suggestions form. Listen to your users, and if you can make a system change that will save them twenty minutes a day, then go for it. Keep this feedback system in place through the entire CMS life, even after migration is completed. Your CMS users may not be technical, but they will get to see a whole lot more of the user interface than the implementation team in the coming months and years. Listen to what they think of it, and change it if it's not right.

Let's Go To Work

Now it's time for the real migration to start. Migration of content from your old site to the new site is a process of pasting content into the CMS, ensuring the new page conforms to the Site Style Guide, and publishing the revised page to the live site. Before you groan under the weight of the impending work, here's some good news. Some files and databases *can* be automatically transferred. Hooray!

For example, if you have a large database of PDF files on your old site, you may be able to transfer this database into the CMS without having to manually upload every PDF into the new system. It may require some clever scripting or automation on behalf of the implementation team, so sit down with them and the CRD and work out what can be automatically transferred across.

For the rest of your content, it's time to start transferring by hand. Your CRD specifies who is responsible for the migration of each section of content. Exactly how you move the content will depend upon your CMS, but cutting-and-pasting is most likely to be the order of the day.

Take the title of the original page, consider it, and if need be come up with a more appropriate new one. Enter this into the CMS. Next, work through the page content paragraph by paragraph, transferring it into your CMS, and reading and changing as you go. Check any external links within the page. Recreate any internal links to other pages in the site. If these linked pages haven't yet been migrated or won't be, make a note in the CRD that your page needs revisiting later in the migration process for link creation.

Perspectives: My Content Has No Structure

You may have some existing content that is in a semi-structured format. Perhaps your old site uses templates that provide a clear distinction between separate paragraphs on a web page, or partially separates content from presentation using CSS. If this is the case, investigate pre-processing your HTML pages before your authors begin manual migration. It may be that you can automate the first 20% of the migration process, copying paragraph text into the CMS ready for a migrator to review, add images, and complete metadata.

The general rule for attempting auto-migration is this: you can't get structured information out of unstructured sources. Any script you write won't be able to magically "detect" some structure that isn't explicit in the document already.

In short, if you have some existing structure, you may be able to preserve it and make a short-cut into content migration. But if not, there really is no way to cheat.

Picture Perfect

Your original page probably contained some images. Are these images appropriate for the new site? Do they match the site style? Are they the correct size and image format as specified in your Site Style Guide? Do they have styling or borders from the old site style that are no longer appropriate? Do they need optimizing or cleaning up?

Depending on the answers to these questions, you may need to track down the image originals or source better images for your new site. This is a good time to create an '*originals*' folder for images that have not yet been reduced in size or optimized, for future reference. There is nothing worse than wasting time by saving an optimized version of an already-optimized image. Time will always be a factor, but try and apply as much care to each image as if it was being created for the first time.

As you re-assess your old site you will inevitably come across images with names such as "`1.jpg`". They're not very helpful! How much time you need to spend renaming images depends on how your CMS stores and presents images for authors to use but, whatever its approach, this is a chance to tidy and improve your naming conventions. Make file names lowercase and as descriptive as possible. Perhaps include the image width and height in your image file name to distinguish between different uses of the same image (for example, a full size image and a thumbnail).

It's Better with Meta

The final stage in a page's migratory journey is the addition of metadata. As we saw in Chapter 2, metadata is officially a Good Thing. CMS or otherwise, your pages should all be tagged with appropriate and useful metadata. Migration is your best and only chance to make sure metadata is applied to your existing content.

Unless you are very lucky, your existing content won't be tagged. I doubt every page in your old site has keywords, a description, and a unique title, let alone any other metadata that would help you to reuse your content in intelligent ways. Don't feel too bad about this. Unless you had a meta-tagging policy in place from day one, this isn't surprising. And I can guess the kind of reaction you would get if you randomly approached content authors to take time out of their lives to re-assess every single page they've ever written. They may have left the company anyway, and if not, that might push them over the edge.

Imagine you have no CMS. There are (commercial) systems available to assist the meta-tagging process for HTML pages, and these systems have my respect for their efforts. However, where these tagging systems fall down is not their ability to manage the HTML tagging process, but the simple fact that no one can be bothered to go through and do it.

But, wait. We're migrating content, and it's a manual process. So we have an excuse to take time out to meta-tag the data as we go. It's probably the only chance we're ever going to get. Let's make the most of it.

This stage of the migration process should enforce the addition of metadata before the revised page can be published. If you're going to tidy up, you might as well get it all right in one go. You won't get the chance to do it again.

For new content, the situation isn't as bad. The same mandatory process should be used. It's just that in the future, you'll only be doing one page at a time, not the entire site. Maybe this is a good time to buy the content migration team some nice gifts.

It's not always easy to come up with appropriate `<meta>` tags for content. To take keywords as an example, don't go overboard. Choose about twenty-five words maximum. A few carefully thought-out keywords or phrases give a much better overview of a page than a hundred brainstormed words in some random order.

Remember (and help your migrators to remember) that they are creating `<meta>` tags about a given page, not the site as a whole. General site keywords should go on the site home page. Internet search engines are getting clever, and some will check if your tags match the content of the page – if they do, you will rank higher.

Keywords don't have to just be words; for metadata purposes they can be phrases too. Place the most important phrases at the start. If the keywords are for the benefit of a search engine, your keywords need to match what *users* would search for, which is not necessarily the same as how *you* would describe the subject in question. If your company is known as "Moe's Drinking Establishments Inc.", users might well search for 'Moe's Bar', so this phrase should appear first.

Consider creating a thesaurus of valid / approved metadata during migration, to ensure consistency throughout the site. Take a look at *http://www.wordtracker.com* – a useful commercial site to suggest popular keywords that users enter into search engines. The site *http://labs.google.com/sets* performs a similar task for free, suggesting related keywords for a given topic.

Checked? Check!

Once the page is assessed, revised, and entered into the CMS, it should be fed into the workflow process and ultimately published. (You may be able to skip parts of the workflow if users with higher permissions in the workflow chain are performing the migration, but this is a good opportunity to check that your workflow for new content is appropriate in practice.)

Well done. Your page is now live. Time to move on to the next one?

Not quite. Each and every page you migrate *must* be checked in its final published form. Just because it looked good in the CMS authoring interface doesn't mean it will look right when it is published. Don't just publish and hope. We're trying to reduce the number of errors, not add more.

Take a long and careful look at your finished page. If there are template issues or layout problems on the live version of the page, let the implementation team know as soon as possible. (Make sure your page conforms to the Site Style Guide before you do.)

When migrating vast amounts of content, there is a temptation to assume that the live version of the page will be right, just because the old one was. In other words, your content migrators might not be 100% diligent. The best way to counter this and make life easier for them in the bargain is to get content migrators to work in pairs. Whilst one migrates, another checks the result with a fresh pair of eyes. The responsibility of ensuring content quality is shared, and the hassle of migration is halved.

Winding Down Your Old Site

Whilst you're working through the mass of content, there's something you should remember. Your old site. It's still there. You may be building a beautiful new replacement, but Joe Surfer is still looking at the old site in the meantime. We've established that the old site had enough problems without us letting it get out of date as well. You need to keep the old site up to date whilst the new one is being created.

Do I hear sobbing? Don't worry. I have a useful phrase for you: "Content slowdown". It sounds great, especially when explaining to managers how your old site will be kept up to date with the bare minimum of effort on your part.

Content slowdown means keeping your old site up to date by only updating time-critical content such as press releases, new job vacancies, or share price information. Any new features or content reviews are put to one side for inclusion in the new site. You should ensure management buy-in for the slowdown before beginning the migration process, to manage their expectations of what will happen to the old site whilst migration takes place.

Any content changes that do make it on to the old site will need to be replicated on the new site too. Just because you are migrating doesn't mean your content won't change from the snapshot taken in the CRD. You'll need to update the CRD (and inform migrators) when changes to existing content are requested during the migration process.

The big rule for migrating your site is to set a (realistic) deadline, and stick to it. Set cut-off dates for areas of content after which the old site will not be updated, slowdown or otherwise.

I'm going to contradict myself now. It may be that it just isn't possible to re-assess all content before the deadline. If you are stuck between a rock and a hard place, migrate the content anyway, and come back and assess it later. It is much better to put a migrated site live with most content assessed than to never go live at all. The longer you take, the more content will need to be changed, and the more content will need duplicating on the old and new sites. If you do have to go live without re-assessing the old content, it probably isn't going to be any worse than before. Just make sure essential pages are up to date.

It's All Just Too Much!

It may be that your site is just too big to migrate everything into a CMS whilst also maintaining an existing live version of the site. This is often the case for large intranets, or well-established sites with a lot of legacy content – I'd suggest more than a few thousand pages as a guideline definition of 'big'. If this is the case, don't worry. It's much better (and more advisable) to migrate the site in several separate parts. Successfully putting some of the site live in its new form is much better than failing to migrate anything at all.

If your site is this large, it helps to think of the site in terms of several (maybe even several hundred) "micro-sites". A **micro-site** is a discrete section of the overall site covering a specific subject or department. You might know these as "site areas", or "departments" – the principle is the same. It's all about dividing your overall site into smaller chunks that can be treated as separate migration projects.

Very large sites may naturally lend themselves to this kind of segmentation, and may even exist as a series of micro-sites already. That said, take this as a good opportunity to check that the existing site division is the right one. Large sites, especially intranets, tend to grow as a collection of micro-sites under an umbrella navigation system. This organic growth does not guarantee that the current micro-site split is the right one. Migration is a great opportunity to restructure your site and amalgamate (or further split) micro-sites into a more appropriate structure.

If your micro-sites share similar functionality, it may make sense to create a CMS-powered "empty shell" site and roll out this site shell for each micro-site, one by one. You may have to adapt your site shell in each case to meet specific requirements, but at least you won't have to re-invent the wheel each time.

Once you are clear on the correct micro-site split, decide upon the order in which you will tackle the micro-sites. Try and choose an important, high-profile micro-site for your first migration project. Although this might sound daunting, getting this site live successfully will increase buy-in and confidence in your CMS project and have other micro-site owners queuing up for content management.

It's better to tackle these micro-sites one at a time (or have several migration teams, each tackling one micro-site at a time). Focus on one site, get it complete and live, and then (and only then) move on to the next one. Issue a schedule showing the order in which the micro-sites will be migrated, with dates for each one.

If your site is *really* huge, with hundreds of micro-sites, it helps to implement a registration process for micro-site owners. Having a process for site owners to sign up for CMS implementation helps manage their expectations as to when they can get their hands on your beautiful system.

While You're There...

Metadata isn't the only thing we can tidy up whilst migrating. It's a great opportunity to remove a whole load of other barnacles from your site.

Did you have a standard site structure before your CMS? Or did your navigation grow in a random, inconsistent way, not unlike a fungus? Either way, your content might not fit into the old site structure any more, so sort it out and restructure your site in a more appropriate way.

If you have chosen to split your site into a collection of micro-sites in order to manage your migration process in several stages, then now is the time to introduce some form of umbrella navigation system across the new collection of sites. This is a project in itself, especially if it must be able to expand to encompass future new micro-sites, but CMS migration is a great opportunity to at least kick-start the challenge of taking a wider look at your navigation strategy.

Finally, some content will require archiving, especially if you have had no content-archiving process in place in the past. Use migration as an opportunity to take old content and files and index it appropriately. Create an archiving process for the future to avoid this happening again.

Are We Nearly There Yet?

OK. Your content has been successfully migrated, and you are now ready for the world to see your new web site. However, before you shout about it, there are a few final points to consider.

Going Live with the New System

If you have a CMS-powered site going live, you will need to switch your old site off and your new site on at some special "go-live" moment. There are a few ways you can do this, depending on your server setup and the kind of site you have.

Let's assume your web site has the **domain name** *www.glasshaus.com*. This domain name is just a name, nothing more – in itself it doesn't give any clue as to where in the world the glasshaus web site lives. The site has a much more useful identifier – its *IP* (*Internet Protocol*) address. This is a number (of the form 204.148.170.150 – it could be any four numbers between 0 and 255) that defines exactly where on the Internet the web site lives. So, how does a web browser translate *www.glasshaus.com* into 204.148.170.150 and find the glasshaus site?

When Joe Surfer enters the domain name into their browser, their browser needs to find out whereabouts on the Internet *www.glasshaus.com* is to be found. To do this, it asks your ISP's **Domain Name Server** (**DNS**) where the given domain lives. Your ISP's DNS asks another DNS, which in turn asks another, until the chain reaches the server that stores the definitive information about *www.glasshaus.com*. This server announces "It's over here!", returns the IP address for "over here", and passes it back down the chain to your browser.

Now, what happens if "over here" changes to be "over there"? To put it another way, what happens if the glasshaus site moves from its old server to a new one, with a different IP address? You would imagine that the same chain of events described above would happen, and you'd find out the new location.

Not quite. The first time your ISP's DNS server seeks out *www.glasshaus.com* and gets the "over here!" response, it also gets told "and don't ask me again!" This might sound rather rude, but it's actually very sensible. DNS servers get asked for information that really doesn't change very often – web sites don't actually move around that much. In order to reduce the load on these DNS servers, they supply a "time to live" for each request they get – it could be an hour, a day, a week – whatever is deemed appropriate by the domain name owner. This tells anyone who asks for the "over here" information that the answer is valid for a certain length of time, and doesn't need rechecking during this time.

Installing a CMS might require moving your site to a new server. This might mean changing the IP address of your site, and therefore changing your domain name to point to this new IP address instead of the old location. If this is the case, make sure the time-to-live of your domain name is set to something short (ten minutes, or maybe an hour) in the run-up to the site going live. That way, when you ask for your domain name to be switched to point at the new server, Joe Surfer will get pointed to the new site within ten minutes of making the switch.

Well, that's the theory (and in most cases it's true), but there are some ISPs out there that are just plain rude. They don't bother updating their DNS servers even if the time to live for a domain is short. It's their way of reducing the load on *their* DNS server in the chain. Some ISPs do this, and there's really nothing you can do about it. Even if you switch your domain name as described, surfers who use the rude ISP won't get pointed to the new site location until their ISP decides it's time to refresh their DNS. Experience suggests this can sometimes be every few weeks.

The only sure-fire way to make sure surfers get pointed to the correct version of your site as soon as it goes live, is to keep it at the same IP address as your old site. This is not as easy as it sounds. If your site is hosted internally, speak to your IT department, who may be able to make it happen. If your site is hosted externally, speak to the hosting company, and get confirmation in advance that they will be able to use the same IP address and make the switch within a given time window.

What if you can't keep you old IP address? How do you avoid Joe Surfer being sent to the wrong site? There are two solutions. One is to leave the old site live for several weeks (the longer the better), until you can be pretty sure that even rude DNS servers will have updated. Unfortunately, during this time your old site will become even more out of date, unless you fancy updating two sites for a while.

The alternative is to replace the old site location with a "bounce page" that transfers users to the new site by using its IP address rather than its domain name. So, if the new glasshaus site has an IP address of `204.148.170.150`, the bounce page will send the user to *http://204.148.170.150/*. This doesn't look great, and you'll need to be sure that your site can be viewed using its IP address without confusing your CMS, but it does ensure that everyone sees the new version from day one.

> Note that the IP address may not be unique to your site if other sites are hosted on the same server.

In short: going live with a new CMS-powered site isn't just a case of FTPing some new files over the old ones. And if you've spent eight chapters-worth of effort getting your new site live, we want people to be able to see it as soon as it goes live.

Good news: If your site is an intranet, and the DNS is handled internally, none of the above should be a problem. If in doubt, speak to your friendly IT manager.

Don't Forget To Remember

Remember earlier on, when you didn't have time to re-assess all of your content before the site went live? Don't let content owners off the hook once the site is live. That content still needs revisiting. If content owners didn't do the migration themselves (which is likely if they didn't have time to re-assess the content), use their CMS training session as an opportunity to go through the re-assessment. And make sure they finish it.

Watch Those Bad Habits

A few weeks into the CMS implementation, make sure your authors are comfortable with the CMS process and haven't picked up any bad habits. It's easy to correct any mistakes in the early stages and focus the content author's mind on the CMS process; it's a lot more difficult to go back and correct twelve month's worth of errors stemming from a misunderstanding of (or lack of confidence in) publishing content through the system. If time permits, it's good to get into the habit of catching up with the authors every few weeks until the content creation and publication process is running smoothly.

Summary

CMS implemented? Check. Content migrated? Check. Celebratory pizza? Check. The hard work is now officially over, and your authors are happily creating, editing, and publishing content without needing to pester an HTML expert, or designer, or programmer.

But hang on a moment. What if your average working day before the CMS involved making lots of content changes? It was fairly grungy work and the authors really should have done it anyway, but hey, it kept you busy. You can't spend *all* your time browsing the Internet. So now you have a CMS, what do you do all day?

I wouldn't worry. Just think of all of the things you never had time to do – implementing a cool new piece of functionality, or promoting your site properly for a change. In fact, all the things that make the most of your skills as an HTML wizard, or designer, or programmer (and not just a copy-and-paste monkey). CMS implementation is your chance to get back to doing the things you do best.

Not that you should forget the CMS. Your CMS implementation was great, but not so great that you can't come up with loads of ways to make it even better and your authors' lives even easier. Even if you can't come up with ways of improving the system, rest assured that your users can. The user feedback loop you put in place whilst migrating should stay in place for as long as the system is used. If you get constant requests from authors for something they can't do in the CMS, like form creation or image map generation, then create tools and templates to empower them to do it themselves. Give a user a form generation toolkit, and they'll love you forever.

With any luck, you will end up being the victim of your CMS's success. When other people see what a fantastic job you've done of the first implementation, and how quick and easy it is for the site's owners to update content, they'll be queuing at your door for a CMS of their own. This is the point where you ask for a pay rise.

Index

A Guide to the Index

The index is arranged in word-by-word order (so that New York would appear before Newark). Unmodified main entries represent the principal treatment of a topic and acronyms have been preferred to their expansions as main entries on the grounds that they are easier to recall. Comments specifically about the index should be sent to billj@glasshaus.com.

Symbols

50/50 rule for costs, 119, 120

A

access to pages
   built CMS systems, 137
   controlling using metadata, 43
accessibility, 69, 70, 91
   older browsers, 70
   power users and, 72
   Section 508 Guidelines, 70
accessing the system
   access rights for users and groups, 108
   questions to ask of CMS vendors, 106
   user ACLs, CMS technical infrastructure
      component, 15
adaptability to change, 19
Adobe Acroread text extractor, 137
Adobe Photoshop, 113
Allen, Dean, on cleaning HTML generated from
   Word, 35
Amazon.com
   design flexibility, 68
   e-commerce web site example, 65
   usability, 70
Apache Software Foundation
   Apache Batik tool, 144
   Apache Cocoon, 130, 133, 142
   Apache Lucene content indexing tool, 137
   Apache Velocity template engine, 130
   Apache Xalan processor, 142
API (Application Programming Interfaces)
   adding or manipulating CMS content with, 14
approver role in creating page content, 39

archiving
   automatic assignment of expiry dates, 110
   content on migration, 185
ASCII text as a CMS authoring source, 35
ASP (Active Server Pages)
   dynamic rendering, 80
   technology for building CMS solutions, 129
ASP (Application Service Providers)
   versions of bought-in CMS products, 100
ASP.NET
   technology for building CMS solutions, 129
   use of Custom Controls, 141
ASPImage image manipulation tool, 143
asset management, 27
   browser-based user interfaces for, 14
   building new assets, 46, 47
   built CMS, 133
   component activity of the CMS process, 12
   distinct from DAM, 13
   information asset management introduced, 28
   questions to ask of CMS vendors, 103
   taking stock of the existing system, 29
auctioning, template modules for, 114
audience members
   see also responsiveness; users.
   audience research, 89, 93
   defining audience needs, 89
   focusing on target audiences, 84
   interface requirements differ from authoring, 82
   managing expectations, 82
   sources of information about, 96
   user profiles, 94
   view of site differs from authors', 96
auditing, 110
Australia, 178
authentication
   built CMS systems, 137
   personalization and, 77

author servers, 115
authoring interface
    creating workflows, 107
    functionality for built CMS, 133
    link to style guide, 177
    questions to ask of CMS vendors, 103
authoring with templates
    questions to ask of CMS vendors, 110
authors
    audience members view of site differs from, 96
    basic and advanced authors, 47, 48
    CMS encourages publication by, 38
    communication with web professionals, 47
    complexity of roles, 108
    involving in Site Style Guide creation, 176
    owners of the site content, 178
    remote access requirement, 106
    risk of alienation, 8
    role in creating page content, 37
    training, 179
        reinforcing good habits, 187
    training need, 121
automatic migration, 180
availability an audience evaluation criterion, 83
AvantGo and publishing to PDAs, 145
AxKit open-source CMS, 133

B

backlogs in coding, effect on site popularity, 8
backup, specifying responsibility for, 156
backup system, 84, 88
baking
    caching embedded applications not possible, 79
    custom page generation by applications, 118
    frying and
        as extemes of rendering, 79
        checking link validity, 106
    frying and, introduced, 14
    link management for baked pages, 136
    updating templates, 67
barcodes, metadata as CMS equivalent, 41
Batik tool, Apache, 144
BBC Online, 65
BDFQ (Big Document Full of Questions), 102
    introduced, 100
benefits of CMS, importance of publicizing, 18
bespoke systems see building your own CMS.
best practice and Site Style Guide, 175
binary content see non-text content.
<blink> tag, 57, 69
Blogger web log software, 66
boilerplate material, 45
bostich.com personal site, 66
bottlenecks
    dependencies on specific people or resources, 88
    web site coding as a source of, 8

bought-in solutions, 99
    dangers of over-specifying, 120
    implementation responsibilities, 150
    licensing and implementation costs, 119
    questions to be asked of vendors, 102
bounce pages, managing domain names on
    migration, 186
brand identity problems, 9
branding, global page area, 157
breadcrumb trails, 57, 103
browser settings, 89
browser-based interfaces
    adding CMS content, 14
    assumed, for built CMS solution, 129
    ease of rollout, compared with desktop, 106
    usability and good design, 103
browsers
    automatic language detection, 138
    degrading well on unsupported browsers, 90
    latest browsers and need for multiple
        templates, 145
    Netscape 4.7 accessibility problems, 70
    other than web browsers, 89
    providing templates for different browsers, 64
    suitable for web-based CMS clients, 50
    target audience and browser support, 89
    testing plans for, 163
    XSLT template creation on, 142
Buckoo movie generator, 144
budgeting, implementation concept phase, 153
    budget signoff, 154
building your own CMS, 125
    asset management, 133
    content transformation, 139
    defining a product roadmap, 133
    implementation responsibilities, 150
    importance of documentation, 128
    importance of separating building and
        implementation stages, 126
    preparation stage, 127
    publishing, 144
    technology choice, 129
business environment
    CMS organizational context, 15
    CMS should accommodate changes in, 18
buying a CMS see bought-in solutions.

C

caching pages
    benefits of static rendering, 79
    checking the cache when rendering reponses, 78
    frequent search results, 80
    performance improvement from, 145
    third-party services, 80
can-we-talk.com, 71
capacity problems, allocation in production CMS, 86

capitalization and Site Style Guide, 176
card-sort tests, 33
CEO details, 173
certificates, allowing time to acquire, 156
change management procedure, 162
    Content Review Document, 183
character sets *see* multilingual content.
charging basis for CMS products, 11
chat site template modules, 114
checking migrated pages, 182
chunking data, 45
clean up Word HTML command, 35
ClearCase version control system, 139
client
    characteristics of, 152, 163
    role in CMS implementation, 152
client interfaces
    see also authoring inrterfaces; browser-based
        interfaces; desktop interfaces.
    customizable, 48
    entering metadata, 50
    inexperienced authors and, 48
    restricting formatting options, 50
client references
    bought-in CMS systems, 119
CNN (Cable News Network), traffic management on
    September 11, 2001, 80
Cocoon, Apache, 130, 133, 142
code testing, 164
ColdFusion, Macromedia
    Flash movie generation, 144
    image manipulation tools, 143
    technology for building CMS solutions, 131
    use of custom tags, 141
collaborative efforts
    CMS needs binding agreements, 16
    modern web site design, 10, 12
    separation of content and design assists, 21
COM integration and ASP, 129
commercial CMS solutions *see* bought-in solutions.
commitment to CMS, seriousness of strategic
    decision, 10
community site template patterns, 66
competitors' sites as source of design ideas, 58
complementary documents, storage of
    metadata in, 44
concept phase of implementation, 153
    detailing unresolved requirements, 162
    SIS document in, 155
    timeline, 153
concurrent users, limiting numbers, 83
consistency
    data reuse for ensuring, 45
    design features of a site, 57
    enforcing during migration, 175
    global branding and, 157
    image generation, 113
    problems with badly-managed web sites, 8

content
    see also separation of content and design.
    anticipating growth, 17
    criteria for migrating, 172
    possible types of content, 75
    potential growth on corporate sites, 6
    proprietary formats favor building your own
        CMS, 127
    providing different templates for the same
        content, 64
    providing extra space for, 63
    retention times, 83
    reuse and HTML inclusion, 134
    risk of staleness, 8
content area
    component of web pages, 157
    specifying heights for text areas, 159
content from non-Web sources, 34
content gaps, 174
content indexing tools, 137
content inventories, 29
    recommended stages in performing, 31
    responsibility of posting departments, 31
content management
    built or bought-in tools, 19
    choice between tools and systems, 15
    CMS includes both tools and organizational
        context, 15
    not restricted to web sites, 7, 13
    people-centric and people-intensive activity, 15
    principles, 17
Content Review Document *see* CRD.
content slowdown, 183
content syndication, 77
content transformation, 55
    component activity of the CMS process, 12
    functionality for built CMS, 139
    graphics and multimedia, 143
    modeling, in the publishing process, 91
    questions to ask of CMS vendors, 110
    role of templates, 59
contentEditable property, IE 5.5+, 134
contextual naming of web pages, 33
conversion of text into web pages, 35
cookie-based security, 137
cool web sites and changing fashion, 58
copy style and Site Style Guide, 177
corporate design and WYSIWYG editors, 134
corporate information pages, 173
costs
    implementation, deriving from SIS document, 166
    licensing and implementation compared, 119
CRD (Content Review Document), 172
    preparing for migration, 172
    timing of preparation, 180
    updating after change requests, 183
    web or spreadsheet based, 174

cross-browser compatibility, publishing process model, 92

CSS (Cascading Style Sheets)
  printer-friendly layouts and, 145
  separation of content and presentation and, 68
  template creation with HTML and, 140

cultural conventions, 90, 178

customer communication encouraged by CMS, 38

customized templates, 63
  template modules may consist of, 114
  use of custom tags, 140

customized web pages, using metadata for, 43

customizing CMS systems
  see also implementation.
  customizing bought-in CMS, 101

customizing forms, re-stringing data for reuse, 46

CVS version control system, 139

CX_GIFGD image manipulation tool, 143

D

DAM (Digital Asset Managment), distinct from CMS asset management, 13

data dictionaries, 42, 44

data reuse, 134
  two approaches to, 45

databases
  database-driven sites and uninformative URLs, 23
  possibility of automatic migration, 180
  searching for site content, 137
  sources of additional content, 34
  specifying in the SIS document, 156
  storage of metadata in, 44

deadlines for migration, sticking to, 183

debugging templates, 112

defining the process, asset management stage, 29

definition of CMS, 12

deliverables
  inclusion in project plan, 165
  specifying in SIS, 155

demonstrations of bought-in CMS solutions, 101

dependency avoidance, 86
  dependencies on specific people or resources, 88

design
  see also visual design.
  specifying in SIS document, 157
    navigation system, 158

design guidelines
  defining in implementation concept phase, 154

Designer role in CMS implementation, 152

desktop clients, 50
  adding content with, 14
  compared to web-based, 50
    ease of rollout, 106

Developer role in CMS implementation, 152

development environment, separation of publishing from, 87
  set-up in production phase of implementation, 167

devices, publishing to multiple targets, 84, 116

directory servers, linking to a CMS, 108

disabled users, 91

disaster planning, 88

discussion forum template modules, 114

diveintomark.org personal site, 66, 72

DNS (Domain Name Service)
  effects of reverse-DNS lookup, 94
  managing domain names on migration, 185

document management functionality, Lotus Notes, 131

documentation
  see also CRD; SIS; Site Style Guide.
  bought-in CMS systems, 121
  building your own CMS, 128
  specifying in the SIS document, 163

domain names
  allowing time to acquire, 156
  managing on migration, 185

DoS (Denial of Service) attacks, 85

downtime
  outages, 84
  scheduling routine operations, 87
  third-party monitoring for, 88

drafts, identifying status of, 39

Dreamweaver, Macromedia
  adding content with, 14
  copying Word documents, 35
  page-oriented nature of, 21
  site mapping function, 32

duplication, avoiding with content repositories, 139

dynamic publishing systems, perfomance improvements, 81

dynamic rendering see frying.

E

e-commerce
  template modules for, 114
  template patterns for, 65

editor role in creating page content, 38

e-mail, using for workflow management, 51, 107

embedded applications, 76
  dynamic rendering suits, 79
  monitoring CMS use through, 94

embedding web pages generated from other applications, 118

empty shell sites, 184

encryption, 85

error messages, helpfulness and embedded applications, 76

error propagation and working upstream, 22
evolt.org site, 66
executive summary, SIS, 156
expectations
    avoiding unreasonable expectations, 18
    raised expectations of web developers, 7
experience, web authors, 47
expiry dates, assigning automatically, 110
external software development, building a
    CMS, 128

F

fault tolerance an audience evaluation criterion, 84
feedback from logging, 93
feedback from users
    building a CMS, 128
    user testing, 180
feedback loops, 41
file attachments, searching for site content, 137
firewalls, 85
Flash, Macromedia, 114
    generating custom movies, 144
    updatable Flash movie content, 114
flexibility
    architecting the system for, 17
    assigning access rights, 108
    requires multiple templates, 60
    templates and, 17, 19
        reducing the burden of updating templates, 68
    workflow managment requirement, 107
focus groups see audience members.
folders and site navigation problems, 105
font rendering capabilities, 113
font support in image manipulation tools, 143
footers as example of modular design principle, 62
form creation template modules, 114
frames, an outdated design technique, 56
fraud prevention, an audience evaluation
    criterion, 85
free CMS see open source CMS.
frying
    baking and
        as extemes of rendering, 79
        checking link validity, 106
        introduced, 14
    custom page generation from applications, 118
    increases need for load testing, 165
    suits embedded applications, 79
    updating templates, 67

G

global branding and global functionality
    component of web pages, 157
global page properties, 158
global thinking, 177
google.com as source of metadata keywords, 182
GPL (General Public Licence, GNU), 132
granularity and web site numbers, 31
graph drawing
    paragraph templates and, 111
    template modules for, 114
graphics and multimedia
    building your own CMS, 143
    motion graphics an outdated design
        technique, 57
    questions to ask of CMS vendors, 112
grouping data for reuse, 45
grouping pages, navigation problems with
    folders, 105
grouping users and access rights, 108
growth in content, anticipating, 17

H

handcrafted web sites
    scalability problems, 9
hand-held devices
    HTML viewers for, 145
    including in testing plans, 164
    mobile devices, 90
    PDA templates, 64, 145
    WAP pages, 64, 117
helpful error messages and embedded
    applications, 76
hierarchical structure, web sites, 23, 136
    administration using, 104
hit counters in assessing web page popularity, 32
holidays, 165
home pages, indicators of capacity problems, 86
hosting environment, specifying in SIS
    document, 156
Ht://Dig content indexing tool, 137
HTML
    allowing in client text fields, 50, 103, 134
    hand coding not appropriate for modern sites, 9
    publishing markup languages other than, 116
    separation of content and presentation and, 68
    site-wide templates, 140
    template creation with CSS and, 140
    viewers for hand-held devices, 145
HTTP cache headers, 145
human involvement, CMS as people-centric and
    people-intensive activity, 15
hype about CMS, 102

I

IDE (Integrated Development Environments) and template creation, 112

IE (Internet Explorer) 5.5+ contentEditable property, 134

IIS (Internet Information Services) caching behavior, 80

image manipulation tools, building your own CMS, 143

ImageMagick, 143

images, 113
  see also graphics.
  image map creation by CMS systems, 106
  migration, 181
  should be stored in their original form, 113, 181
  specifying treatment in SIS document, 160

immaturity of CMS market, 11

implementation, 149
  CMS, choices to be made, 16
  concept phase, 153
  costs, 166
    compared with those of licensing, 119
  production phase, 166
  separate stage from building your own CMS, 126

implementation team
  automatic migration and, 180
  kick-off meetings, 154
  production briefing, 167
  production problem management, 167
  SIS review, 155

import and export, content syndication, 77

index order of pages
  allowing authors to change, 135
  promotion of least used, 94

informality of online text compared with print, 175

information site template patterns for, 65

infrastructure, CMS, 16
  technical infrastructure, 14

integrated voice response, 7

interfaces
  see also authoring interface; client interface; user interfaces.
  audience evaluation criterion, 84
  template creation interfaces, 112

International Herald Tribune web site, 65

internationalization, 7
  CMS can facilitate, 177
  multilingual content and, 109, 138

Interwoven as example of a top-end CMS system, 100

intranets
  content from non-Web sources, 34
  web-based CMS clients on, 50

inventory process
  content inventories, 29
  introduced, 29

inverted-L layout, 60

invitations to tender, 100

IP (Internet Protocol) addresses, managing on migration, 185

irs.gov site, 66

J

Java
  applets, 105
  Java 2D image manipulation libraries, 143
  open source CMS based on, 133
  technology for building CMS solutions, 130

Java Outline Editor, 136

JavaScript
  navigation and rendering speed, 79
  usability and, 72

JAWS screen reader, 71

JDBC, 20

JGenerator movie generator, 144

JScript language for ASP-based CMS, 129

JSP (JavaServer Pages) use of Taglibs custom tags, 141

K

knowledge transfer *see* training.

L

languages other than English, 178

language-specific sites
  automatic language detection, 138
  compared to multilingual sites, 109

last accessed date, 31

last mile caches, 80

Last Modified fields, 22

LDAP, 20, 108

left-hand navigation, permitting removal of, 63

legacy system integration favors building your own CMS, 127

legal requirements, 91
  web site changes following, 7

libswf PHP module and Flash movie generation, 144

licensing
  basis of, for CMS products, 11
  costs, compared with those of implementation, 119
  costs, ongoing license fees, 121
  free CMS systems, 132
  support obligations, 168

link management
    automatic updating, 106
    built CMS, 136
    facility offered by some CMS tools, 23
    questions to ask of CMS vendors, 105
    site navigation and, 14
links and the Site Style Guide, 177
liquid design, 160
littleyellowdifferent.com personal site, 66
LiveStats reporting tool, 94
load balancing, 165
    built CMS solutions, 146
load testing, 165
localization, 90
    locale effects on content, 93
logging
    audience research from access logs, 93
    information and misinformation from, 94
Lotus Notes
    distributed authoring, 145
    technology for building CMS solutions, 131
low quality site consequences, 9
Lucene content indexing tool, 137
Lynx text browser, providing templates for, 64

M

Macromedia Corporation see ColdFusion;
    Dreamweaver; Flash.
maintenance of web sites, 9
    automating using CMS, 10
    root causes of problems, 9
manageability of web sites, 31
managers' role as content approvers, 39
managing web sites, problems associated with
    growth, 6
mapping web sites, content inventories and, 32
markup languages other than HTML, 116
<meta> tags, 44
    commercial systems to help add, 182
metadata, 42
    access control using, 43
    below page level, 44
    CMS author interfaces, 134
    CMS content description with, 14
    desirable metadata to collect, 43
    enforcing addition during migration, 181
    entering on CMS client interfaces, 50
    importance in a CMS, 42, 76
    Last Modified fields, 22
    modes of storage, 44
    page creation user interface, 49
    questions to ask of CMS vendors, 110
    responsibility for creating, 44
    specifying in SIS documents, 158
    thesaurus of approved metadata, 182
    virtual structures using, 23

micro-sites, 184
Microsoft Corporation see IE; IIS.
Microsoft Excel, save as web page commands, 35
Microsoft FrontPage
    copying Word documents, 35
    learning curve, 48
    page-oriented nature of, 21
    site mapping function, 32
Microsoft Indexing Service, 137
Microsoft Visio site mapping function, 32
Microsoft Word
    adding content with, 14
    save as web page commands, 35
Midgard open source CMS, 133
migration, 171
    automatic migration, 181
    checking migrated pages, 182
    criteria for migrating content, 172
    discovering content gaps before, 174
    images, 181
    splitting large web sites, 184
    timing of the migration process, 180
    winding down the old site, 183
milestones, inclusion in project plan, 165
misleading logs, 95
mobile devices see hand-held devices.
modularity as a design principle, 62
modules
    see also template modules.
    questions to ask of CMS vendors, 114
monitor resolution, 72
monitoring CMS use, 17
    fixing content retention times, 83
    learning from the results, 93
monitoring performance, 108
    downtime, 88
motion graphics
    see also Flash movies.
    outdated design technique, 57
Moveable Type web log software, 66
MSXML processor, 142
multilingual content
    built CMS solutions, 138
    languages other than English, 178
    questions to ask of CMS vendors, 108
    web site planning and, 7
multimedia encoding for text-based languages, 117
multiple targets
    deciding on support for, 84
    publishing built CMS to, 145
    questions to ask of CMS vendors, 116
multiple templates, printer-friendly layouts, 145
mutlithreading and multiprocessor support, 119
MVC (Model-View-Controller) model, 130

N

naming conventions
  images, 181
  pages within a web site, 32
    numbering compared to contextual naming, 33
navigation
  card-sort tests and, 33
  component of web pages, 157, 158
  generating navigation graphics automatically, 113
  problems with folders in the site tree, 104
  providing excessive navigation, 57
  rendering as an expanding tree, 105
  rendering site structures as navigation
    systems, 104
  repeated and contextual approaches, 62
  tools for building navigation, 136
navigation-based file location, 33
Netscape 4.7 accessibility problems, 70
new functionality, dealing with requests for, 168
New York Times web site, 65
news sites
  re-stringing data for reuse, 46
  template patterns for, 65
Nielsen, Jakob, usability author, 72
non-clickable items, 105
non-text content
  see also images; motion graphics.
  encoding for text-based languages, 117
  storing previous versions for rollbacks, 110
numbering systems compared to contextual naming
  for web pages, 33

O

ODBC, 20
one developer syndrome, 128
one-to-many publishing, 117
ongoing license fees, 121
ontology, 76
OpenCMS product, 133
open source CMS systems, 133
  advantages and disadvantages, 132
  availability complicates selling on, 126
outages see downtime.

P

page caching, 145
page creation, 35
  changing the existing process, 37
  content from different applications, 118
  feedback loops, 41
  metadata use for customized pages, 43
  role of approvers, 39
  role of authors, 37
  role of editors, 38
  status of a page, 39, 40
  streamlining the process, 40
  understanding the existing process, 36
page reuse and templates, 17
page templates, 111
  special page templates, 161
  specifying in SIS document, 158
page types
  identifying, in content inventories, 34
  versions for different target devices, 116
paragraph formatting
  online text compared with print, 175
  Site Style Guide and, 176
paragraph templates, 111
  authoring interfaces and, 134
  modular design and, 63
  specifying in SIS document, 160
parallel workflow, 107
parnerships with CMS vendors, 100
patient records, 91
PDA (Personal Digital Assistants), templates for,
  64, 145
PDF (Portable Document Format) pages, 117
  displaying oversized content, 63
PDFLIB PDF generation tool, 145
perceptions see responsiveness.
Perforce version control system, 139
performance improvement
  built CMS solutions, 145
performance statictics
  bought-in CMS, 119
Perl
  open source CMS based on, 133
  technology for building CMS solutions, 131
personal site template patterns, 66
personalization and authentication, 77
personalized content, customizing templates for
  audience groups, 64
Photoshop, Adobe, 113
PHP
  libswf module, 144
  open source CMS based on, 133
  Sablotron XSLT processor and, 142
  technology for building CMS solutions, 131
pixel measurements, specifying page layouts, 159
pizza, 167, 169, 187
planning
  importance for successful CMS
    implementation, 16
  planning for failures, 88
  planning to survive change, 18
popularity assessment for web pages, 32
pop-up windows, displaying oversized content, 63
post-production phase of implementation, 168
power users, 72

pre-production phase of implementation, 166
previewing
    authoring interfaces and, 134
    templates should match the live site, 106
print documents
    publishing from the Web to, 90
    style doesn't translate to online, 175
printer-friendly layouts, 117, 145
problems addressed by CMS, 6
processes, CMS viewed as a set of, 15
product roadmaps, 121
    definition for built CMS, 133
production environment, committing changes, 87
production phase of implementation, 166, 167
production problem management, 167
production processes, need for and hand
    coding, 10
Project Manager
    management time estimates, 166
    role in CMS implementation, 151
project plan as attachment to SIS document, 165
proof of concept installations, assessing bought-in
    systems, 102
proprietary formats favor building your own
    CMS, 127
prototyping when building a CMS, 128
publishing, 75
    component activity of the CMS process, 12
    functionality for built CMS, 144
    interface requirements differ from authoring, 82
    involvement of team and system, 82, 86
    one-to-many publishing, 117
    operating in a production environment, 86
    publishing to multiple target devices, 89, 116
    questions to ask of CMS vendors, 114
    rendering sequence, 78
publishing opportunities, content from non-Web
    sources, 34
purchasing CMS systems see bought-in solutions.
Python
    open source CMS based on, 133
    technology for building CMS solutions, 132

R

Radio web log software, 66
RCS (Revision Control System, GNU), 139
recovery techniques, 84, 88
remote access requirement for content authors,
    106, 177
rendering, baking and frying as extemes of, 79
    points in between, 80
rendering sequence, 78
repeating information, attaching dynamically, 45
replication
    impracticable on built CMS solutions, 144
    Lotus Notes functionality, 131

reporting tools, misleading inferences by, 95
repositories, CMS
    avoiding duplication with, 139
    JSR-170 proposed standard for, 20
    physical form of, 14
requests for proposals, 100
requirements specification see SIS.
resource allocation, production phase of
    implementation, 167
responsibilities
    associated with building your own CMS, 127
    author training, 179
    backup and support, 156
    CMS implementation, 150
    CMS support, 122
    content management by departments, 179
    CRD preparation, 173
    security upgrades, 85
    web site maintenance, 8
responsiveness
    audience evaluation criterion, 83
    audience perception of, 81
        content dependency, 79
        importance, 83
re-stringing data for reuse, 46
restructuring sites on migration, 184
reusable data, 45, 134
right-hand navigation, permitting removal of, 63
Robocopy replication tool, 145
robustness advantage of working upstream, 22
roles
    access rights for users and groups, 108, 137
        specifying in SIS document, 156
    building your own CMS, 127
    implementation responsibilities, 150
    page creation process, 36, 41
    purchase process for bought-in CMS, 102
routine operations, scheduling to minimize
    downtime, 87
Rsync replication tool, 145
rule-of-thumb for cost estimation, 119

S

Sablotron processor, 142
sausage example of link management, 106
save as web page commands, 35
scalability
    adding more servers, 119
    anticipating growth, 17
    audience evaluation criterion, 83
    handcrafted web site problems, 9
    load testing, 165
    publishing to multiple servers, 144
    separation of content and design assists, 21
    working upstream of integration, 22
screen readers, 71

scripting
  technologies for building a CMS
    ASP, 129
    ASP.NET, 129
    MacroMedia ColdFusion, 131
    Java, 130
    PHP, 131
  template development and, 112, 141
    combining with XSLT use, 142
search engines, 91
search functionality
  built CMS, 136
  caching frequent search results, 80
  special page templates for, 161
Section 508 accessibility guidelines, 70
security
  see also accessing the system.
  authentication, 77, 137
  asset management and, 40
  audience evaluation criterion, 85
  built CMS solutions, 137
  publishing to multiple servers, 144
  techniques can burden users, 85
selling a built CMS, 126
separation of building and implementation, 126
separation of content and design, 21, 68, 93
  advantages for easy redesign, 10
  allowing in client text fields, 134
  CMS assists with, 10
  hand coding as cause of dependencies, 10
  managing code, 23
  managing structure, 23
  principle of CMS selection, 17
  publishing dependencies, 86
  template creation in built CMS systems, 140
  using Java and MVC, 130
  value to publishing system, 93
  working upstream, 22
separation of publishing and development, 87
September 11, 2001, CNN traffic management, 80
server logs metadata example, 42
server reports, content inventory first stage, 31
servers
  allocation in production CMS, 86
  development, should mirror live environment, 167
  generating SVG on, 144
  loading effects of baking and frying, 14
  monitoring CMS use, 94
  need for load testing, 165
  publishing to multiple servers, 115, 144
  questions to ask of CMS vendors, 118
  XSLT template creation on, 142
shelf life of design techniques, 59
shopping basket template modules, 114
shortcutting the CMS process, 17, 18
simulated user testing, 164

SIS (System Implementation Specification)
  document
  approval, 166
  basis for budgeting, 153
  change management procedure, 162
  client involvement in creating, 152
  client requirements specifications and, 154
  CRD distinguished from, 173
  creating, 155
  deriving implementation costs from, 166
  implementation team review, 155
  introduced, 149
  involvement of Project Manager, 151
  product of implementation concept phase, 153
  project plan as attachment, 165
  scope of document, 155
  specifying testing plans, 163
  specifying the hosting environment, 156
  stages in the implementation concept phase
    and, 155
site maps
  adding, 103
  special page templates, 161
site structures
  index order of pages, 135
  management, built CMS, 135
  management, specifying in SIS document, 156
  questions to ask of CMS vendors, 103
  site navigation and, 14
Site Style Guide, 175
  consistent branding and, 9
  involving authors in creation, 176
  online version, 177
  preparing for migration, 172
  signoff, 177
  suggested content, 176
skills required in building your own CMS, 127
slashdot community site, 66
snapshots of entire sites, 110, 139
software integration, 117
SourceSafe version control system, 139
special offers, metadata use for, 43
special page templates, 161
specifying requirements *see* SIS.
spell checking, 135
spreadsheets for building the CRD, 174
SSI (Server Side Includes) as a modular design
  principle, 62
SSL (Secure Sockets Layer), 85, 156
standard content
  attaching dynamically, 45
  WYSIWYG editors and corporate design, 134
standardization
  aspects of standards-compliance, 20
  building a CMS on standards, 17
  ISO 9000 compliance, 7
  speeding design work, 70

static publishing systems, perfomance
 improvements, 81
static rendering see baking.
strategic vision, site audience and message, 10
style guides see Site Style Guide.
Sun Microsystems see Java.
support
 see also training.
 bought-in CMS systems, 121, 122
 post-production phase, 168
 responsibilities associated with building your own
  CMS, 127
 specifying responsibility for, 156
SVG (Scalable Vector Graphics), 143
Swish-E content indexing tool, 137
syndication, 77
system development departments
 role in building a CMS, 127
System Implementation Specification see SIS.
system integration
 non web-enabled systems, 118
 questions to ask of CMS vendors, 117
systems and integration testing, 165
 migrating real content during, 180

T

target audience, 84
 browser support and, 89
team leader appointment during content
 inventories, 31
technical infrastructure of CMS, 14
Technical Lead Developer role in CMS
 implementation, 151
technological progress
 assumptions about the future, 19
 web site changes following, 7
template creation
 approaches for built CMS, 139
 dedicated servers for, 116
 embedding code, 141
 questions to ask of CMS vendors, 112
 use of custom tags, 140
 using XML/XSLT, 141
template creation interface, assessing bought-in
 systems, 102
template engines
 Apache Velocity, 130
 CMS technical infrastructure component, 14
 page and paragraph templates, 111
template modules, 114
 viewed as collections of custom templates, 161
template patterns, 65

templates
 authorizing departures from default, 63
 consistent branding and, 9
 customizing templates, 63
  for users, 64
 designing for flexibility, 19
 designing for page reuse and flexibility, 17
 developing and debugging, 112
 different templates for the same content, 64
 error propagation and correction, 22
 example layout illustrating use of, 111
 identifying page types in content inventories, 34
templates (Cont'd)
 limiting access rights, 108
 modeling, in the publishing process, 91
 previewing templates should match the live
  site, 106
 printer-friendly layouts, 145
 role in content transformation, 59
 role in publishing system reponses, 78
 separating authors from, 48
 specifying in SIS document, 157, 158
 updating, 67
 version control, 139
 XSLT and, 20
templating see content transformation, 13
testing plans
 operating in a production environment, 86
 specifying in the SIS document, 163
 time estimates, 166
texas.gov site, 66
text
 conversion into web pages, 35
 problems in specifying heights, 159
text browsers, 64, 71
text editors as CMS authoring source, 35
textism web site, 35
thesaurus of approved metadata, 182
thinking out of the box, 101
threaded discussions, CMS links to, 76
time limits on workflow stages, 108
time to live
 assigning for page content, 110
 managing domain names on migration, 186
timescales, bought -in and built CMS solutions, 126
To-Do lists, 51
tone setting by Site Style Guide, 176
training
 author training, 179
  reinforcing good habits, 187
 specifying in the SIS document, 163
 web developers and authors, 120
transformation see content transformation.
tree metaphor
 limitations of, for site navigation, 104
 site structures and, 136

U

umbrella navigation, 184
UML (Unified Modeling Language) publishing process model, 91
Unicode, 138
unresolved requirements in concept phase of implementation, 162
unused files, locating on a web server, 31
upgrades, bought-in CMS solutions, 121
URLs as source of contextual information, 23
usability, 69
    importance for e-commerce sites, 65
    myths surrounding, 72
    site navigation and, 33
user ACL (Access Control Lists), CMS technical infrastructure component, 15
user authentication, built CMS systems, 137
user expectations and web site development, 7
user interfaces
    see also authoring interfaces; client interfaces.
    authoring interface usability, 103
    authors, simplicity desirable, 38
    browser-based, adding content using, 14
    simplicity of CMS, 48
    web-based and desktop compared, 49
user profiles, 94
user testing, 164, 180
users
    see also authors; audience members.
    customizing templates for, 64
    limiting numbers of concurrent users, 83
    myths surrounding usability, 72
    role in CMS implementation, 152
users and their rights
    built CMS solutions, 137
    questions to ask of CMS vendors, 108

V

VBScript language for ASP-based CMS, 129
Velocity template engine, Apache, 130
vendors
    business models and licensing, 11
    difficulty of comparing, 11
    importance of workflow in evaluating, 36
    product support limited, 11
    proof of concept installations, 102
    questions to be asked of vendors, 102
    responsibility for author training, 179
version control
    built CMS solutions, 139
    CMS technical infrastructure component, 15
    integrating with RCS, 139
    questions to ask of CMS vendors, 109
    storing previous versions for rollbacks, 110

Vignette
    example of a top-end CMS system, 100
    template creation options, 112
Virginia, effects of reverse-DNS lookup, 94
virtual structures
    distinct from physical file systems, 23
    shelf life of design techniques, 59
visual design, 56
    see also images.
    inverted-L layout, 60
    monitor resolution and, 72
    need for balance, 60
    outdated techniques, 57
    suitability to the site's purpose, 58

W

W3C (World Wide Web Consortium), 69
WAP (Wireless Application Protocol) pages, 117
    providing templates for, 64
Wayback Machine web site, 59
web developer
    availability of web developers favors building a CMS, 125
    benefits of hardware and networking knowledge, 87
    one developer syndrome, 128role in CMS implementation, 152
    training for, 120
web development technical complexities, 7
web logs, 66
web pages
    automatic assignment of expiry dates, 110
    component areas identified, 157
    decisions on metadata, 44
    embedding code using scripting languages, 129
    example layout
        illustrating content from different applications, 118
        illustrating inverted-L design, 60, 61
        illustrating use of templates, 111, 159
    global page properties, 158
    growth in overall Web content, 1
    identifying page types, 34
    last accessed date, 31
    more current than printed equivalents, 7
    numbering compared to contextual naming, 33
web professionals
    communication with authors, 47
    defining success, 89
    role in connection with building a CMS, 127
    role in purchase process for bought-in CMS, 100, 102
web sites
    automating maintenance using CMS, 10
    factors by which audiences evaluate, 82
    maintenance problems, 8
    splitting large sites, 184
    winding down the old site, 183

web-based clients, compared to desktop, 50
webmonkey.com site, 69
webstandards.org site, 66
WebTrends reporting tool, 94
whatdoiknow.org personal site, 66
wordtracker as source of metadata keywords, 182
workflow, 35
    built CMS solutions, 138
    changing the existing process, 37
    CMS technical infrastructure component, 15
    Lotus Notes functionality, 131
    managing, 51
    need for enforcement of agreements, 16
    questions to ask of CMS vendors, 107
    role of authors, 47
    workflow tools and, 13
working upstream, advantages, 22
Wvware text extractor, 137
WYSIWYG editing, 134
    user interface for adding content, 103

X

Xalan processor, Apache, 142
XHTML (Extensible HTML), 142
    separation of content and presentation and, 68
XML (Extensible Markup Language)
    separation of content and presentation and, 68
    standard for CMS, 20
    storage of metadata as, 44
    web publishing using Cocoon, 130
XPDF text extractor, 137
XS DHTML editor, 134
XSLT (Extensible Stylesheet Language for
    Transformations), 20
    combining with scripting for template
        development, 142
    output for hand-held devices, 145
    separation of content and presentation and, 68
    template creation using XML and, 141
        transformations on server or browser, 142

Z

Zope open source CMS, 132, 133
    hierarchy management facility, 136

Notes

Notes

Notes

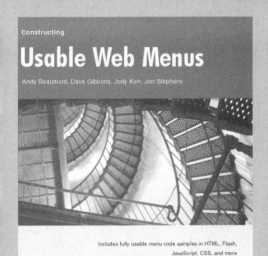

Also from glasshaus:

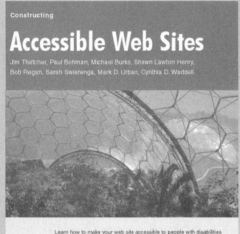

Constructing Accessible Web Sites

Paul Bohman, Michael Burks,
Shawn Lawton Henry, Jim Thatcher,
Mark Urban, Sarah Swierenga

1-904151-00-0

April 2002

US: $49.99
C: $74.95
UK: £36.99

Accessibility is about making a web site accessible to those with aural, visual or physical disabilities - or rather, constructing web sites that don't exclude these people from accessing the content or services being provided.

The purpose of this book is to enable web professionals to create and retrofit accessible web sites quickly and easily. It includes discussion of the technologies and techniques that are used to access web sites, and the legal stipulations and precedents that exist in the US and around the world. The main body of the book is devoted to the business of making web sites and their content accessible: testing techniques, web development tools, and advanced techniques. The book concludes with a quick reference checklist for creating accessible web sites.

This is a practical book with lots of step-by-step examples, supported with a Section 508 checklist enabling developers to refer to the book as they work as well as a complete list of accessibility testing and approval sites.

Also from glasshaus:

Practical JavaScript
for the Usable Web

Paul Wilton, Stephen Williams, Sing Li

1-904151-05-1

March 2002

US: $39.99

C: $52.95

UK: £28.99

This is a new kind of JavaScript book. It's not cut'n'paste, it's not a reference, and it's not an exhaustive investigation of the JavaScript language. It is about client-side, web focused, and task-oriented JavaScript.

JavaScript is a core skill for web professionals, and as every web professional knows, client-side JavaScript can produce all sorts of glitches and bugs. 'Practical JavaScript for the Usable Web' takes a two pronged approach to learning the JavaScript that you need to get your work done: teaching the core client-side JavaScript that you need to incorporate usable interactivity into your web applications, including many short functional scripts, and building up a complete application with shopping cart functionality.

When you have finished working with this book, you will have a thorough grounding in client-side JavaScript, and be able to construct your own client-side functionality quickly, easily, and without falling into any of the usability traps that this technology leaves wide open.

Also from glasshaus:

web professional to web professional

Usability: The Site Speaks for Itself

**Kelly Braun, Max Gadney,
Matt Haughey, Adrian Roselli,
Don Synstelien, Tom Walter,
David Wertheimer**

1-904151-03-5

May 2002

US: $49.99

C: $77.99

UK: £36.99

This book features case studies in usability and information architecture from the makers of **eBay**, **SynFonts** (a Flash-driven font foundry e-commerce site), the **BBC News Online** site, **Economist.com** web site, **evolt.org** (a peer-to-peer web professional site), and **MetaFilter**.

There are no hard-and-fast rules for usability on the Web, which is why this book steers away from the rigid prescriptions of gurus. Instead, it looks at six very different, but highly usable sites. The web professionals behind these sites discuss the design of each from their inception to today, how they solicited and responded to feedback, how they identified and dealt with problems, and how they met the audience's needs and expectations.

> "Our industry could use more books like this"
> - Jeffery Zeldman

Also from glasshaus:

glasshaus
web professional to web professional

Cascading Style Sheets:
Separating Content from Presentation

Owen Briggs, Steven Champeon,
Eric Costello, Matt Patterson

1-904151-04-3

US $ 34.99
C: $54.99
UK: £25.99

May 2002

This is a focused guide to using Cascading Style Sheets (CSS) for the visual design of web pages. It's practical, there's no fluff, and the core CSS skills are balanced by techniques for using the technology in today's browsers.

With CSS, we can lay out HTML data on a web page without either misusing tags or using hacks to get the page looking right. The complete separation of content from presentation enables web professionals to change the entire design of a site by modifying one stylesheet, rather than updating every document that the web site contains.

CSS is one of the trio of core client-side web professional skills: HTML for markup, JavaScript for dynamism, and CSS for style. All web professionals who want to take their page design to the next level, with all the advantages that CSS brings, will need this book.

Also from glasshaus:

glasshaus
web professional to web professional

Dreamweaver MX:
PHP Web Development

Bruno Mairlot, Gareth Downes-Powell
Tim Green

1-904151-11-6

US: $39.99
C : $61.99
UK: £28.99

July 2002

This book is all about making dynamic PHP web sites with Dreamweaver MX . It covers PHP, enough to get the reader up to speed with the technology, and how to use Dreamweaver MX to produce PHP code quickly and efficiently. It also covers site design and databases and SQL. It uses an example project, a hotel reservation system, that is built up through the chapters to demonstrate the concepts explained

Web Professionals have been calling for years for Dreamweaver/ UltraDev to support PHP, as it's the premier free open-source server-side scripting language. With Macromedia's landmark new release of Dreamweaver, PHP is fully supported in the familiar Dreamweaver visual environment.

It's is a no-fluff 400 pages, so you can learn enough PHP to make real dynamic web pages, spending less time reading and more time on the job.

Aimed at web professionals who want to use Dreamweaver MX to produce PHP web sites. It doesn't assume any knowledge of PHP, and it doesn't hold your hand when talking about Dreamweaver, so experience of Dreamweaver would be useful. It assumes knowledge of HTML and Web design.

Also from glasshaus:

Tools of the Trade

Dynamic Dreamweaver MX

Rachel Andrews, Omar Elbaga, Alan Foley, Bob Regan, Rob Turnbull

Overview of Dreamweaver MX fundamentals
Creating standards-compliant XHTML and CSS code using Dreamweaver MX
Accessibility features of Dreamweaver MX
Dynamic web page creation via server-side scripting
Using Server Behaviors to create advanced dynamic web applications with ease

glasshaus
web professional to web professional

Dynamic Dreamweaver MX

Rob Turnbull, Bob Regan, Omar Elbaga, Paul Boon, Rachel Andrew

1-904151-10-8

US: $29.99

C : $21.99

UK: £46.99

July 2002

This book gets you up to speed on using Macromedia Dreamweaver MX, the new version of Macromedia's premier visual web site design tool, to produce dynamic, creative, visually stunning sites that comply with web standards and accessibility guidelines. It gets straight to the heart of the matter so you spend less time reading, and more time building your site.

- **Rachel Andrew** is a member of the Web Standards Project's Dreamweaver Task Force, responsible for improving Dreamweaver's standards compliance and accessibility

- **Omar Elbaga** started out as a fine artist and moved to computer graphic arts. He is also a member of Team Macromedia

- **Alan Foley** is an Assistant Professor of Instructional Technology who teaches and consults on web accessibility and usability issues

- **Bob Regan** is the Senior Product Manager for Accessibility at Macromedia

- **Rob Turnbull** is also a member of Team Macromedia

glasshaus

web professional to web professional

glasshaus writes books for you. Any suggestions, or ideas about how you want information given in your ideal book will be studied by our team. Your comments are always valued at glasshaus.

Free phone in USA 800-873 9769
Fax (312) 893 8001

UK Tel.: (0121) 687 4100   Fax: (0121) 687 4101

Content Management Systems – Registration Card

Name _____

Address _____

_____

_____

City _____ State/Region_____

Country _____ Postcode/Zip_____

E-Mail _____

Occupation _____

How did you hear about this book?

❏ Book review (name) _____

❏ Advertisement (name) _____

❏ Recommendation _____

❏ Catalog _____

❏ Other _____

Where did you buy this book?

❏ Bookstore (name) _____ City_____

❏ Computer store (name) _____

❏ Mail order _____

❏ Other _____

What influenced you in the purchase of this book?

❏ Cover Design ❏ Contents ❏ Other (please specify):

How did you rate the overall content of this book?

❏ Excellent ❏ Good ❏ Average ❏ Poor

What did you find most useful about this book? _____

_____

What did you find least useful about this book? _____

_____

Please add any additional comments. _____

_____

What other subjects will you buy a computer book on soon?

_____

What is the best computer book you have used this year?

_____

> **Note:** This information will only be used to keep you updated about new glasshaus titles and will not be used for any other purpose or passed to any other third party.

Check here if you DO NOT want to receive support for this book ■

glasshaus

web professional to web professional

Note: If you post the bounce back card below in the UK, please send it to:

glasshaus, Arden House, 1102 Warwick Road,
Acocks Green, Birmingham B27 6HB. UK.

Computer Book Publishers